The Panchatantra

The Panchatantra

Translated from the Sanskrit by

Arthur W. Ryder

GYAN

Published by

Gyan Publishing House
5, Ansari Road
Daryaganj, New Delhi-110002
Phone: 011-47034999, 9811692060
E-mail: books@gyanbooks.com

Distribution Network
gyanbooks.com
India, USA, Canada, UK, Australia, France

ISBN: 978-81-212-7961-1 (PB)
First Published, 1925

2nd Impression 2023

Printed at: Gyan Press, Delhi.

THE PANCHATANTRA
Translator: ARTHUR W. RYDER

The Panchatantra

The Panchatantra

Translated from the Sanskrit by

Arthur W. Ryder

PHOENIX BOOKS

THE UNIVERSITY OF CHICAGO PRESS / CHICAGO & LONDON

TABLE OF CONTENTS

BOOK II—THE WINNING OF FRIENDS

BOOK III—CROWS AND OWLS

BOOK IV—LOSS OF GAINS

BOOK V—ILL-CONSIDERED ACTION

INTRODUCTIONS

TRANSLATOR'S INTRODUCTION

I

One Vishnusharman, shrewdly gleaning
All worldly wisdom's inner meaning,
In these five books the charm compresses
Of all such books the world possesses.

—Introduction to the *Panchatantra*

The *Panchatantra* contains the most widely known stories in the world. If it were further declared that the *Panchatantra* is the best collection of stories in the world, the assertion could hardly be disproved, and would probably command the assent of those possessing the knowledge for a judgment. Assuming varied forms in their native India, then traveling in translations, and translations of translations, through Persia, Arabia, Syria, and the civilized countries of Europe, these stories have, for more than twenty centuries, brought delight to hundreds of millions.

Since the stories gathered in the *Panchatantra* are very ancient, and since they can no longer be ascribed to their respective authors, it is not possible to give an accurate report of their genesis, while much in their subsequent history will always remain obscure. Dr. Hertel, the learned and painstaking editor of the text used by the present translator, believes that the original work was composed in Kashmir, about 200

B.C. At this date, however, many of the individual stories were already ancient. He then enumerates no less than twenty-five recensions of the work in India. The text here translated is late, dating from the year 1199 A.D.

It is not here intended to summarize the history of these stories in India, nor their travels through the Near East and through Europe. The story is attractive—whose interest is not awakened by learning, for example, that in this work he makes the acquaintance of one of La Fontaine's important sources? Yet here, as elsewhere, the work of the "scholars" has been of somewhat doubtful value, diverting attention from the primary to the secondary, from literature itself to facts, more or less important, about literature. The present version has not been made by a scholar, but by the opposite of a scholar, a lover of good books, eager, so far as his powers permit, to extend an accurate and joyful acquaintance with the world's masterpieces. He will therefore not endeavor to tell the history of the *Panchatantra*, but to tell what the *Panchatantra* is.

II

Whoever learns the work by heart,
Or through the story-teller's art
  Becomes acquainted,
His life by sad defeat—although
The king of heaven be his foe—
  Is never tainted.

—INTRODUCTION TO THE *Panchatantra*

The *Panchatantra* is a *niti-shastra*, or textbook of *niti*. The word *niti* means roughly "the wise conduct of life." Western civilization must endure a certain shame in realizing that no precise equivalent of the term is found in English, French, Latin, or Greek. Many words are therefore necessary to explain what *niti* is, though the idea, once grasped, is clear, important, and satisfying.

First of all, *niti* presupposes that one has considered, and rejected, the possibility of living as a saint. It can be practiced only by a social being, and represents an admirable attempt to answer the insistent question how to win the utmost possible joy from life in the world of men.

The negative foundation is security. For example, if one is a mouse, his dwelling must contain recesses beyond the reach of a cat's paw. Pleasant stanzas concerning the necessity of security are scattered throughout the work. Thus:

> The poor are in peculiar need
> Of being secret when they feed;
> The lion killed the ram who could
> Not check his appetite for food.

or again:

> In houses where no snakes are found,
> One sleeps; or where the snakes are bound:
> But perfect rest is hard to win
> With serpents bobbing out and in.

The mere negative foundation of security requires a considerable exercise of intelligence, since the world swarms with rascals, and no sensible man can imagine them capable of reformation.

> Caress a rascal as you will,
> He was and is a rascal still:
> All salve- and sweating-treatments fail
> To take the kink from doggy's tail.

Yet roguery can be defeated; for by its nature it is stupid.

> Since scamp and sneak and snake
> So often undertake
> A plan that does not thrive,
> The world wags on, alive.

Having made provision for security, in the realization that

> A man to thrive
> Must keep alive,

one faces the necessity of having money. The *Panchatantra*, being very wise, never falls into the vulgar error of supposing money to be important. Money must be there, in reasonable amount, because it is unimportant, and what wise man permits things unimportant to occupy his mind? Time and again the *Panchatantra* insists on the misery of poverty, with greatest detail in the story of "Gold's Gloom" in the second book, never perhaps with more point than in the stanza:

> A beggar to the graveyard hied
> And there "Friend corpse, arise," he cried;
> "One moment lift my heavy weight
> Of poverty; for I of late

Grow weary, and desire instead
Your comfort; you are good and dead."
The corpse was silent. He was sure
'Twas better to be dead than poor.

Needless to say, worldly property need not be, indeed should not be, too extensive, since it has no value in possession, but only in use:

In case of horse or book or sword,
Of woman, man or lute or word,
The use or uselessness depends
On qualities the user lends.

Now for the positive content of *niti*. Granted security and freedom from degrading worry, then joy results from three occupations—from resolute, yet circumspect, use of the active powers; from intercourse with like-minded friends; and above all, from worthy exercise of the intelligence.

Necessary, to begin with, for the experience of true joy in the world of men, is resolute action. The difficulties are not blinked:

There is no toy
Called easy joy;
But man must strain
To body's pain.

Time and again this note is struck—the difficulty and the inestimable reward of sturdy action. Perhaps the most splendid expression of this essential part of *niti* is found in the third book, in the words which the crow, Live-Strong, addresses to his king, Cloudy:

A noble purpose to attain
Desiderates extended pain,
Asks man's full greatness, pluck, and care,
And loved ones aiding with a prayer.
Yet if it climb to heart's desire,
What man of pride and fighting fire,
Of passion and of self-esteem
Can bear the unaccomplished dream?
His heart indignantly is bent
(Through its achievement) on content.

Equal stress is laid upon the winning and holding of intelligent friends. The very name of the second book is "The Winning of Friends"; the name of the first book is "The Loss of Friends." Throughout the whole work, we are never permitted to be long oblivious of the rarity, the necessity, and the pricelessness of friendship with the excellent. For, indeed,

The days when meetings do not fail
  With wise and good
Are lovely clearings on the trail
  Through life's wild wood.

So speaks Slow, the turtle; and Swift, the crow, expresses it thus:

They taste the best of bliss, are good,
  And find life's truest ends,
Who, glad and gladdening, rejoice
  In love, with loving friends.

Last of all, and in a sense including all else, is the use of the intelligence. Without it, no human joy is possible, nothing beyond animal happiness.

For if there be no mind
  Debating good and ill,
And if religion send
  No challenge to the will,
If only greed be there
  For some material feast,
How draw a line between
  The man-beast and the beast?

One must have at disposal all valid results of scholarship, yet one must not be a scholar. For

Scholarship is less than sense;
Therefore seek intelligence.

One must command a wealth of detailed fact, ever alert to the deceptiveness of seeming fact, since oftentimes

The firefly seems a fire, the sky looks flat;
Yet sky and fly are neither this nor that.

One must understand that there is no substitute for judgment, and no end to the reward of discriminating judgment:

To know oneself is hard, to know
  Wise effort, effort vain;
But accurate self-critics are
  Secure in times of strain.

One must be ever conscious of the past, yet only as it offers material for wisdom, never as an object of brooding regret:

For lost and dead and past
  The wise have no laments:
Between the wise and fools
  Is just this difference.

This is the lofty consolation offered by a woodpecker to a hen-sparrow whose eggs have been crushed by an elephant with the spring fever. And the whole matter finds its most admirable expression in the noble words of Cheek, the jackal:

What is learning whose attaining
Sees no passion wane, no reigning
  Love and self-control?
Does not make the mind a menial,
Finds in virtue no congenial
  Path and final goal?
Whose attaining is but straining
For a name, and never gaining
  Fame or peace of soul?

This is *niti*, the harmonious development of the powers of man, a life in which security, prosperity, resolute action, friendship, and good learning are so combined as to produce joy. It is a noble ideal, shaming many tawdry ambitions, many vulgar catchwords of our day. And this noble ideal is presented in an artistic form of perfect fitness, in five books of wise and witty stories, in most of which the actors are animals.

III

Better with the learnèd dwell,
Even though it be in hell
Than with vulgar spirits roam
Palaces that gods call home.

—*Panchatantra*, Book II

The word *Panchatantra* means the "Five Books," the Pentateuch. Each of the five books is independent, consisting of a framing story with numerous inserted stories, told, as fit circumstances arise, by one or another of the characters in the main narrative. Thus, the first book relates the broken friendship of the lion Rusty and the bull Lively, with some thirty inserted stories, told for the most part by the two jackals, Victor and Cheek. The second book has as its framing story the tale of the friendship of the crow, the mouse, the turtle, and the deer, whose names are Swift, Gold, Slow, and Spot. The third book has as framing story the war between crows and owls.

These three books are of considerable length and show great skill in construction. A somewhat different impression is left by Books IV and V. The framing story of Book IV, the tale of the monkey and the crocodile, has less interest than the inserted stories, while Book V can hardly be said to have a framing story, and it ends with a couple of grotesque tales, somewhat different in character from the others. These two shorter books, in spite of the charm of their contents, have the appearance of being addenda, and in some of the older recensions are reduced in bulk to the verge of extinction.

The device of the framing story is familiar in oriental works, the instance best known to Europeans being that of the *Arabian Nights*. Equally characteristic is the use of epigrammatic verses by the actors in the various tales. These verses are for the most part quoted from sacred writings or other sources of dignity and authority. It is as if the animals in some English beast-fable were to justify their actions by quotations from Shakespeare and the Bible. These wise verses it is which make the real character of the *Panchatantra.* The stories, indeed, are charming when regarded as pure narrative; but it is the beauty, wisdom, and wit of the verses which lift the *Panchatantra* far above the level of the best story-books. It hardly needs to be added that in the present version, verse is always rendered by verse, prose by prose. The titles of the individual stories, however, have been supplied by the translator, since the original has none.

The large majority of the actors are animals, who have, of course, a fairly constant character. Thus, the lion is strong but dull of wit, the jackal crafty, the heron stupid, the cat a hypocrite. The animal actors present, far more vividly and more urbanely than men could do, the view of life here recommended—a view shrewd, undeceived, and free of all sentimentality; a view that, piercing the humbug of every false ideal, reveals with incomparable wit the sources of lasting joy.

ARTHUR W. RYDER

BERKELEY, CALIFORNIA
July, 1925

INTRODUCTION

One Vishnusharman, shrewdly gleaning
All worldly wisdom's inner meaning,
In these five books the charm compresses
Of all such books the world possesses.

And this is how it happened.

In the southern country is a city called Maidens' Delight. There lived a king named Immortal-Power. He was familiar with all the works treating of the wise conduct of life. His feet were made dazzling by the tangle of rays of light from jewels in the diadems of mighty kings who knelt before him. He had reached the far shore of all the arts that embellish life. This king had three sons. Their names were Rich-Power, Fierce-Power, Endless-Power, and they were supreme blockheads.

Now when the king perceived that they were hostile to education, he summoned his counselors and said: "Gentlemen, it is known to you that these sons of mine, being hostile to education, are lacking in discernment. So when I behold them, my kingdom brings me no happiness, though all external thorns are drawn. For there is wisdom in the proverb:

Of sons unborn, or dead, or fools,
Unborn or dead will do:

They cause a little grief, no doubt;
But fools, a long life through.

And again:

To what good purpose can a cow
That brings no calf nor milk, be bent?
Or why beget a son who proves
A dunce and disobedient?

Some means must therefore be devised to awaken their intelligence."

And they, one after another, replied: "O King, first one learns grammar, in twelve years. If this subject has somehow been mastered, then one masters the books on religion and practical life. Then the intelligence awakens."

But one of their number, a counselor named Keen, said: "O King, the duration of life is limited, and the verbal sciences require much time for mastery. Therefore let some kind of epitome be devised to wake their intelligence. There is a proverb that says:

Since verbal science has no final end,
Since life is short, and obstacles impend,
Let central facts be picked and firmly fixed,
As swans extract the milk with water mixed.

"Now there is a Brahman here named Vishnusharman, with a reputation for competence in numerous sciences. Intrust the princes to him. He will certainly make them intelligent in a twinkling."

When the king had listened to this, he summoned Vishnusharman and said: "Holy sir, as a favor to me you must make these princes incomparable masters of the art of practical life. In return, I will bestow upon you a hundred land-grants."

And Vishnusharman made answer to the king: "O King, listen. Here is the plain truth. I am not the man to sell good learning for a hundred land-grants. But if I do not, in six months' time, make the boys acquainted with the art of intelligent living, I will give up my own name. Let us cut the matter short. Listen to my lion-roar. My boasting arises from no greed for cash. Besides, I have no use for money; I am eighty years old, and all the objects of sensual desire have lost their charm. But in order that your request may be granted, I will show a sporting spirit in reference to artistic matters. Make a note of the date. If I fail to render your sons, in six months' time, incomparable masters of the art of intelligent living, then His Majesty is at liberty to show me His Majestic bare bottom."

When the king, surrounded by his counselors, had listened to the Brahman's highly unconventional promise, he was penetrated with wonder, intrusted the princes to him, and experienced supreme content.

Meanwhile, Vishnusharman took the boys, went home, and made them learn by heart five books which he composed and called: (I) "The Loss of Friends," (II) "The Winning of Friends," (III) "Crows and Owls," (IV) "Loss of Gains," (V) "Ill-considered Action."

These the princes learned, and in six months' time they answered the prescription. Since that day this work on the art of intelligent living, called *Panchatantra*, or the "Five Books," has traveled the world, aiming at the awakening of intelligence in the young. To sum the matter up:

> Whoever learns the work by heart,
> Or through the story-teller's art
> Becomes acquainted,
> His life by sad defeat—although
> The king of heaven be his foe—
> Is never tainted.

BOOK I
THE LOSS OF FRIENDS

BOOK I

THE LOSS OF FRIENDS

Here then begins Book I, called "The Loss of Friends." The first verse runs:

> The forest lion and the bull
> Were linked in friendship, growing, full:
> A jackal then estranged the friends
> For greedy and malicious ends.

And this is how it happened.

In the southern country was a city called Maidens' Delight. It rivaled the city of heaven's King, so abounding in every urban excellence as to form the central jewel of Earth's diadem. Its contour was like that of Kailasa Peak. Its gates and palaces were stocked with machines, missile weapons, and chariots in great variety. Its central portal, massive as Indrakila Mountain, was fitted with bolt and bar, panel and arch, all formidable, impressive, solid. Its numerous temples lifted their firm bulk near spacious squares and crossings. It wore a moat-girdled zone of walls that recalled the high-uplifted Himalayas.

In this city lived a merchant named Increase. He possessed a heap of numerous virtues, and a heap of money, a result of the accumulation of merit in earlier lives.

As he once pondered in the dead of night, his conclusions took this form: "Even an abundant store of wealth, if pecked at, sinks together like a pile of soot. A very little, if added to, grows like an ant-hill. Hence, even though money be abundant, it should be increased. Riches unearned should be earned. What is earned, should be guarded. What is guarded, should be enlarged and heedfully invested. Money, even if hoarded in commonplace fashion, is likely to go in a flash, the hindrances being many. Money unemployed when opportunities arise, is the same as money unpossessed. Therefore, money once acquired should be guarded, increased, employed. As the proverb says:

Release the money you have earned;
 So keep it safely still:
The surplus water of a tank
 Must find a way to spill.

Wild elephants are caught by tame;
With capital it is the same:
In business, beggars have no scope
Whose stock-in-trade is empty hope.

If any fail to use his fate
For joy in this or future state,
His riches serve as foolish fetters;
He simply keeps them for his betters."

Having thus set his mind in order, he collected merchandise bound for the city of Mathura, assembled his servants, and after saying farewell to his parents when asterism and lunar station were auspicious, set forth from the city, with his people following and with blare of conch-shell and beat of drum preceding. At the first water he bade his friends turn back, while he proceeded.

To bear the yoke he had two bulls of good omen. Their names were Joyful and Lively; they looked like white clouds, and their chests were girded with golden bells.

Presently he reached a forest lovely with grisleas, acacias, dhaks, and sals, densely planted with other trees of charming aspect; fearsome with elephants, wild oxen, buffaloes, deer, grunting-cows, boars, tigers, leopards, and bears; abounding in water that issued from the flanks of mountains; rich in caves and thickets.

Here the bull Lively was overcome, partly by the excessive weight of the wagon, partly because one foot sank helpless where far-flung water from cascades made a muddy spot. At this spot the bull somehow snapped the yoke and sank in a heap. When the driver saw that he was down, he jumped excitedly from the wagon, ran to the merchant not far away, and humbly bowing, said: "Oh, my lord! Lively was wearied by the trip, and sank in the mud."

On hearing this, merchant Increase was deeply dejected. He halted for five nights, but when the poor bull did not return to health, he left caretakers with a supply of fodder, and said: "You must join me later, bringing Lively, if he lives; if he dies, after performing the last sad rites." Having given these directions, he started for his destination.

On the next day, the men, fearing the many drawbacks of the forest, started also and made a false report to their master. "Poor Lively died," they said, "and we performed the last sad rites with fire and everything else." And the merchant, feeling grieved for a mere moment, out of gratitude performed a ceremony that included rites for the departed, then journeyed without hindrance to Mathura.

In the meantime, Lively, since his fate willed it and further life was predestined, hobbled step by step to the bank of the Jumna, his body invigorated by a mist of spray from the cascades. There he browsed on the emerald tips of grass-blades, and in a few days grew plump as Shiva's bull, high-humped, and full of energy. Every day he tore the tops of ant-hills with goring horns, and frisked like an elephant.

But one day a lion named Rusty, with a retinue of all kinds of animals, came down to the bank of the Jumna for water. There he heard Lively's prodigious bellow. The sound troubled his heart exceedingly, but he concealed his inner feelings while beneath a spreading banyan tree he drew up his company in what is called the Circle of Four.

Now the divisions of the Circle of Four are given as: (1) the lion, (2) the lion's guard, (3) the under-strappers, (4) the menials. In all cities, capitals, towns, hamlets, market-centers, settlements, border-posts, land-grants, monasteries, and communities there is just one occupant of the lion's post. Relatively few are active as the lion's guard. The understrappers are the indiscriminate throng. The menials are posted on the outskirts. The three classes are each divided into members high, middle, and low.

Now Rusty, with counselors and intimates, enjoyed a kingship of the following order. His royal office, though lacking the pomp of umbrella, flyflap, fan, vehicle, and amorous display, was held erect by sheer pride in the sentiment of unaffected pluck. It showed unbroken haughtiness and abounding self-esteem. It manifested a native zeal for unchecked power that brooked no rival. It was ignorant of cringing speech, which it delegated to those who like that sort of thing. It functioned by means of impatience, wrath, haste, and hauteur. Its manly goal was fearlessness, disdaining fawning, strange to obsequiousness, unalarmed. It made use of no wheedling artifices, but glittered in its reliance on enterprise, valor, dignity. It was independent, unattached, free from selfish worry. It advertised the reward of manliness by its pleasure in benefiting others. It was unconquered, free from constraint and meanness, while it had no thought of elaborating defensive works. It kept no account of revenue and expenditure. It knew no deviousness nor time-serving, but was prickly with the energy earned by loftiness of spirit. It wasted no deliberation on the conventional six expedients, nor did it hoard weapons or jewelry. It had an uncommon appetite for power, never adopted subterfuges, was never an object of suspicion. It paid no heed to wives or ambush-layers, to their torrents of tears or their squeals. It was without reproach. It had no artificial training in the use of weapons, but it did not disappoint expectations. It found satisfactory food and shelter without dependence on servants. It had no timidity about any foreign forest, and no alarms. Its head was high. As the proverb says:

> The lion needs, in forest station,
> No trappings and no education,
>   But lonely power and pride;
> And all the song his subjects sing,
> Is in the words: "O King! O King!"
>   No epithet beside.

And again:

> The lion needs, for his appointing,
> No ceremony, no anointing;
> His deeds of heroism bring
> Him fortune. Nature crowns him king.
>
> The elephant is the lion's meat,
> With drops of trickling ichor sweet;
> Though lack thereof should come to pass,
> The lion does not nibble grass.

Now Rusty had in his train two jackals, sons of counselors, but out of a job. Their names were Cheek and Victor. These two conferred secretly, and Victor said: "My dear Cheek, just look at our master Rusty. He came this way for water. For what reason does he crouch here so disconsolate?" "Why meddle, my dear fellow?" said Cheek. "There is a saying:

> Death pursues the meddling flunkey:
> Note the wedge-extracting monkey."

"How was that?" asked Victor. And Cheek told the story of

THE WEDGE-PULLING MONKEY

There was a city in a certain region. In a grove near by, a merchant was having a temple built. Each day at the noon hour the foreman and workers would go to the city for lunch.

Now one day a troop of monkeys came upon the half-built temple. There lay a tremendous anjana-log, which a mechanic had begun to split, a wedge of acacia-wood being thrust in at the top.

There the monkeys began their playful frolics upon tree-top, lofty roof, and woodpile. Then one of them, whose doom was near, thoughtlessly bestrode the log, thinking: "Who stuck a wedge in this queer place?" So he seized it with both hands and started to work it loose. Now what happened when the wedge gave at the spot where his private parts entered the cleft, that, sir, you know without being told.

"And that is why I say that meddling should be avoided by the intelligent. And you know," he continued, "that we two pick up a fair living just from his leavings."

"But," said Victor, "how can you give first-rate service merely from a desire for food with no desire for distinction? There is wisdom in the saying:

> In hurting foes and helping friends
> The wise perceive the proper ends
> Of serving kings. The belly's call
> To answer, is no job at all.

And again:

> When many lives on one depend,
> Then life is life indeed:
> A crow, with beak equipped, can fill
> His belly's selfish need.

> If loving kindness be not shown
> To friends and souls in pain,
> To teachers, servants, and one's self,
> What use in life, what gain?
> A crow will live for many years
> And eat the offered grain.

> A dog is quite contented if
> He gets a meatless bone,
> A dirty thing with gristle-strings
> And marrow-fat alone—
> And not enough of it at that
> To still his belly's moan.

> The lion scorns the jackal, though
> Between his paws, to smite
> The elephant. For everyone,
> However sad his plight,
> Demands the recompense that he
> Esteems his native right.

Dogs wag their tails and fawn and roll,
  Bare mouth and belly, at your feet:
Bull-elephants show self-esteem,
  Demand much coaxing ere they eat.

A tiny rill
Is quick to fill,
  And quick a mouse's paws;
So seedy men
Are grateful, when
  There is but little cause.

For if there be no mind
  Debating good and ill,
And if religion send
  No challenge to the will,
If only greed be there
  For some material feast,
How draw a line between
  The man-beast and the beast?

Or more accurately yet:

Since cattle draw the plow
  Through rough and level soil,
And bend their patient necks
  To heavy wagons' toil,
Are kind, of sinless birth,
  And find in grass a feast,
How can they be compared
  With any human beast?"

"But at present," said Cheek, "we two hold no job at court. So why meddle?" "My dear fellow," said Victor, "after a little the jobless man does hold a job. As the saying goes:

The jobless man is hired
For careful serving;
The holder may be fired,
If undeserving.

No character moves up or down
At others' smile or others' frown;
But honor or contempt on earth
Will follow conduct's inner worth.

And once more:

It costs an effort still
To carry stones uphill;
They tumble in a trice:
So virtue, and so vice."

"Well," said Cheek, "what do you wish to imply?" And Victor answered: "You see, our master is frightened, his servants are frightened, and he does not know what to do." "How can you be sure of that?" asked Cheek, and Victor said: "Isn't it plain?

An ox can understand, of course,
The spoken word; a driven horse
Or elephant, exerts his force;

But men of wisdom can infer
Unuttered thought from features' stir—
For wit rewards its worshiper.

And again:

From feature, gesture, gait,
From twitch, or word,
From change in eye or face
Is thought inferred.

So by virtue of native intelligence I intend to get him into my power this very day."

"Why," said Cheek, "you do not know how to make yourself useful to a superior. So tell me. How can you establish power over him?"

"And why, my good fellow, do I not know how to make myself useful?" said Victor. "The saintly poet Vyasa has sung the entry of the Pandu princes into Virata's court. From his poem I learned the whole duty of a functionary. You have heard the proverb:

> No burden enervates the strong;
> To enterprise no road is long;
> The well-informed all countries range;
> To flatterers no man is strange."

But Cheek objected: "He might perhaps despise you for forcing yourself into a position that does not belong to you." "Yes," said Victor, "there is point in that. However, I am also a judge of occasions. And there are rules, as follows:

> The Lord of Learning, speaking to
> A false occasion,
> Will meet with hatred, and of course
> Lack all persuasion.

And again:

> The favorite's business comes to be
> A sudden source of king's *ennui*,
> When he is thoughtful, trying scents,
> Retiring, or in conference.

And once again:

On hours of talk or squabbling rude,
Of physic, barber, flirting, food,
A gentleman does not intrude.

Let everyone be cautious
   In palaces of kings;
And let not students rummage
   In their professor's things:
For naughty meddlers suffer
   Destruction swift and sure,
Like evening candles, lighted
   In houses of the poor.

Or put it this way:

On entering a palace,
   Adjust a modest dress;
Go slowly, bowing lowly
   In timely humbleness;
And sound the kingly temper,
   And kingly whims no less.

Or this way:

Though ignorant and common,
   Unworth the honoring,
Men win to royal favor
   By standing near the king:
For kings and vines and maidens
   To nearest neighbors cling.

And once again:

The servant in his master's face
Discerns the signs of wrath and grace,
And though the master jerk and tack,
The servant slowly mounts his back.

And finally:

The brave, the learnèd, he who wins
  To bureaucratic power—
These three, alone of all mankind,
  Can pluck earth's golden flower.

"Now let me inform you how power is gained by dancing attendance on a master.

Win the friendly counselors,
  To the monarch dear,
Win persuasive speakers; so
  Gain the royal ear.

On the undiscerning mob
  'Tis not wise to toil:
No man reaps a harvest by
  Plowing barren soil.

Serve a king of merit, though
  Friendless, destitute;
After some delay, you pluck
  Long-enduring fruit.

Hate your master, and you fill
  Servant's meanest state:
Not discerning whom to serve,
  'Tis yourself you hate.

Treat the dowager, the queen,
  And the king-to-be,
Chaplain, porter, counselor,
  Most obsequiously.

One who seeks the van in fights,
  In the palace clings,
In the city walks behind,
  Is beloved of kings.

One who flatters when addressed,
  Does the proper things,
Acts without expressing doubts,
  Is beloved of kings.

One, the royal gifts of cash
  Prudently who flings,
Wearing gifts of garments, he
  Is beloved of kings.

One who never makes reply
  That his master stings,
Never boisterously laughs,
  Is beloved of kings.

One who never hearkens to
  Queenly whisperings,
In the women's quarters dumb,
  Is beloved of kings.

One who, even in distress,
  Never boasts and sings
Of his master's favor, he
  Is beloved of kings.

One who hates his master's foe,
  Loves his friend, and brings
Pain or joy to either one,
  Is beloved of kings.

One who never disagrees,
  Blames, or pulls the strings
Of intrigue with enemies,
  Is beloved of kings.

One who finds in battle, peace
Free from questionings,
Thinks of exile as of home,
Is beloved of kings.

One who thinks of dice as death,
Wine as poison-stings,
Others' wives as statues, he
Is beloved of kings."

"Well," said Cheek, "when you come into his presence, what do you intend to say first? Please tell me that." And Victor replied:

"Answers, after speech begins,
Further answers breed,
As a seed, with timely rain,
Ripens other seed.

And besides:

A clever servant shows his master
The gleam of triumph or disaster
From good or evil courses springing,
And shows him wit, decision-bringing.

The man possessing such a wit
Should magnify and foster it;
Thereby he earns a livelihood
And public honor from the good.

And there is a saying:

Let anyone who does not seek
His master's fall, unbidden speak;
So act at least the excellent:
The other kind are different."

"But," said Cheek, "kings are hard to conciliate. There is a saying:

In sensuous coil
And heartless toil,
In sinuous course
And armored force,
In savage harms
That yield to charms—
In all these things
Are snakes like kings.

Uneven, rough,
And high enough—
Yet low folk roam
Their flanks as home,
And wild things haunt
Them, hungry, gaunt—
In all these things
Are hills like kings.

The things that claw, and the things that gore
Are unreliable things;
And so is a man with a sword in his hand,
And rivers, and women, and kings."

"Quite true," said Victor. "However:

The clever man soon penetrates
The subject's mind, and captivates.

Cringe, and flatter him when angry;
Love his friend and hate his foe;
Duly advertise his presents—
Trust no magic—win him so.

And yet:

If a man excel in action,
Learning, fluent word,

Make yourself his humble servant
While his power is stirred,
Quick to leave him at the moment
When he grows absurd.

Plant your words where profit lies:
Whiter cloth takes faster dyes.

Till you know his power and manhood,
Effort has no scope:
Moonlight's glitter vainly rivals
Himalaya's slope."

And Cheek replied: "If you have made up your mind, then seek the feet of the king. Blest be your journeyings. May your purpose be accomplished.

Be heedful in the presence of the king;
We also to your health and fortune cling."

Then Victor bowed to his friend, and went to meet Rusty.

Now when Rusty saw Victor approaching, he said to the doorkeeper: "Away with your reed of office! This is an old acquaintance, the counselor's son Victor. He has free entrance. Let him come in. He belongs to the second circle." So Victor entered, bowed to Rusty, and sat down on the seat indicated to him.

Then Rusty extended a right paw adorned with claws as formidable as thunderbolts, and said respectfully: "Do you enjoy health? Why has so long a time passed since you were last visible?" And Victor replied: "Even though my royal master has no present need of me, still I ought to report at the proper time. For there is nothing that may not render service to a king. As the saying goes:

To clean a tooth or scratch an ear
  A straw may serve a king:
A man, with speech and action, is
  A higher kind of thing.

"Besides, we who are ancestral servants of our royal master, follow him even in disasters. For us there is no other course. Now the proverb says:

Set in fit position each
  Gem or serving-man;
No tiaras on the toes,
  Just because you can.

Servants leave the kings who their
  Qualities ignore,
Even kings of lofty line,
  Wealthy, served of yore.

Lacking honor from their equals,
  Jobless, *déclassé*,
Servants give their master notice
  That they will not stay.

And again:

If set in tin, a gem that would
  Adorn a golden frame,
Will never scream nor fail to gleam,
  Yet tells its wearer's shame.

The king who reads a servant's mind—
  Dull, faithless, faithful, wise—
May servants find of every kind
  For every enterprise.

"And as for my master's remark: 'It is long since you were last visible,' pray hear the reason of that:

Where just distinction is not drawn
   Between the left and right,
The self-respecting, if they can,
   Will quickly take to flight.

If masters no distinction make
   Among their servants, then
They lose the zealous offices
   Of energetic men.

And in a market where it seems
   That no distinctions hold
Between red-eye and ruby, how
   Can precious gems be sold?

There must be bonds of union
   In all their dealings, since
No prince can lack his servants
   Nor servants lack a prince.

"Yet the nature of the servant also depends on the master's quality. As the saying goes:

In case of horse or book or sword,
Of woman, man or lute or word,
The use or uselessness depends
On qualities the user lends.

"And another point. You do wrong to despise me because I am a jackal. For

Silk comes from worms, and gold from stone;
From cow's hair sacred grass is grown;
The water-lily springs from mud;
From cow-dung sprouts the lotus-bud;

The moon its rise from ocean takes;
And gems proceed from hoods of snakes;
From cows' bile yellow dyestuffs come;
And fire in wood is quite at home:
The worthy, by display of worth,
Attain distinction, not by birth.

And again:

Kill, although domestic born,
  Any hurtful mouse:
Bribe an alien cat who will
  Help to clean the house.

And once again:

How use the faithful, lacking power?
  Or strong, who evil do?
But me, O King, you should not scorn,
  For I am strong and true.

Scorn not the wise who penetrate
  Truth's universal law;
They are not men to be restrained
  By money's petty straw:
When beauty glistens on their cheeks
  By trickling ichor lent,
Bull-elephants feel lotus-chains
  As no impediment."

"Oh," said Rusty, "you must not say such things. You are our counselor's son, an old retainer." "O King," said Victor, "there is something that should be said." And the king replied: "My good fellow, reveal what is in your heart."

Then Victor began: "My master set out to take water. Why did he turn back and camp here?" And

Rusty, concealing his inner feelings, said: "Victor, it just happened so." "O King," said the jackal, "if it is not a thing to disclose, then let it be.

> Some things a man should tell his wife,
> Some things to friend and some to son;
> All these are trusted. He should not
> Tell everything to everyone."

Hereupon Rusty reflected: "He seems trustworthy. I will tell him what I have in mind. For the proverb says:

> You find repose, in sore disaster,
> By telling things to powerful master,
> To honest servant, faithful friend,
> Or wife who loves you till the end.

Friend Victor, did you hear a great voice in the distance?" "Yes, master, I did," said Victor. "What of it?"

And Rusty continued: "My good fellow, I intend to leave this forest." "Why?" said Victor. "Because," said Rusty, "there has come into our forest some prodigious creature, from whom we hear this great voice. His nature must correspond to his voice, and his power to his nature."

"What!" said Victor. "Is our master frightened by a mere voice? You know the proverb:

> Water undermines the dikes;
> Love dissolves when malice strikes;
> Secrets melt when babblings start;
> Simple words melt dastard hearts.

So it would be improper if our master abruptly left the forest which was won by his ancestors and has been so long in the family. For they say:

> Wisely move one foot; the other
> Should its vantage hold;
> Till assured of some new dwelling,
> Do not leave the old.

"Besides, many kinds of sounds are heard here. Yet they are nothing but noises, not a warning of danger. For example, we hear the sounds made by thunder, wind among the reeds, lutes, drums, tambourines, conch-shells, bells, wagons, banging doors, machines, and other things. They are nothing to be afraid of. As the verse says:

> If a king be brave, however
> Fierce the foe and grim,
> Sorrows of humiliation
> Do not wait for him.

And again:

> Bravest bosoms do not falter,
> Fearing heaven's threat:
> Summer dries the pools; the Indus
> Rises, greater yet.

And once again:

> Mothers bear on rare occasions
> To the world a chief,
> Glad in luck and brave in battle,
> Undepressed in grief.

And yet again:

> Do not act as does the grass-blade.
> Lacking honest pride,

Drooping low in feeble meanness,
Lightly brushed aside.

My master must take this point of view and reinforce his resolution, not fear a mere sound. As the saying goes:

I thought at first that it was full
Of fat; I crept within
And there I did not find a thing
Except some wood and skin."

"How was that?" asked Rusty. And Victor told the story of

THE JACKAL AND THE WAR-DRUM

In a certain region was a jackal whose throat was pinched by hunger. While wandering in search of food, he came upon a king's battle ground in the midst of a forest. And as he lingered a moment there, he heard a great sound.

This sound troubled his heart exceedingly, so that he fell into deep dejection and said: "Ah me! Disaster is upon me. I am as good as dead already. Who made that sound? What kind of a creature?"

But on peering about, he spied a war-drum that loomed like a mountain-peak, and he thought: "Was that sound its natural voice, or was it induced from without?" Now when the drum was struck by the tips of grasses swaying in the wind, it made the sound, but was dumb at other times.

So he recognized its helplessness, and crept quite near. Indeed, his curiosity led him to strike it himself on both heads, and he became gleeful at the thought: "Aha! After long waiting food comes even to me. For this is sure to be stuffed with meat and fat."

Having come to this conclusion, he picked a spot, gnawed a hole, and crept in. And though the leather covering was tough, still he had the luck not to break his teeth. But he was disappointed to find it pure wood and skin, and recited a stanza:

> Its voice was fierce; I thought it stuffed
> With fat, so crept within;
> And there I did not find a thing
> Except some wood and skin.

So he backed out, laughing to himself, and said:

> I thought at first that it was full
> Of fat, ...

and the rest of it.

"And that is why I say that one should not be troubled by a mere sound." "But," said Rusty, "these retainers of mine are terrified and wish to run away. So how am I to reinforce my resolution?" And Victor answered: "Master, they are not to blame. For servants take after the master. You know the proverb:

> In case of horse or book or sword,
> Of woman, man or lute or word,
> The use or uselessness depends
> On qualities the user lends.

"Then summon your manhood and remain on this spot until I return, having ascertained the nature of the creature. Then act as seems proper." "What!" said Rusty, "are you plucky enough to go there?" And Victor answered: "When the master commands, is there any difference between 'possible' and 'impossible' to the good servant? As the proverb says:

> Good servants, when their lords command,
> Behold no fear on any hand,
> Cross pathless seas if he desire
> Or gladly enter flaming fire.
>
> The servant who, his lord commanding,
> Should strive to reach an understanding
> On labors hard or easy, he
> King's counselor should never be."

"If you feel so, my dear fellow," said Rusty, "then go. Blest be your journeyings."

So Victor bowed low and set out in the direction of the sound made by Lively. And when he was gone, terror troubled Rusty's heart, so that he thought: "Ah, I made a sad mistake in trusting him to the point of revealing what is in my mind. Perhaps this Victor will betray me by taking wages from both parties, or from spite at losing his job. For the proverb says:

> A servant suffering from a king
> Dishonor after honoring,
> Though born and trained to service, will
> Be eager to destroy him still.

"So I will go elsewhere and wait, in order to learn his purpose. Perhaps Victor might even bring the thing along and try to kill me. As the saying goes:

> The trustful strong are caught
> By weaker foes with ease;
> The wary weak are safe
> From strongest enemies."

Thus he set his mind in order, went elsewhere, and waited all alone, spying on Victor's procedure.

Meanwhile Victor drew near to Lively, discovered that he was a bull, and reflected gleefully: "Well, well! This is lucky. I shall get Rusty into my power by dangling before him war or peace with this fellow. As the proverb puts it:

> All counselors draw profit from
> A king in worries pent,
> And that is why they always wish
> For him, embarrassment.

> As men in health require no drug
> Their vigor to restore,
> So kings, relieved of worry, seek
> Their counselors no more."

With these thoughts in mind, he returned to meet Rusty. And Rusty, seeing him coming, assumed his former attitude in an effort to put a good face on the matter. So when Victor had come near, had bowed low, and had seated himself, Rusty said: "My good fellow, did you see the creature?" "I saw him," said Victor, "through my master's grace." "Are you telling the truth?" asked Rusty. And Victor answered: "How could I report anything else to my gracious master? For the proverb says:

> Whoever makes before a king
> Small statements, but untrue,
> Brings certain ruin on his gods
> And on his teacher, too.

And again:

> The king incarnates all the gods,
> So sing the sages old;
> Then treat him like the gods: to him
> Let nothing false be told.

And once again:

> The king incarnates all the gods,
> Yet with a difference:
> He pays for good or ill at once;
> The gods, a lifetime hence."

"Yes," said Rusty, "I suppose you really did see him. The great do not become angry with the mean. As the proverb says:

> The hurricane innocuous passes
> O'er feeble, lowly bending grasses,
> But tears at lofty trees: the great
> Their prowess greatly demonstrate."

And Victor replied: "I knew beforehand that my master would speak thus. So why waste words? I will bring the creature into my gracious master's presence." And when Rusty heard this, joy overspread his lotus-face, and his mind felt supreme satisfaction.

Meanwhile Victor returned and called reproachfully to Lively: "Come here, you villainous bull! Come here! Our master Rusty asks why you are not afraid to keep up this meaningless bellowing." And Lively answered: "My good fellow, who is this person named Rusty?"

"What!" said Victor, "you do not even know our master Rusty?" And he continued with indignation: "The consequences will teach you. He has a retinue of all kinds of animals. He dwells beside the spreading banyan tree. His heart is high with pride. He is lord of life and wealth. His name is Rusty. He is a mighty lion."

When Lively heard this, he thought himself as good as dead, and he fell into deep dejection, saying: "My dear fellow, you appear to be sympathetic and eloquent. So if you cannot avoid conducting me there, pray cause the master to grant me a gracious safe-conduct." "You are quite right," said Victor. "Your request shows *savoir faire*. For

The earth has a limit,
  The mountains, the sea;
The deep thoughts of kings are
  Without boundary.

Do you then remain in this spot. Later, when I have held him to an agreement, I will conduct you to him."

Then Victor returned to Rusty and said: "Master, he is no ordinary creature. He has served as the vehicle of blessèd Shiva. And when I questioned him, he said: 'Great Shiva was satisfied with me and bade me crop the grass beside the Jumna. Why make a long story of it? The blessèd one has given me this forest as a playground.' "

At this Rusty was frightened, and he said: "I knew it, I knew it. Only by special favor of the gods do creatures wander in a wild wood, bellowing like that, and fearlessly cropping the grass. But what did you say?"

"Master," said Victor, "I said: 'This forest is the domain of Rusty, vehicle of Shiva's passionate wife. Hence you come as a guest. You must meet him, must spend your time in brotherly love, must eat, drink, work, play, and make your home with him.' All this he promised, adding: 'You must make your master grant me a safe-conduct.' As to that, the master is the sole judge."

At this Rusty was delighted and said: "Splendid, my intelligent servant, splendid! You must have taken counsel with my own heart before speaking. I grant him a safe-conduct. You must hasten to conduct him here, but not until he too has bound himself by oath toward me. Yes, there is sound sense in the saying:

> Polished, fully tested,
> Sturdy too, and straight
> Are the pillars proper
> To a house—or state.

Again:

> Wit is shown in hours of crisis:
> Doctors' wit, in sore disease;

Counselors', in patching friendship—
All are wise in hours of ease."

Now Victor thought, as he set out to meet Lively: "Well, well! The master is gracious to me and ready to do my bidding. So there is none more blest than I. For

Four things are nectar: milky food;
A fire in chilly weather;
An honor granted by the king;
And loved ones, come together."

So he found Lively, and said respectfully: "My friend, I won the old master's favor for you, and made him give you a safe-conduct. You may go without anxiety. Still, though you have favor in the eyes of the king, you must act in agreement with me. You must not play the haughty master. I for my part, in alliance with you, will take the rôle of counselor, and bear the whole burden of administration. Thus we shall both enjoy royal affluence. For

A sinful chase—yet men can stalk
The treasures of the crown:
One starts the quarry from its lair;
Another strikes it down.

And again:

Whoever is too haughty to
Pay king's retainers honor due,
Will find his feet are tottering—
So merchant Strong-Tooth with the king."

"How was that?" asked Lively. And Victor told the story of

MERCHANT STRONG-TOOTH

There is a city called Growing City on the earth's surface. In it lived a merchant named Strong-Tooth who directed the whole administration. So long as he handled city business and royal business, all the inhabitants were satisfied. Why spin it out? Nobody ever saw or heard of his like for cleverness. For there is much wisdom in the proverb:

> Suppose he minds the king's affairs,
>   The common people hate him;
> And if he plays the democrat,
>   The prince will execrate him:
> So, since the struggling interests
>   Are wholly contradictory,
> A manager is hard to find
>   Who gives them both the victory.

While he occupied this position, he once had a daughter married. To the wedding he invited all the townspeople and the king's entourage, paid them much honor, feasted them, and regaled them with gifts of garments and the like. And when the wedding was over, he conducted the king home with his ladies and showed him reverence.

Now the king had a house-cleaning drudge named Bull, who took a seat that did not belong to him—this in the very palace, and in the presence of the king's professor. So Strong-Tooth administered a cuffing and drove him out. From that moment the humiliation so rankled in Bull's inner soul that he had no rest even at night. Yet he thought: "After all, why should I grow thin? It does me no good. For I cannot possibly hurt him. And there is sense in the saying:

> Indulge no angry, shameless wish
> To hurt, unless you can:
> The chick-pea, hopping up and down,
> Will crack no frying-pan."

Now one morning, as he was sweeping near the bed where the king lay half awake, he said: "What impudence! Strong-Tooth kisses the queen." When the king heard this, he jumped up in a hurry, crying: "Come, come, Bull! Is that thing true that you were muttering? Has the queen been kissed by Strong-Tooth?"

"O King," answered Bull, "I was awake all night because I am passionately fond of gambling. So sleep overpowered me even when I was busy with my sweeping. I do not know what I said."

But the jealous king thought: "Yes, he has free entrance to my palace. So has Strong-Tooth. Perhaps he actually saw the fellow hugging the queen. For the proverb says:

> Whate'er a man desires, sees, does
> In broad daylight,
> Still mindful, he will say or do
> Asleep at night.

And again:

> Whatever secrets, good or ill,
> Men in their bosoms keep,
> Are soon betrayed when they are drunk
> Or talking in their sleep.

In any case, what doubt can there be where a woman is concerned?

> With one she tries the gossip's art;
>   Her glances with a second flirt;
> She holds another in her heart:
>   Whom does she love enough to hurt?

And again:

> The logs will glut the hungry fire,
> The rivers glut the sea's desire,
> And Death with life be glutted, when
> The flirt has had enough of men.

> No chance, no corner dark,
>   No man to woo;
> Then, holy sage, you find
>   A woman true.

And once again:

> The blunderhead who thinks:
>   'My love loves me,'
> Is ever in her power;
>   A tame bird, he."

After all this lamentation, he withdrew his favor forthwith from Strong-Tooth. Not to make a long story of it, he forbade his entrance at court.

When Strong-Tooth saw that the monarch's favor was suddenly withdrawn, he thought: "Ah me! There is wisdom in the stanza:

> Whom does not fortune render proud?
>   Whom does not death lay low?
> To what *roué* do passions not
>   Bring never ceasing woe?

What beggar can be dignified?
  Whose heart no woman stings?
Who, trapped by scamps, comes safely off?
  Who is beloved of kings?

And again:

Who ever saw or heard
A gambler's truthful word,
A neat and cleanly crow,
A woman going slow
In love, a kindly snake,
A eunuch's pluck awake,
A drunkard's love of science,
A king in friends' alliance?

And yet I never committed an unfriendly act against the king—or anyone else—not even in a dream, not even by mere words. So why does the king withdraw his favor from me?"

Now one day Bull, the sweeper, saw Strong-Tooth stopped at the palace gate, and he laughed aloud, saying to the doorkeepers: "Be careful, doorkeepers! This fellow Strong-Tooth's temper has been spoiled by the king's favor and he dispenses arrests and releases. If you stop him, you will get a cuffing, just like me."

And Strong-Tooth reflected on hearing this: "I see. It was Bull's doing. Well, there is sense in the proverb:

Though foolish, base, and lacking pride,
A servant at the monarch's side
Will have his honor satisfied.

Though fashioned on a cowardly plan
And mean, a royal servant can
Resent affronts from any man."

After this lamentation he went home, abashed and deeply stirred. Then he summoned Bull in the evening, gave him two garments as an honorable present, and said: "My good fellow, I did not drive you out by order of the king. It was because I saw you, in the chaplain's presence, sitting where you did not belong, that I humiliated you."

Now Bull received the two garments as if they were the Kingdom of Heaven, and feeling intense satisfaction, he said: "Friend merchant, I forgive you. You will soon see the reward of the honor shown me in the king's favor and such things." With this he departed in high glee. For there is wisdom in the saying:

A little thing will lift him high,
A little make him fall:
'Twixt balance-beam and scamp there is
No difference at all.

On the next day Bull entered the palace, and did his sweeping. And while the king lay half awake, he said: "What intelligence! When our king sits at stool, he eats a cucumber."

Now the king, hearing this, rose in amazement and said: "Come, come, Bull! What twaddle is this? But I remember that you are a house-servant and do not kill you. Did you ever see me engaged in that occupation?"

"O King," said Bull, "I was awake all night because I am passionately fond of gambling. So drowsiness overcame me in the very act of doing my sweeping. I do not know what I was muttering. Pardon me, master. I was really asleep."

Then the king thought: "Why, from the day of my birth I never ate a cucumber while engaged in that occupation. And since this blockhead has talked unimaginable nonsense about me, it must be the same with Strong-Tooth. This being so, I made a mistake in taking the poor man's honors from him. Nothing of the sort is conceivable with such men. And in his absence all the king's business and city business is at loose ends."

After thus considering the matter from every point of view, he summoned Strong-Tooth, presented him with gems from his own person and with garments, and reinstated him.

"And that is why I say:

> Whoever is too haughty to
> Pay king's retainers honor due, ...

and the rest of it." "My dear fellow," said Lively, "your argument is quite convincing. Let it be as you say."

After this Victor took him to Rusty and said: "O King, here is Lively. I have brought him hither. The future rests with the king." Then Lively bowed respectfully and stood before the king in a modest attitude. Thereupon Rusty extended over him a right paw plump, firm, massive, adorned with claws as formidable as thunderbolts, and said with deference: "Do you enjoy health? Why do you dwell in this wild wood?"

Thus questioned, Lively related accurately his separation from merchant Increase and the others. And Rusty, after listening to the story, said: "Have no fear, comrade. Protected by my paws, lead your own life in this forest. Furthermore, you must always take your amusements in my vicinity. For this forest has many drawbacks, since it swarms with numerous savage creatures." And Lively made answer: "Very well, O King."

Then the king of beasts went down to the bank of the Jumna, drank and bathed his fill, and plunged again into the forest, wherever inclination led him.

Thus the time passed, the mutual affection of the two increasing daily. Now Lively had assimilated solid intelligence by mastering numerous authoritative works, so that in a very few days he planted discernment in Rusty, dull as was his mind. He weaned him from forest habits and taught him village manners. Why spin it out? Lively and Rusty did nothing but hold secret confabulations every day.

This being so, all the other animals of the retinue were kept at a distance. As for the two jackals, they did not even have the entrée. More than that, as soon as they lacked the lion's prowess, the whole company of animals, not excluding the two jackals, suffered grievously from hunger and huddled together. As the proverb puts it:

> A king, though proud and pure of birth,
>   Will see his servants flee
> A court where no rewards are won,
>   As birds a withered tree.

And again:

> They may be honored gentlemen,
>   They may devoted be,
> Yet servants leave a monarch who
>   Forgets the salary.

While, on the other hand:

> A king may scold
> Yet servants hold,
> If he but pay
> Upon the day.

Indeed, all the creatures in this world, adopting cajolery or one of the other three devices, live by eating one another. For example:

> Some eat the countries; these are kings;
> The doctors, those whom sickness stings;
> The merchants, those who buy their things;
>   And learnèd men, the fools.
>
> The married are the clergy's meat;
> The thieves devour the indiscreet;
> The flirts their eager lovers eat;
>   And Labor eats us all.
>
> They keep deceitful snares in play;
> They lie in wait by night and day;

And when occasion offers, prey
Like fish on lesser fish.

Now Cheek and Victor, robbed of their master's favor, took counsel together—for their throats were pinched with hunger. And Victor said: "Cheek, my noble friend, we two seem to have lost our job. For Rusty takes such delight in Lively's conversation that he neglects his business. And the whole court is scattered every which way. What is to be done?"

And Cheek replied: "Even if the master does not take your advice, still you should admonish him to correct his faults. For the proverb says:

Good counselors should warn a king
Although he pay no heed
(As Vidur warned the monarch blind)
To cease from evil deed.

And again:

Good counselors or drivers may not duck
From kings or elephants that run amuck.

Besides, in introducing this grass-nibbler to the master you were handling live coals." And Victor answered: "You are right. The fault is mine, not the master's. As the saying goes:

The jackal at the ram-fight;
And we, when tricked by June;
The meddling friend—were playing
A self-defeating tune."

"How was that?" asked Cheek. And Victor told three stories in one, called

GODLY AND JUNE

In a certain district there was a monastery in a secluded spot. In it lived a holy man named Godly, who in course of time acquired a great sum of money by selling finely woven garments, the numerous offerings of the faithful for whom he performed sacrifices. As a result, he trusted no man, and kept his treasure under his arm by night and day. For there is wisdom in the proverb:

> Money causes pain in getting;
> In the keeping, pain and fretting;
> Pain in loss and pain in spending:
> Damn the trouble never ending!

Now a rogue named June, who took other people's money from them, observed the treasure under his arm, and reflected: "How am I to take this treasure from him? In the first place, I cannot pierce the wall of the cell, which is compactly built of solid stone. And I cannot enter the door, which is too high. I will talk to him, win his confidence, and become his disciple, for he will be in my power when I have his confidence. As the proverb says:

> None lacking shrewdness flatter well;
> None but a lover plays the swell;
> No saints are found in judgment seats;
> No clear, straightforward speaker cheats."

Having thus made up his mind, he drew near to Godly, uttered the words: "Glory to Shiva. Amen," fell flat on his face, and spoke with deference: "O holy sir! All life is vanity. Youth slips by like a mountain torrent. The days of our life are like a fire in chaff. Delights of the flesh are as the shadow of a cloud. Union with son, friend, servant, wife, is but a dream. All this I discern clearly. What shall I do that I may safely cross the sea of many lives?"

On hearing this, Godly said respectfully: "My son, blest are you, being thus indifferent to the world in early youth. What says the proverb?

> 'Tis only saints in youth
> That can be saints in truth:
> Ah, who is not a saint
> When ebbing passions faint?

And again:

> First mind, then body ages
> In case of holy sages:
> The body ages first,
> Mind never, in the worst.

"And as for your search to find a means of safely crossing the sea of many lives, just listen to this:

> A hangman with his matted hair,
> Or serf, or other man, through prayer
> To holy Shiva, changes caste,
> Becomes pure Brahman at the last.
>
> Six syllables, a little prayer;
> A single blossom resting there
> On Shiva's symbol—and on earth
> No further pain, no later birth."

When he had listened to this, June clasped the holy man's feet and said deferentially: "This being so, holy sir, pray do me the favor of imposing a vow."

"My son," answered Godly, "I am ready to oblige you. But you must not enter my cell by night. For renunciation is recommended to ascetics, to you and to me as well. As the proverb puts it:

Ascetics come to grief through greed;
And kings, who evil counsels heed;
Children through petting, wives through wine,
Through wicked sons a noble line;
A Brahman through unstudied books,
A character through haunting crooks;
A farm is ruined through neglect;
And friendship, lacking kind respect;
Love dies through absence; fortunes crash
Through naughtiness; and hoarded cash
Through carelessness or giving rash.

So, after taking the vow, you must sleep in a hut of thatch at the monastery gate."

"Holy sir," said the other, "your prescription is the law of my life. I shall need it in the next world." So, the sleeping arrangements being made, Godly graciously gave him initiation and granted discipleship. June for his part made the holy man very happy by rubbing his hands and feet, bringing writing-paper, and other services. Still, Godly kept his treasure under his arm.

As the time passed in this manner, June reflected: "Dear me! Do what I will, he does not trust me. So shall I kill him with a knife in broad daylight? Or give him poison? Or butcher him like a beast?"

While he was reflecting thus, the son of a pupil of Godly's came from the village, bearing an invitation.

And he said: "Holy sir, pray come to my house for the ceremony of the sacred thread." And when Godly heard this, he started with June.

Now as he traveled, he came to a river, seeing which he took the treasure from under his arm, wrapped it carefully in his patched ascetic robe, worshiped the appropriate gods, and said to June: "June, I must step aside. Please keep careful watch of this robe and of the necessary until I return." With these words he moved away. And as soon as he was out of sight, June seized the treasure and decamped.

THE JACKAL AT THE RAM-FIGHT

Now Godly sat down perfectly carefree, for his disciple's countless virtues had lulled his suspicions. As he rested, he saw a herd of rams, and two of them fighting. These two would angrily draw apart and dash together, their slablike foreheads crashing so that blood flowed freely. This spectacle attracted a jackal whose soul was in the fetters of carnivorous desire, and he stood between the two, lapping up the blood.

When Godly observed this, he thought: "Well, well! This is a dull-witted jackal. If he happens to be between just when they crash, he will certainly meet death. This inference seems inescapable to me."

Now the next time, being greedy as ever to lap up the blood, the jackal did not move away, was caught between the crashing heads, and was killed. Then

Godly said: "The jackal at the ram-fight," and grieving for him, started to resume his treasure.

He returned in no haste, but when he failed to find June, he hurried through a ceremony of purification, then examined his robe. Finding the treasure gone, he fell to the ground in a swoon, murmuring: "Oh, oh! I am robbed." In a moment he came to himself, rose again, and started to scream: "June, June! Where did you go after cheating me? Give me answer!" With this repeated lamentation he moved slowly on, picking up his disciple's tracks and muttering: "And we, when tricked by June."

THE WEAVER'S WIFE

Now as he walked along, Godly spied a weaver who with his wife was on his way to a neighboring city for liquor to drink, and he called out: "Look here, my good fellow! I come to you a guest, brought by the evening sun. I do not know a soul in the village. Let me receive the treatment due a guest. For the proverb says:

> No stranger may be turned aside
> Who seeks your door at eventide;
> Nay, honor him and you shall be
> Transmuted into deity.

And again:

> Some straw, a floor, and water,
> With kindly words beside:
> These four are never wanting
> Where pious folk abide.

And once again:

> The sacred fires by kindly word
> And Indra by the chair is stirred,
> Krishna by water for the feet,
> The Lord of All by things to eat."

On hearing this, the weaver said to his wife: "Go, my dear. Take this guest to the house. Treat him hospitably, giving him water for the feet, food, a bed, and so on. And stay in the house yourself. I will bring plenty of wine and meat for you." With this he went farther.

So the wife started home with Godly, and she showed a laughing countenance, for she was a whore and had a certain swain in mind. Indeed, there is sense in the verse:

> When night is dark
> And dark the day,
> When streets are mired
> With sticky clay,
> When husband lingers
> Far away,
> The flirt becomes
> Supremely gay.
>
> The wench cares not
> A straw to miss
> The covered couch,
> The husband's kiss,
> The pleasant bed;
> In place of this
> She ever seeks
> A stolen bliss.

And again:

For stranger men
  The slut will see
The ruin of
  Her family,
The world's reproach,
  The jailer's key—
Will risk a death
  She cannot flee.

Then she went home, offered Godly a rickety cot and said: "My holy sir, a woman friend has come from the village and I must speak to her. I will be back directly. Meanwhile, you may stay in our house. But please be careful." With this she put on her best things and started to find her swain.

At this moment she ran into her husband, clasping a jug of wine. He was reeling drunk, his hair was towsled, and he stumbled at every step. She ran when she saw him, entered the house, took off her finery, and appeared as usual.

Now the weaver had seen her flee, had observed the finery, and since he had previously heard the gossip that went the rounds about her, his heart was troubled and anger overcame him. So he entered the house and said: "You wench! You whore! Where were you going?"

And she replied: "I have not been out since I left you. What is this drunken twaddle? There is sense in the proverb:

After wine and fever, these
  Selfsame symptoms come:

Shaking, falling to the ground,
  Mad delirium.

And again:

The setting sun and drunken man
  Are both a fiery red;
They sink in naked helplessness;
  Their dignity is dead."

When he had taken the scolding and had noticed her change of dress, he said: "Whore! I have heard gossip about you for a long time. Today I have seen the proof. I am going to give you what you deserve." So he beat her limp with a club, tied her firmly to a post, and fell into a drunken slumber.

At this juncture her friend, the barber's wife, learning that the weaver was asleep, came in and said: "My dear, he is waiting for you over there—you know who. Go at once." But the weaver's wife replied: "Just see what a fix I am in. How can I go? You must return and tell my adorer that I cannot possibly meet him there at this moment."

"My dear," said the barber's wife, "do not say things like that. For a wench of spirit this is no way to behave. As the saying goes:

Those who earn the name of blessèd
  Show a camel-like persistence
When they pluck the fruit of pleasure,
  Counting neither toil nor distance.

And again:

As the other world is doubtful
  And as scandal misses truth,

When you've hooked another's lover,
Best enjoy the fruit of youth.

And once again:

Fate may rob him of his manhood,
He may handsome be or ugly,
Yet a wench, whate'er it cost her,
Entertains her lover snugly."

"Very fine indeed," said the weaver's wife. "But tell me how I am to go when I am tied fast. And here lies my husband—the brute!" "My dear," said the barber's wife, "he is helpless with drink and will not wake until the sun's rays reach him. I will set you free and take your place myself. But you must hurry back when you have entertained your admirer."

This she did, and a moment later the weaver rose a little mollified, and said drunkenly: "Come, you nagger! If you will stay at home after today and stop nagging, I will set you free." The barber's wife said nothing, fearing that her voice would betray her. Even when he repeated his offer, she made no answer. Then he became angry and cut off her nose with a sharp knife. And he said: "Whore! Now you can stay there. I shall not be nice to you again." So he fell asleep, muttering. Now Godly, having lost his money, was so tormented by hunger that he could not sleep, and was a witness of all that the women did.

Presently the weaver's wife, after enjoying the full delight of love with her swain, came home and said to the barber's wife: "Well, are you all right? I hope that brute did not get up while I was gone."

And the barber's wife answered: "The rest of me is all right. But I've lost my nose. Set me free quick, before he wakes up. I want to go home. If not, he will do something worse next time, cut off ears and things."

So the wench freed the barber's wife, took her former position, and cried reproachfully: "Oh, you dreadful simpleton! I am a true wife, a model of faithfulness. What man is able to violate or disfigure me? Listen, ye guardian deities of the world!

> Earth, heaven, and death, the feeling mind,
> Sun, moon, and water, fire and wind,
> Both twilights, justice, day and night
> Discern man's conduct, wrong or right.

So, if I am a faithful wife, may these gods make my nose grow again as it was before. More than that, if I have had so much as a secret desire for a strange man, may they reduce me to ashes."

After this explosion, she said to him directly: "Look, you villain! By virtue of my faithfulness my nose has grown as it was before." And when he took a torch and examined her, he found her nose as it was originally, and a great pool of blood on the floor. At this he was amazed, released her from the cords, and flattered her with a hundred wheedling endearments.

Now Godly had seen the whole business. And he was amazed and said:

> "Learn science with the gods above
> Or imps in nether space,

Yet women's wit will rival it:
   How keep them in their place?

Behold the faults with woman born:
Impurity, and heartless scorn,
Untruth, and folly, reckless heat,
Excessive greediness, deceit.

Be not enslaved by women's charm,
Nor wish them growth in power to harm:
Their slaves, of manly feeling stripped,
Are tame, pet crows whose wings are clipped.

Honey in a woman's words,
   Poison in her breast:
So, although you taste her lip,
   Drub her on the chest.

This palace filled with vice, this field where sprouts
Suspicion's crop, this whirling pool of doubts,
This town of recklessness, sin's aggregate,
This house where frauds by hundreds lie in wait,
This basketful of riddling sham and quip
O'er guessing which our best and bravest trip,
This woman, this machine, this nectar-bane—
Who set it here, to make religion vain?

A bosom hard is praised, a forehead low,
A fickle glance, a mumbling speech and slow,
Thick hips, a heart that constant tremors move,
A natural twist in hair, and twists in love.
Their virtues are a pack of vices. Then
Let beasts adore the fawn-eyed things, not men.

For reasons good they laugh or weep;
They trust you not, your trust they keep:
These graveyard urns, oh, haunt them not!
Keep kin and conduct free from spot.

The lion o'er whose awful face
  Falls fierce the towsled mane,
The elephant upon whose cheeks
  Streams ichor's glistening rain,
The men of wit or courage who
  In books or battles gleam,
In presence of their females, all
  Turn into cowards supreme.

And once more:

This gunja-fruit (oh, what was God about?)
Is poisonous within, and sweet without."

In these meditations the night dragged drearily for the holy man. Meanwhile the go-between went home with her nose cut off, and reflected: "What is to be done now? How is this great deficiency to be concealed?"

The night during which she pondered thus, her husband spent in the king's palace, practicing his trade. At dawn he came home and, being eager to begin his thriving business with the townspeople, he stopped at the door and called to her: "My dear, bring me my razor-case at once. The townspeople need my services."

Hereupon an idea occurred to the noseless woman. She remained in the house, but sent him a single razor. And the barber, angry because the entire case had not been delivered, flung the razor in her direction. This gave the wench her opportunity. Lifting her hands to heaven, she dashed from the house, screaming with all her might: "Oh, oh, oh! The ruffian! I was always a faithful wife. Look! He cut off my nose. Save me, save me!"

Hereupon the police arrived, thrashed the barber limp, tied him fast, and took him to court with his wife whose nose was gone. And the judges asked him: "Why did you do this ghastly thing to your wife?" Then, his wits being so addled by astonishment that he could give no answer, the jurymen quoted law:

"The guilty man is terrified
By reason of his crime. His pride
Is gone, his powers of speaking fail,
His glances rove, his face is pale.

And again:

The sweat appears upon his brow,
He stumbles on, he knows not how,
His face is pale, and all he utters
Is much distorted; for he stutters.

The culprit always may be found
To shake, and gaze upon the ground:
Observe the signs as best you can
And shrewdly pick the guilty man.

While, on the other hand:

The innocent is self-reliant;
His speech is clear, his glance defiant;
His countenance is calm and free;
His indignation makes his plea.

The prisoner is obviously guilty. The legal penalty for assaulting a woman is death. Let him be impaled."

But Godly, seeing him led to the place of execution, went to the officers of justice and said: "Gentlemen, you make a mistake in putting this wretched barber to death. His conduct has been correct. Pray listen to these words of mine:

> The jackal at the ram-fight;
> And we, when tricked by June;
> The meddling friend—were playing
> A self-defeating tune."

So the officers said: "How was that, holy sir?" Then Godly related to them the three stories, complete in every detail. And they were all astonished as they listened. They set the barber free, and said:

> "Slay not a woman, Brahman, child,
> An invalid or hermit mild:
> In case of major dereliction,
> Disfigurement is the infliction.

Now she has lost her nose through her own act. As additional punishment from the king, let her ears be cut off." When this had been done, Godly, strengthening his spirit by the two examples, returned to his own monastery.

"And that is why I say:

> The jackal at the ram-fight, ...

and the rest of it."

"Well," said Cheek, "such being the case, what are you and I to do?" And Victor answered: "Even in these circumstances, I shall have a flash of intelligence, showing me how to separate Lively from the king. Besides, he has fallen into serious vice, has our master Rusty. For

Mad folly stings
The greatest kings,
  Who then embrace a vice;
But servants' care
Should check them there
  By means of learning nice."

"Into what vice has our master Rusty fallen?" asked Cheek. And Victor replied: "There are seven vices in the world, namely:

Drink, women, hunting, scolding, dice,
Greed, cruelty: these seven are vice.

These, however, really make a single vice, called 'attachment,' with seven subdivisions." Then Cheek inquired: "Is there only a single fundamental vice, or are there others also?"

And Victor expounded: "There are in the world five situations fundamentally vicious." And when Cheek asked: "How are they differentiated?" Victor continued: "They are called: (1) deficiency, (2) corruption, (3) attachment, (4) devastation, (5) mistaken policy.

"To begin at the beginning, the vice called 'deficiency' means the non-existence of one or another of these: king, counselor, people, fortress, treasure, punitive power, friends.

"Secondly, when subjects, whether foreign or native, become restless, whether individually or *en masse*, there arises the vicious situation called 'corruption.'

" 'Attachment' was explained above, in the words:

Drink, women, hunting, ...

and the rest of it. Here there is a love-group (drink, women, hunting, dice) and a wrath-group (scolding, and the rest). A man thwarted in the love-group becomes obnoxious to the wrath-group. The love-group requires no elucidation. The wrath-group, however, threefold as already described, needs some further characterization. 'Scolding' is ill-considered imputation of fault on the part of one bent on injuring an antagonist. 'Cruelty' means ruthless and unwarranted refinements in putting to death, imprisonment, mutilation. 'Greed' is covetousness pushed to a merciless point. These are the seven subdivisions of the vice of attachment.

"Next, there are eight kinds of devastation: by act of God, fire, water, disease, plague, panic, famine, devil-rain (which is a mere name for excessive rain). This disposes of the vice called 'devastation.'

"Finally, there is mistaken policy. Where a man makes a mistaken use of the six expedients—peace, war, change of base, entrenchment, alliance, duplicity—adopting war instead of peace, or peace instead of war, or making similar mistakes in regard to the other expedients, there we have the vice of mistaken policy.

"Now our master Rusty has fallen into the very first vice, that of deficiency. For he has been so captivated by Lively that he pays not the smallest heed to counselor or any other of the six supports of his throne. He adopts rather completely a vegetarian morality. So what is the use of a lengthy discussion? Rusty must by all means be detached from Lively. No lamp, no light."

"How will you detach him?" objected Cheek. "You have not the power." "My dear fellow," said Victor, "there is a verse to fit the situation, namely:

> In cases where brute force would fail,
> A shrewd device may still prevail:
> The crow-hen used a golden chain,
> And so the dreadful snake was slain."

"How was that?" asked Cheek. And Victor told

HOW THE CROW-HEN KILLED THE BLACK SNAKE

In a certain region grew a great banyan tree. In it lived a crow and his wife, occupying the nest which they had built. But a black snake crawled through the hollow trunk and ate their chicks as fast as they were born, even before baptism. Yet for all his sorrow over this violence, the poor crow could not desert the old familiar banyan and seek another tree. For

> Three cannot be induced to go—
> The deer, the cowardly man, the crow:
> Three go when insult makes them pant—
> The lion, hero, elephant.

At last the crow-hen fell at her husband's feet and said: "My dear lord, a great many children of mine have been eaten by that awful snake. And grief for my loved and lost haunts me until I think of moving. Let us make our home in some other tree. For

> No friend like health abounding;
> And like disease, no foe;
> No love like love of children;
> Like hunger-pangs, no woe.

And again:

> With fields o'erhanging rivers,
> With wife on flirting bent,
> Or in a house with serpents,
> No man can be content.

We are living in deadly peril."

At this the crow was dreadfully depressed, and he said: "We have lived in this tree a long time, my dear. We cannot desert it. For

> Where water may be sipped, and grass
> Be cropped, a deer might live content;
> Yet insult will not drive him from
> The wood where all his life was spent.

Moreover, by some shrewd device I will bring death upon this villainous and mighty foe."

"But," said his wife, "this is a terribly venomous snake. How will you hurt him?" And he replied: "My dear, even if I have not the power to hurt him, still I have friends who possess learning, who have mastered the works on ethics. I will go and get from them some shrewd device of such nature that the villain—curse him!—will soon meet his doom."

After this indignant speech he went at once to another tree, under which lived a dear friend, a jackal. He courteously called the jackal forth, related all his sorrow, then said: "My friend, what do you consider opportune under the circumstances? The killing of our children is sheer death to my wife and me."

"My friend," said the jackal, "I have thought the matter through. You need not put yourself out. That villainous black snake is near his doom by reason of his heartless cruelty. For

> Of means to injure brutal foes
> You do not need to think,
> Since of themselves they fall, like trees
> Upon the river's brink.

And there is a story:

> A heron ate what fish he could,
> The bad, indifferent, and good;
> His greed was never satisfied
> Till, strangled by a crab, he died."

"How was that?" asked the crow. And the jackal told the story of

THE HERON THAT LIKED CRAB-MEAT

There was once a heron in a certain place on the edge of a pond. Being old, he sought an easy way of catching fish on which to live. He began by lingering at the edge of his pond, pretending to be quite irresolute, not eating even the fish within his reach.

Now among the fish lived a crab. He drew near and said: "Uncle, why do you neglect today your usual meals and amusements?" And the heron replied: "So long as I kept fat and flourishing by eating fish, I spent my time pleasantly, enjoying the taste of you. But a great disaster will soon befall you. And as I am old, this will cut short the pleasant course of my life. For this reason I feel depressed."

"Uncle," said the crab, "of what nature is the disaster?" And the heron continued: "Today I overheard the talk of a number of fishermen as they passed near the pond. 'This is a big pond,' they were saying, 'full of fish. We will try a cast of the net tomorrow or the day after. But today we will go to the lake near the city.' This being so, you are lost, my food supply is cut off, I too am lost, and in grief at the thought, I am indifferent to food today."

Now when the water-dwellers heard the trickster's report, they all feared for their lives and implored the heron, saying: "Uncle! Father! Brother! Friend! Thinker! Since you are informed of the calamity, you also know the remedy. Pray save us from the jaws of this death."

Then the heron said: "I am a bird, not competent to contend with men. This, however, I can do. I can transfer you from this pond to another, a bottomless one." By this artful speech they were so led astray that they said: "Uncle! Friend! Unselfish kinsman! Take me first! Me first! Did you never hear this?

> Stout hearts delight to pay the price
> Of merciful self-sacrifice,
> Count life as nothing, if it end
> In gentle service to a friend."

Then the old rascal laughed in his heart, and took counsel with his mind, thus: "My shrewdness has brought these fishes into my power. They ought to be eaten very comfortably." Having thus thought it through, he promised what the thronging fish implored, lifted some in his bill, carried them a certain distance to a slab of stone, and ate them there. Day after day he made the trip with supreme delight and satisfaction, and meeting the fish, kept their confidence by ever new inventions.

One day the crab, disturbed by the fear of death, importuned him with the words: "Uncle, pray save me, too, from the jaws of death." And the heron reflected: "I am quite tired of this unvarying fish diet. I should like to taste him. He is different, and choice." So he picked up the crab and flew through the air.

But since he avoided all bodies of water and seemed planning to alight on the sun-scorched rock, the crab asked him: "Uncle, where is that pond without any bottom?" And the heron laughed and said: "Do you see that broad, sun-scorched rock? All the water-dwellers have found repose there. Your turn has now come to find repose."

Then the crab looked down and saw a great rock of sacrifice, made horrible by heaps of fish-skeletons. And he thought: "Ah me!

> Friends are foes and foes are friends
> As they mar or serve your ends;
> Few discern where profit tends.

Again:

> If you will, with serpents play;
> Dwell with foemen who betray:
> Shun your false and foolish friends,
> Fickle, seeking vicious ends.

Why, he has already eaten these fish whose skeletons are scattered in heaps. So what might be an opportune course of action for me? Yet why do I need to consider?

> Man is bidden to chastise
> Even elders who devise
> Devious courses, arrogant,
> Of their duty ignorant.

Again:

> Fear fearful things, while yet
>   No fearful thing appears;
> When danger must be met,
>   Strike, and forget your fears.

So, before he drops me there, I will catch his neck with all four claws."

When he did so, the heron tried to escape, but being a fool, he found no parry to the grip of the crab's nippers, and had his head cut off.

Then the crab painfully made his way back to

the pond, dragging the heron's neck as if it had been a lotus-stalk. And when he came among the fish, they said: "Brother, why come back?" Thereupon he showed the head as his credentials and said: "He enticed the water-dwellers from every quarter, deceived them with his prevarications, dropped them on a slab of rock not far away, and ate them. But I—further life being predestined—perceived that he destroyed the trustful, and I have brought back his neck. Forget your worries. All the water-dwellers shall live in peace."

"And that is why I say:

> A heron ate what fish he could, ...

and the rest of it."

"My friend," said the crow, "tell me how this villainous snake is to meet his doom." And the jackal answered: "Go to some spot frequented by a great monarch. There seize a golden chain or a necklace from some wealthy man who guards it carelessly. Deposit this in such a place that when it is recovered, the snake may be killed."

So the crow and his wife straightway flew off at random, and the wife came upon a certain pond. As she looked about, she saw the women of a king's court playing in the water, and on the bank they had laid golden chains, pearl necklaces, garments, and gems. One chain of gold the crow-hen seized and started for the tree where she lived.

But when the chamberlains and the eunuchs saw the theft, they picked up clubs and ran in pursuit. Meanwhile, the crow-hen dropped the golden chain in the snake's hole and waited at a safe distance.

Now when the king's men climbed the tree, they found a hole and in it a black snake with swelling hood. So they killed him with their clubs, recovered the golden chain, and went their way. Thereafter the crow and his wife lived in peace.

"And that is why I say:

> In cases where brute force would fail, ...

and the rest of it. Furthermore:

> Some men permit a petty foe
> Through purblind heedlessness to grow,
> Till he who played a petty rôle
> Grows, like disease, beyond control.

Indeed, there is nothing in the world that the intelligent cannot control. As the saying goes:

> Intelligence is power. But where
> Could power and folly make a pair?
> The rabbit played upon his pride
> To fool him; and the lion died."

"How was that?" asked Cheek. And Victor told the story of

NUMSKULL AND THE RABBIT

In a part of a forest was a lion drunk with pride, and his name was Numskull. He slaughtered the animals without ceasing. If he saw an animal, he could not spare him.

So all the natives of the forest—deer, boars, buffaloes, wild oxen, rabbits, and others—came together, and with woe-begone countenances, bowed heads, and knees clinging to the ground, they undertook to beseech obsequiously the king of beasts: "Have done, O King, with this merciless, meaningless slaughter of all creatures. It is hostile to happiness in the other world. For the Scripture says:

> A thousand future lives
> Will pass in wretchedness
> For sins a fool commits
> His present life to bless.

Again:

> What wisdom in a deed
> That brings dishonor fell,
> That causes loss of trust,
> That paves the way to hell?

And yet again:

> The ungrateful body, frail
> And rank with filth within,
> Is such that only fools
> For its sake sink in sin.

"Consider these facts, and cease, we pray, to slaughter our generations. For if the master will remain at home, we will of our own motion send him each day for his daily food one animal of the forest. In this way neither the royal sustenance nor our families will be cut short. In this way let the king's duty be performed. For the proverb says:

The king who tastes his kingdom like
  Elixir, bit by bit,
Who does not overtax its life,
  Will fully relish it.

The king who madly butchers men,
  Their lives as little reckoned
As lives of goats, has one square meal,
  But never has a second.

A king desiring profit, guards
  His world from evil chance;
With gifts and honors waters it
  As florists water plants.

Guard subjects like a cow, nor ask
  For milk each passing hour:
A vine must first be sprinkled, then
  It ripens fruit and flower.

The monarch-lamp from subjects draws
  Tax-oil to keep it bright:
Has any ever noticed kings
  That shone by inner light?

A seedling is a tender thing,
  And yet, if not neglected,
It comes in time to bearing fruit:
  So subjects well protected.

Their subjects form the only source
  From which accrue to kings
Their gold, grain, gems, and varied drinks,
  And many other things.

The kings who serve the common weal,
  Luxuriantly sprout;
The common loss is kingly loss,
  Without a shade of doubt."

After listening to this address, Numskull said: "Well, gentlemen, you are quite convincing. But if an animal does not come to me every day as I sit here, I promise you I will eat you all." To this they assented with much relief, and fearlessly roamed the wood. Each day at noon one of them appeared as his dinner, each species taking its turn and providing an individual grown old, or religious, or grief-smitten, or fearful of the loss of son or wife.

One day a rabbit's turn came, it being rabbit-day. And when all the thronging animals had given him directions, he reflected: "How is it possible to kill this lion—curse him! Yet after all,

In what can wisdom not prevail?
In what can resolution fail?
What cannot flattery subdue?
What cannot enterprise put through?

I can kill even a lion."

So he went very slowly, planning to arrive tardily, and meditating with troubled spirit on a means of killing him. Late in the day he came into the presence of the lion, whose throat was pinched by hunger in consequence of the delay, and who angrily thought as he licked his chops: "Aha! I must kill all the animals the first thing in the morning."

While he was thinking, the rabbit slowly drew

near, bowed low, and stood before him. But when the lion saw that he was tardy and too small at that for a meal, his soul flamed with wrath, and he taunted the rabbit, saying: "You reprobate! First, you are too small for a meal. Second, you are tardy. Because of this wickedness I am going to kill you, and tomorrow morning I shall extirpate every species of animal."

Then the rabbit bowed low and said with deference: "Master, the wickedness is not mine, nor the other animals'. Pray hear the cause of it." And the lion answered: "Well, tell it quick, before you are between my fangs."

"Master," said the rabbit, "all the animals recognized today that the rabbits' turn had come, and because I was quite small, they dispatched me with five other rabbits. But in mid-journey there issued from a great hole in the ground a lion who said: 'Where are *you* bound? Pray to your favorite god.' Then I said: 'We are traveling as the dinner of lion Numskull, our master, according to agreement.' 'Is that so?' said he. 'This forest belongs to me. So all the animals, without exception, must deal with me—according to agreement. This Numskull is a sneak thief. Call him out and bring him here at once. Then whichever of us proves stronger, shall be king and shall eat all these animals.' At his command, master, I have come to you. This is the cause of my tardiness. For the rest, my master is the sole judge."

After listening to this, Numskull said: "Well, well, my good fellow, show me that sneak thief of a lion, and be quick about it. I cannot find peace of mind until I have vented on him my anger against the animals. He should have remembered the saying:

Land and friends and gold at most
  Have been won when battles cease;
If but one of these should fail,
  Do not think of breaking peace.

Where no great reward is won,
  Where defeat is nearly sure,
Never stir a quarrel, but
  Find it wiser to endure."

"Quite so, master," said the rabbit. "Warriors fight for their country when they are insulted. But this fellow skulks in a fortress. You know he came out of a fortress when he held us up. And an enemy in a fortress is hard to handle. As the saying goes:

A single royal fortress adds
  More military force
Than do a thousand elephants,
  A hundred thousand horse.

A single archer from a wall
  A hundred foes forfends;
And so the military art
  A fortress recommends.

God Indra used the wit and skill
  Of gods in days of old,
When Devil Gold-mat plagued the world,
  To build a fortress-hold.

And he decreed that any king
Who built a fortress sound,
Should conquer foemen. This is why
Such fortresses abound."

When he heard this, Numskull said: "My good fellow, show me that thief. Even if he is hiding in a fortress, I will kill him. For the proverb says:

The strongest man who fails to crush
At birth, disease or foe,
Will later be destroyed by that
Which he permits to grow.

And again:

The man who reckons well his power,
Nor pride nor vigor lacks,
May single-handed smite his foes
Like Rama-with-the-axe."

"Very true," said the rabbit. "But after all it was a mighty lion that I saw. So the master should not set out without realizing the enemy's capacity. As the saying runs:

A warrior failing to compare
Two hosts, in mad desire
For battle, plunges like a moth
Headforemost into fire.

And again:

The weak who challenge mighty foes
A battle to abide,
Like elephants with broken tusks,
Return with drooping pride."

But Numskull said: "What business is it of yours? Show him to me, even in his fortress." "Very well," said the rabbit. "Follow me, master." And he led the way to a well, where he said to the lion: "Master, who can endure your majesty? The moment he saw you, that thief crawled clear into his hole. Come, I will show him to you." "Be quick about it, my good fellow," said Numskull.

So the rabbit showed him the well. And the lion, being a dreadful fool, saw his own reflection in the water, and gave voice to a great roar. Then from the well issued a roar twice as loud, because of the echo. This the lion heard, decided that his rival was very powerful, hurled himself down, and met his death. Thereupon the rabbit cheerfully carried the glad news to all the animals, received their compliments, and lived there contentedly in the forest.

"And that is why I say:

> Intelligence is power, ...

and the rest of it."

"But," said Cheek, "that is like a palm-fruit falling on a crow's head—a quite exceptional case. Even if the rabbit was successful, still a man of feeble powers should not deal fraudulently with the great." And Victor retorted: "Feeble or strong, one must make up his mind to vigorous action. You know the proverb:

> Unceasing effort brings success;
> 'Fate, fate is all,' let dastards wail:
> Smite fate and prove yourself a man;
> What fault if bold endeavor fail?

Furthermore, the very gods befriend those who ever strive. As the story goes:

The gods befriend a man who climbs
  Determination's height:
So Vishnu, discus, bird sustained
  The weaver in the fight.

And further:

Not even Brahma sees the end
  Of well-devised deceit:
The weaver, taking Vishnu's form,
  Embraced the princess sweet."

"How was that?" asked Cheek. "Are undertakings successful even through deceit, resolutely and well devised?" And Victor told the story of

THE WEAVER WHO LOVED A PRINCESS

In the Molasses Belt is a city called Sugarcane City. In it lived two friends, a weaver and a carpenter. Since they were past masters in their respective crafts, they had earned enough money by their labors so that they kept no account of receipt and expenditure. They wore soft, gaily colored, expensive garments, adorned themselves with flowers and betel-leaves, and diffused odors of camphor, aloes, and musk. They worked nine hours a day, after which they adorned their persons and met for recreation in such places as public squares or temples. They made the rounds of the spots where society gathered—theaters, *conversaziones*, birthday parties, banquets, and the like—then went home at twilight. And so the time passed.

One day there was a great festival, an occasion when the entire population, wearing the finest ornaments that each could afford, began sauntering through the temples of the gods and other public places. The weaver and the carpenter, like the rest, put on their best things, and in squares and courtyards inspected the faces of people dressed to kill. And they caught a glimpse of a princess seated at the window of a stucco palace. The vicinity of her heart was made lovely by a firm bosom with the curve of early youth. Below the slender waist was the graceful swell of the hips. Her hair was black as a raincloud, soft, glossy, with a billowy curl. A golden earring danced below an ear that seemed a hammock where Love might swing. Her face had the charm of a new-blown, tender water-lily. Like a dream she took captive the eyes of all, as she sat surrounded by girl friends.

And the weaver, ravished by lavish loveliness, since the love-god with five fierce arrows pierced his heart, concealed his feelings by a supreme effort of resolution, and tottered home, seeing nothing but the princess in the whole horizon. With long-drawn, burning sighs he tumbled on the bed (though it had not been made up), and there he lay. He perceived, he thought of nothing but her, just as he had seen her, and there he lay, reciting poetry:

Virtues with beauty dwell:
  So poets sing,
This contradiction not
  Considering:
That she, so cruel-sweet,
  Far, far apart,
Tortures my body still,
  Still in my heart.

Or does this explain it?

One heart my darling took;
  One pines as if to die;
One throbs with feeling pure:
  How many hearts have I?

And yet

If all the world from virtue draws
  A blessing and a gain,
Why should all virtue in my maid,
  My fawn-eyed maiden, pain?

Each guards his home, they say;
Yet in my heart you stay,
Burning your home alway,
Sweet, heartless one!

That these—her bosom's youthful pride,
Her curling hair, her sinuous side,
Her blood-red lip, her waist so small—
Should hurt me, is not strange at all:
But that her cheeks so clear, so bright,
Should torture me, is far from right.

Her bosom, like an elephant's brow,
Swells, saffron-scented. How, ah, how

May I thereon my bosom lay,
When weary love is tired of play,
So, fettered in her arms, to keep
A vigil waking half, half sleep?

If fate has willed
 That I should die,
Are there no means
 Save that soft eye?

You see my love, though far apart,
Before you ever, O my heart!
Should vision cease to satisfy,
Oh, teach your magic to my eye:
For even her presence will distress,
If bought by too great loneliness,
Since none—the merciful are blest—
Of selfishness may stand confessed.

She stole his luster from the moon—
 The moon is dull and cold;
The lily's sheen is in her eyes—
 No charge of theft will hold;
The elephant's majesty she seized—
 Naught knows he of her art;
From me the slender maiden took,
 Ah, strange! a feeling heart.

In middle air I see my love,
On earth below, in heaven above;
In life's last hour, on her I call:
She is, like Vishnu, all-in-all.

All mental states, the Buddha said,
 Are transient; he was wrong:
My meditations on my love
 Are infinitely long.

In such lamentation, his thoughts tossing to and fro, the night dragged drearily away. On the next day at the customary hour, the carpenter, wearing an elegant costume, came as usual to the weaver's house. There he found the weaver with arms and legs sprawled over the unmade bed, heard his long-drawn, burning sighs, and noticed his pallid cheeks and trickling tears. Finding him in this condition, he said: "My friend, my friend, why are you in such a state today?" But the poor weaver, though questioned repeatedly, was too embarrassed to say a word. At last the carpenter grew weary and dropped into poetry:

No friend is he whose anger
Compels a timid languor,
  Nor he whom all must anxiously attend;
But when you trust another
As if he were your mother,
  He is no mere acquaintance, but a friend.

Then, after examining the weaver's heart and other members with a hand skilled in detecting symptoms, he said: "Comrade, if my diagnosis is correct, your condition is not the result of fever, but of love."

Now when his friend voluntarily introduced the subject, the weaver sat up in bed and recited a stanza of poetry:

You find repose in sore disaster
By telling things to clear-eyed master,
To virtuous servant, gentle friend,
Or wife who loves you to the end.

Then he related his whole experience from the moment he laid eyes on the princess. And the carpenter, after some reflection, said: "The king belongs to the warrior caste, while you are a business man. Have you no reverence for the holy law?"

But the weaver replied: "The holy law allows a warrior three wives. The girl may be the daughter of a woman of my caste. That may explain my love for her. What says the king in the play?

> Surely, she may become a warrior's bride;
>   Else, why these longings in an honest mind?
> The motions of a blameless heart decide
>   Of right and wrong, when reason leaves us blind."

Thereupon the carpenter, perceiving his determined purpose, said: "Comrade, what is to be done next?" And the weaver answered: "I don't know. I told you because you are my friend." And to this he would not add a word.

At last the carpenter said: "Rise, bathe, eat. Say farewell to despondency. I will invent something such that you will enjoy with her the delights of love without loss of time."

Then the weaver, hope reviving at his friend's promise, rose and returned to seemly living. And the next day the carpenter came bringing a brand-new mechanical bird, like Garuda, the bird of Vishnu. It was made of wood, was gaily painted in many colors, and had an ingenious arrangement of plugs.

"Comrade," he said to the weaver, "when you

mount the bird and insert a plug, it goes wherever you wish. And the contrivance alights at the spot where you pull out the plug. It is yours. This very night, when people are asleep, adorn your person, disguise yourself as Vishnu—my wit and skill are at your service—mount this Garuda bird, alight on the maidens' balcony of the palace, and make whatever arrangements you like with the princess. I have ascertained that the princess sleeps alone on the palace balcony."

When the carpenter had gone, the weaver spent the rest of the day in a hundred fond imaginings. He took a bath, used incense, powders, ointments, betel, scents for the breath, flowers, and so forth. He put on gay garlands and garments, rich in fragrance. He adorned himself with a diadem and other jewelry. And when the night came clear, he followed the carpenter's instructions.

Meanwhile, the princess lay in her bed alone on the palace balcony bathed in moonbeams. She gazed at the moon, her mind idly dallying with the thought of love. All at once she spied the weaver, disguised as Vishnu and mounted on his heavenly bird. At sight of him she started from her bed, adored his feet, and humbly said: "O Lord, to what end am I honored by this visit? Pray command me. What am I to do?"

To the princess' words the weaver, in dignified and sweetly modulated accents, made stately answer: "Yourself, dear maiden, are the occasion of this visit to earth." "But I am merely a mortal girl," said she.

And he continued: "Nay, you have been my bride, now fallen to earth by reason of a curse. It is I who have so long protected you from contact with a man. I will now wed you by the ceremony used in heaven." And she assented, for she thought: "It is a thing beyond my fondest aspirations." And he married her by the ceremony used in heaven.

So day followed day in the enjoyment of love's delights, each day witnessing a growth in passion. Before dawn the weaver would mount his mechanical Garuda, would bid her farewell with the words: "I depart for Vishnu's heaven," and would always reach his house undetected.

One day the guards at the women's quarters observed indications that the princess was meeting a man, and in fear of their very lives made a report to their master. "O King," they said, "be gracious and confirm our personal security. There is a disclosure to be made." And when the king assented, the guards reported: "O King, we have used anxious care to forbid the entrance of men. Yet indications are observed that Princess Lovely has meetings with a man. Not unto us does it fall to take measures. The king, the king alone is prime mover."

Upon this information the king pondered with troubled spirit:

> You are worried when you hear that she is born;
> Picking husbands makes you anxious and forlorn;
> When she marries, will her husband be a churl?
> It is tough to be the father of a girl.

Again:

At her birth she steals away her mother's heart;
Loving friends, when she is older, fall apart;
Even married, she is apt to bring a stain:
Having daughters is a business full of pain.

Again:

When a poem or daughter comes out,
The author is troubled with doubt,
  With a doubt that his questions betray;
Will she reach the right hands?
Will she please as she stands?
  And what will the critics say?

Having thus considered the matter from every point of view, he sought the queen and said: "My dear queen, pray give careful attention to what these chamberlains have to say. Who is this offender whom the death-god seeks today?"

Now when they had related the facts, the queen hastened in great perturbation to the maiden's apartments and found her daughter with lips sore from kissing and with telltale traces on her limbs. And she cried: "You wicked girl! You are a disgrace to the family! How could you throw your character away? Who is the man that comes to you? The death-god has looked upon him. Dreadful as things are, at least tell the truth." Then the princess, with shamefaced, drooping glances, recounted the whole story of the weaver disguised as Vishnu.

Thereupon the queen, with laughing countenance and thrilling in every limb, hastened to the king and said: "O King, you are indeed fortunate. It is blessèd Vishnu who comes each night in person to our daughter's side. He has married her by the ceremony used in heaven. This very night you and I are to hide in the window niche and have sight of him. But with mortals he does not exchange words."

On hearing this, the king was glad at heart, and somehow lived through the day, which seemed a hundred years. When night came, the king and queen stood hidden in the window niche and waited, their gaze fixed on the sky. Presently the king descried one descending from heaven, mounted on Garuda, grasping the conch-shell, discus, mace, marked with the familiar symbols. And feeling as if drenched by a shower of nectar, he said to the queen: "There is none other on earth so blest as you and I, whose child blessèd Vishnu seeks with love. All the desires nearest our hearts are granted. Now, through the power of our son-in-law, I shall reduce the whole world to subjection."

At this juncture envoys arrived to collect the yearly tribute for King Valor, monarch of the south, lord of nine million, nine hundred thousand villages. But the king, proud of his new relationship with Vishnu, did not show them the customary honor, so that they grew indignant and said: "Come, King! Pay-day is past. Why have you failed to offer the taxes due? It must be that you have recently come into possession of some unanticipated, supernatural power from some source or other, that you irritate King Valor, who is a flame, a whirlwind, a venomous serpent, a death-god." Upon this the king showed them his bare bottom. And they returned to their own country, exaggerated the matter a hundred thousand fold, and stirred the wrath of their master.

Then the southern monarch, with his troops and retainers, at the head of an army with all four service branches, marched against the king. And he angrily cried:

> This king may climb the heavenly mount,
> May plunge beneath the sea;
> And yet—I promise it—the wretch
> Shall soon be slain by me.

So Valor reached the country by marches never interrupted, and ravaged it. And the inhabitants who survived the slaughter besieged the palace gate of the king of Sugarcane City, and taunted him. But what he heard did not cause the king the slightest anxiety.

On the following day the forces of King Valor arrived and invested Sugarcane City, whereupon hosts of counselors and chaplains interceded with the king: "O King," they said, "a powerful enemy has arrived and invested the city. How can the king show himself so unconcerned?" And the king replied: "You gentlemen may be quite comfortable. I have devised a means of killing this foe. What I am about to do to his army, you, too, will learn tomorrow morning." After this address, he bade them provide adequate defense for the walls and gates.

Then he summoned Lovely and with respectful coaxing said: "Dear child, relying on your husband's power, we have begun hostilities with the enemy. This very night pray speak to blessèd Vishnu when he comes, so that in the morning he may kill this enemy of ours."

So Lovely delivered to him at night her father's message, complete in every particular. On hearing it, the weaver laughed and said: "Dear love, how little a business is this, a mere war with men! Why, in days gone by I have with the greatest ease slain mighty demons by the thousand, and they were armed with magic; there was Hiranyakashipu, and Kansa, and Madhu, and Kaitabha, to name but a few. Go, then, and say to the king: 'Dismiss anxiety. In the morning Vishnu will slay the host of your enemies with his discus.' "

So she went to the king and proudly told him all. Whereat he was overjoyed and commanded the doorkeeper to have proclamation made with beat of drum throughout the city, in these words: "Whatever any shall lay hands on during tomorrow's battle in the camp of Valor slain, whether coined money or grain or gold or elephant or horse or weapon or other object, that shall remain his personal possession." This proclamation delighted the citizens, so that they gossiped together, saying: "This king of ours is a lofty soul, unalarmed even in the presence of the hostile host. He is certain to kill his rival in the morning."

Meanwhile the weaver, forgetting love's allurements, took counsel with his brooding mind: "What am I to do now? Suppose I mount the machine and fly away, then I shall never meet my pearl, my wife, again. King Valor will drag her from the palace after killing my poor father-in-law. Yet if I accept battle, I shall meet death, who puts an end to every heart's desire. But death is mine if I lose her. Why spin it out? Death, sure death, in either case. It is better, then, to die game. Besides, it is just possible that the enemy, if they see me accepting battle and mounted on Garuda, will think me the genuine Vishnu and will flee. For the proverb says:

Let resolution guide the great,
However desperate his state,
However grim his hostile fate:

By resolution lifted high,
With shrewd decision as ally,
He grimly sees grim trouble fly."

When the weaver had thus resolved on battle, the genuine Garuda made respectful representations to the genuine Vishnu in heaven. "O Lord," he said, "in a city on earth called Sugarcane is a weaver who, disguising himself as my Lord, has wedded a princess. As a result, a more powerful monarch of the south has marched to extirpate the king of Sugarcane City. Now the weaver today takes his resolution to befriend his father-in-law. This, then, is what I must refer to your decision. If he meets death in battle, then scandal will arise in the mortal world to the effect that blessèd Vishnu has been killed by the king of the south. Thereafter sacrificial offerings will fail, and other religious ceremonies. Then atheists will destroy the temples of the Lord, while pilgrims of the triple staff, devotees of blessèd Vishnu, will abstain from pious journeyings. Such being the condition of affairs, decision rests with my Lord."

Then blessèd Vishnu, after exhaustive meditation, spoke to Garuda: "O King of the wingèd, your reasoning is just. This weaver has a spark of divinity in him. Therefore he must be the slayer of yonder king. And to bring this about, you and I must befriend him. My spirit shall enter his body, you are to inspire his bird, and my discus, his discus." "So be it," said Garuda, assenting.

Hereupon the weaver, inspired by Vishnu, gave instructions to Lovely: "Dear love, when I set out for battle, let all things be made ready that bring a benediction." He then performed auspicious ceremonies, assumed ornaments seemly for battle, and permitted worshipful offerings of yellow pigment, black mustard, flowers, and the like. But when the friend of day-blooming water-lilies, the blessèd, thousand-beamèd sun arose, adorning the bridal brow of the eastern sky, then to the victorious roll of the war-drums, the king issued from the city and drew near the field of battle, then both armies formed in exact array, then the infantry came to blows. At this moment the weaver, mounted on Garuda, and scattering largess of gold and precious gems, flew from the palace roof toward heaven's vault, while the townspeople, thrilling with wonder, gazed and adored, then beyond the city he hovered above his army, and drew from Vishnu's conch a proud, grand burst of martial sound.

At the blare of the conch, elephants, horses, chariots, foot-soldiers, were dismayed and many garments were fouled. Some with shrill screams fled afar. Some rolled on the ground, all purposive movement paralyzed. Some stood stock still, with terrified gaze fixed unwavering on heaven.

At this point all the gods were drawn to the spot by curiosity to see the fight, and Indra said to Brahma: "Brahma, is this some imp or demon who must needs be slain? For blessèd Vishnu, mounted on Garuda, has gone forth to battle in person." At these words Brahma pondered:

> "Lord Vishnu's discus drinks in flood
> The hostile demons' gushing blood,
> And strikes no mortal flat:
> The jungle lion who can draw
> The tusker's life with awful paw,
> Disdains to crush a gnat.

What means this marvel?" Thus Brahma himself was astonished. That is why I told you:

> Not even Brahma sees the end
> Of well-devised deceit:
> The weaver, taking Vishnu's form,
> Embraced the princess sweet.

While the very gods were thus pondering with tense interest, the weaver hurled his discus at Valor. This discus, after cutting the king in twain, returned to his hand. At the sight, all the kings without exception leaped from their vehicles, and with hands, feet, and head drooping in limp obeisance, they implored him who bore the form of Vishnu: "O Lord,

An army, leaderless, is slain.

Be mindful of this and spare our lives. Command us. What are we to do?"

So spoke the whole throng of kings, until he made answer who bore the form of Vishnu: "Your persons are secure henceforth. Whatever commands you receive from the local king, King Stout-Mail, you must on all occasions unhesitatingly perform." And all the kings humbly received his instructions, saying: "Let it be as our Lord commands."

Thereupon the weaver bestowed on Stout-Mail all his rival's wealth, whether men or elephants or chariots or horses or stores of merchandise or other riches, while he himself, having attained the special majesty of those victorious, enjoyed all known delights with the princess.

"And that is why I say:

The gods befriend a man who climbs
Determination's height, ...

and the rest of it."

Having listened to this, Cheek said: "If you, too, are thus climbing determination's height, then proceed to the accomplishment of your desire. Blest be your journeyings."

Thereupon Victor sought the presence of the lion, who said, when Victor had bowed and seated himself: "Why has so long a time passed since you were last visible?" And Victor answered: "O King, urgent business awaits my master today. Hence I am come, the bearer of tidings unwelcome but wholesome. This is not, indeed, the desire of dependents, who yet bring such tidings when they fear the neglect of immediate and necessary action. As the proverb says:

> When those appointed to advise
> Speak wholesome truth, they cause surprise
> By this remarkable excess
> Of passionate devotedness.

And again:

> A man is quickly found, O King,
> To say the sycophantic thing;
> But one prepared to hear or speak
> Unwelcome truth, is far to seek."

Hereupon Rusty, believing his words worthy of trust, respectfully asked him: "What do you wish to imply?" And Victor answered: "O King, Lively has crept into your confidence with treasonable purpose. On several occasions he has confidentially whispered in my hearing: 'I have examined the strong points and the weak in your master's power—in his prestige, his advisers, and his material resources. I plan to kill him and to seize the royal power myself without difficulty.' This very day this Lively person intends to carry out his design. That is why I am here to warn the master whose service is mine by inheritance."

To Rusty this report was more terrible than the fall of a thunderbolt. He sank into a panic-stricken stupor and said not a word. Then Victor, comprehending his state of mind, continued: "This is the great sadness in the discharge of a counselor's duty. There is wisdom in the saying:

> When a counselor or king
>   Rises higher than he should,
> Fortune strives in vain to make
>   Still her double footing good;
> Being woman, feels the strain;
> Soon abandons one of twain.

For, indeed,

> With broken sliver, loosened tooth,
> Or counselor who fails in truth,
> Pull roots and all; so only, grief
> Will find its permanent relief.

And again:

> No king should ever delegate
> To one sole man the powers of state:
> For folly seizes him, then pride,
> Whereat he grows dissatisfied
> With service; thus impatient grown,
> He longs to rule the realm alone;
> And such impatient longings bring
> Him into plots to kill his king.

Even now, this Lively manages all business as he will, without restraint of any kind. Hence the well-known saying finds application:

A counselor who tramples through
His business, though his heart be true,
May not unheeded go his way,
Since future days the present pay.

But such is the nature of kings. As the poet sings:

Some gentle actions born of love
To thoughts of active hatred move;
Some deeds of traitorous offense
Win guerdon of benevolence;
The kingly mind can no man tame,
As never being twice the same:
Such service makes the spirit faint,
A hard conundrum for a saint."

On hearing this, Rusty said: "After all, he is my servant. Why should he experience a change of heart toward me?" But Victor answered: "Servant or not, there is nothing conclusive in that. For the proverb says:

The man who loves not royalty,
  Just serving while he can
Find nothing better worth his pains,
  Is not a loyal man."

"My dear fellow," said the lion, "even so, I cannot find it in my heart to turn against him. For

However false and fickle grown,
  Once dear is always dear:
Who does not love his body, though
  Decrepit, blemished, queer?

And again:

His actions may be hard to bear,
His speech be harsh to hear;
The heart still clings delighted to
A person truly dear."

"For that very reason," retorted Victor, "there is a serious flaw in the business of getting on in the world. Observe how this person, upon whom the master has concentrated his consideration to the exclusion of the whole company of animals, now desires to become himself the master. As the verse puts it:

The man of birth or man unknown,
If kingly eyes on him alone
Are fixed, aspires to seize the throne.

Therefore, dear though he be, he should be abandoned, being a traitor, like one who has never been dear. There is much wisdom in the saying:

Pursue your aim, abandoning
The fools inclined to sin,
The comrades, brothers, friends, or sons,
Or honorable kin:
You know the song the women sing,
We hear it far and near—
What good are golden earrings, if
They lacerate your ear?

"And if you fancy that he will bring benefit because he is bulky of body, you make a perverse mistake. For

How use a proud bull-elephant
That will not serve the king?
A man is better, fat or lean,
Who does the helpful thing.

"Again, any pity that our lord and king might feel toward him, is quite out of place. For

Whoever leaves the righteous path
  For some unrighteous course,
Will meet calamity in time
  And suffer much remorse.

Whoever will not take from friends
  Most excellent advice,
Will gladden foes, and falling soon,
  Will pay his folly's price.

And again:

On wicked trick intently bent,
  The wilful still lack ear to hear
(So blind their mind) of nice and vice
  The cause in saws appearing clear.

Furthermore:

Where one will speak and one will heed
  What in the end is well,
Although unpleasant at the time,
  There riches love to dwell.

And again:

No king's retainer should devise
A fraud, for spies are kingly eyes:
Then bear with harsh as kind, O King;
The truth is seldom flattering.

Tried servants never should be left,
  And strangers taken;
A kingdom's health by no disease
  Is sooner shaken."

"My good fellow," said the lion, "pray do not say such things. For

> Never publicly defame
> Any once commended name:
> Broken promises are shame.

"Now I formerly gave him a safe-conduct, since he appeared as a suppliant. How then can he prove ungrateful?" But Victor rejoined:

> "No rogue asks reason for his wrath;
> Nor saint, to tread in kindness' path:
> By nature's power, the sweet or sour
> In sugar dwells or nim-tree's flower.

And again:

> Caress a rascal as you will,
> He was and is a rascal still:
> All salve- and sweating-treatments fail
> To take the kink from doggy's tail.

And once again:

> Slight kindness shown to lofty souls
>   A strange enlargement seeks:
> The moonbeams gleam with whiter light
>   On Himalaya's peaks.

While, on the other hand:

> The kindness shown to vicious souls
>   Strange diminution seeks:
> The gleam of moonbeams is absorbed
>   On Sooty Mountain's peaks.
>
> A hundred benefits are lost,
>   If lavished on the mean;
> A hundred epigrams, with their
>   True relevance unseen;

A hundred counsels, when a life
  Obeys no rigid rule;
A hundred cogent arguments
  Are lost upon a fool.

Lost is every gift that goes
  Where it does not fit;
Lost is service lavished on
  Sluggish mind and wit;
Lost upon ingratitude
  Is the kindest plan;
Lost is courtesy on one
  Not a gentleman.

Or put it this way:

Perfume offered to a corpse,
  Lotus-planting dry,
Weeping in the wood, prolonged
  Rain on alkali,
Taking kinks from doggy's tail,
  Drawl in deafened ear,
Decking faces of the blind,
  Sense for fools to hear.

Or this way:

Milk a bull, and think him some
  Heavy-uddered cow;
Blind to lovely maidens, clasp
  Eunuchs anyhow;
Seek in shining scraps of quartz
  Lapis lazuli:
Do not serve an addlepate,
  Bidding sense goodbye.

"Ergo, the master must by no means fail to heed my sound advice. And one thing more:

What tiger, monkey, snake advised,
I did not do; and so
That dreadfully ungrateful man
Has brought me very low."

"How was that?" asked Rusty. And Victor told the story of

THE UNGRATEFUL MAN

In a certain town lived a Brahman whose name was Sacrifice. Every day his wife, chafing under their poverty, would say to him: "Come, Brahman! Lazy-bones! Stony-Heart! Don't you see your babies starving, while you hang about, mooning? Go somewhere, no matter where, find some way, any way, to get food, and come back in a hurry."

At last the Brahman, weary of this refrain, undertook a long journey, and in a few days entered a great forest. While wandering hungry in this forest, he began to hunt for water. And in a certain spot he came upon a well, overgrown with grass. When he looked in, he discovered a tiger, a monkey, a snake, and a man at the bottom. They also saw him.

Then the tiger thought: "Here comes a man," and he cried: "O noble soul, there is great virtue in saving life. Think of that, and pull me out, so that I may live in the company of belovèd friends, wife, sons, and relatives."

"Why," said the Brahman, "the very sound of your name brings a shiver to every living thing. I cannot deny that I fear you." But the tiger resumed:

"To Brahman-slayer, impotent,
To drunkard, him on treason bent,
To sinner through prevarication,
The holy grant an expiation:
While for ingratitude alone
No expiation will atone."

And he continued: "I bind myself by a triple oath that no danger threatens you from me. Have pity and pull me out." Then the Brahman thought it through to this conclusion: "If disaster befalls in the saving of life, it is a disaster that spells salvation." So he pulled the tiger out.

Next the monkey said: "Holy sir, pull me out too." And the Brahman pulled him out too. Then the snake said: "Brahman, pull me out too." But the Brahman answered: "One shudders at the mere sound of your name, how much more at touching you!" "But," said the snake, "we are not free agents. We bite only under orders. I bind myself by a triple oath that you need have no fear of me." After listening to this, the Brahman pulled him out too. Then the animals said: "The man down there is a shrine of every sin. Beware. Do not pull him out. Do not trust him."

Furthermore, the tiger said: "Do you see this mountain with many peaks? My cave is in a wooded ravine on the north slope. You must do me the favor of paying me a visit there some day, so that I may make return for your kindness. I should not like to drag the debt into the next life." With these words he started for his cave.

Then the monkey said: "My home is quite near the cave, beside the waterfall. Please pay me a visit there." With this he departed.

Then the snake said: "In any emergency, remember me." And he went his way.

Then the man in the well shouted time and again: "Brahman! Pull me out too!" At last the Brahman's pity was awakened, and he pulled him out, thinking: "He is a man, like me." And the man said: "I am a goldsmith, and live in Baroch. If you have any gold to be worked into shape, you must bring it to me." With this he started for home.

Then the Brahman continued his wanderings but found nothing whatever. As he started for home, he recalled the monkey's invitation. So he paid a visit, found the monkey at home, and received fruits sweet as nectar, which put new life into him. Furthermore, the monkey said: "If you ever have use for fruit, pray come here at any time." "You have done a friend's full duty," said the Brahman. "But please introduce me to the tiger." So the monkey led the way and introduced him to the tiger.

Now the tiger recognized him and, by way of returning his kindness, bestowed on him a necklace and other ornaments of wrought gold, saying: "A certain prince whose horse ran away with him came here alone, and when he was within range of a spring, I killed him. All this I took from his person and stored carefully for you. Pray accept it and go where you will."

So the Brahman took it, then recalled the goldsmith and visited him, thinking: "He will do me the favor of getting it sold." Now the goldsmith welcomed him with respectful hospitality, offering water for the feet, an honorable gift, a seat, hard food and soft, drink, and other things, then said: "Command me, sir. What may I do for you?" And the Brahman said: "I have brought you gold. Please sell it." "Show me the gold," said the goldsmith, and the other did so.

Now the goldsmith thought when he saw it: "I worked this gold for the prince." And having made sure of the fact, he said: "Please stay right here, while I show it to somebody." With this he went to court and showed it to the king. On seeing it, the king asked: "Where did you get this?" And the goldsmith replied: "In my house is a Brahman. He brought it."

Thereupon the king reflected: "Without question, that villain killed my son. I will show him what that costs." And he issued orders to the police: "Have this Brahman scum fettered, and impale him tomorrow morning."

When the Brahman was fettered, he remembered the snake, who appeared at once and said: "What can I do to serve you?" "Free me from these fetters," said the Brahman. And the snake replied: "I will bite the king's dear queen. Then, in spite of the charms employed by any great conjurer and the antidotes of other physicians, I will keep her poisoned. Only by the touch of your hand will the poison be neutralized. Then you will go free."

Having made this promise, the snake bit the queen, whereupon shouts of despair arose in the palace, and the entire city was filled with dismay. Then they summoned dealers in antidotes, conjurers, scientists, druggists, and foreigners, all of whom treated the case with such resources as they had, but none could neutralize the poison. Finally, a proclamation was made with beat of drum, upon hearing which the Brahman said: "I will cure her." The moment he spoke, they freed him from his fetters, took him to the king, and introduced him. And the king said: "Cure her, sir." So he went to the queen and cured her by the mere touch of his hand.

When the king saw her restored to life, he paid the Brahman honor and reverence, then respectfully asked him: "Reveal the truth, sir. How did you come by this gold?" And the Brahman began at the beginning and related the whole adventure accurately. As soon as the king comprehended the facts, he arrested the goldsmith, while he gave the Brahman a thousand villages and appointed him privy counselor. But the Brahman summoned his family, was surrounded by friends and relatives, took delight in eating and other natural functions, acquired massive merit by the performance of numerous sacrifices, concentrated authority by heedful attention to all phases of royal duty, and lived happily.

"And that is why I say:

What tiger, monkey, snake advised, ...

and the rest of it." And Victor continued:

"Friend or kinsman, teacher, king,
Must be kept from trespassing:
If they cling to evil still,
They will bend you to their will.

"O King, he is obviously a traitor. However,

Tirelessly benevolent,
Save a friend on evil bent:
This is sainthood's perfect song;
Every substitute is wrong.

Again:

Who saves from vice is truly kind;
True wife is she who shares your mind;
True acts are free from every blame;
True joy, from avarice's shame;
True wisdom wins the praise of saints;
True friends involve in no restraints;
True glory knows no haughtiness;
True men are cheerful in distress.

And again:

Rest your sleeping head in fire;
  Pillow it with snakes:
Do not smile at worthy friends
  Who pursue mistakes.

"Now my lord and king associates with Lively, making a vicious mistake that results in the neglect of the three things worth living for—virtue, money, and love. And in spite of my protestations, urged from various points of view, my lord and king goes his wilful way, unheeding. In the future, therefore, when the crash comes, do not blame your servant. You have heard the saying:

No thought of profit or of right
  Can headstrong monarchs stay,
Who, like bull-elephants amuck,
  Pursue their reckless way;
When, puffed with pride, they come to grief
  In thickets of distress,
They blame their servants, and forget
  Their proper naughtiness."

"Such being the case, my good fellow," said the lion, "should I warn him?" "What! Warn him?" said Victor. "What kind of policy would that be? For

He stings or strikes in hasty fear
  When warning has been heard:
'Tis wise to warn an enemy
  By action, not by word."

"After all," said Rusty, "he is a grass-nibbler. I am a carnivore. How can he hurt me?" "Precisely," said Victor. "He is a grass-nibbler. My lord and king is a carnivore. He is food. My lord and king devours food. In spite of all, if the fellow is not likely to work harm through his own power, he will egg on another to it. As the saying goes:

The weak, malicious fool
Can use a keener tool:
It sharpens sword-blades, but
The whetstone cannot cut."

"How can that be?" said the lion. And Victor answered: "Why, you have constantly engaged in battle with unnumbered bull-elephants, wild oxen, buffaloes, boars, tigers, and leopards, until your body is spotted with scars left by the thrust of claw and tusk. Now this Lively, living beside you, is always scattering his excrement far and wide. In it worms will breed. These worms, finding your body conveniently near, will creep into ready-made crevices, and will bore deep. And so you are as good as dead. As the proverb says:

With no stranger share your house;
Leap, the flea, killed Creep, the louse."

"How was that?" asked Rusty. And Victor told the story of

LEAP AND CREEP

In the palace of a certain king stood an incomparable bed, blessed with every cubiculary virtue. In a corner of its coverlet lived a female louse named Creep. Surrounded by a thriving family of sons and daughters, with the sons and daughters of sons and daughters, and with more remote descendants, she drank the king's blood as he slept. On this diet she grew plump and handsome.

While she was living there in this manner, a flea named Leap drifted in on the wind and dropped on the bed. This flea felt supreme satisfaction on examining the bed—the wonderful delicacy of its coverlet, its double pillow, its exceptional softness like that of a broad, Gangetic sand-bank, its delicious perfume. Charmed by the sheer delight of touching it, he hopped this way and that until—fate willed it so—he chanced to meet Creep, who said to him: "Where do *you* come from? This is a dwelling fit for a king. Begone, and lose no time about it." "Madam," said he, "you should not say such things. For

> The Brahman reverences fire,
> Himself the lower castes' desire;
> The wife reveres her husband dear;
> But all the world must guests revere.

Now I am your guest. I have of late sampled the various blood of Brahmans, warriors, business men, and serfs, but found it acid, slimy, quite unwholesome. On the contrary, he who reposes on this bed must have a delightful vital fluid, just like nectar. It must be free from morbidity, since wind, bile, and phlegm are kept in harmony by constant and heedful use of potions prepared by physicians. It must be enriched by viands unctuous, tender, melting in the mouth; viands prepared from the flesh of the choicest creatures of land, water, and air, seasoned furthermore with sugar, pomegranate, ginger, and pepper. To me it seems an elixir of life. Therefore, with your kind permission, I plan to taste this sweet and fragrant substance, thus combining pleasure and profit."

"No," said she. "For fiery-mouthed stingers like you, it is out of the question. Leave this bed. You know the proverb:

> The fool who does not know
> His own resource, his foe,
> His duty, time, and place,
> Who sets a reckless pace,
> Will by the wayside fall,
> Will reap no fruit at all."

Thereupon he fell at her feet, repeating his request. And she agreed, since courtesy was her hobby, and since, when the story of that prince of sharpers, Muladeva, was being repeated to the king while she lay on a corner of the coverlet, she had heard how Muladeva quoted this verse in answer to the question of a certain damsel:

> Whoever, angry though he be,
> Has spurned a suppliant enemy,
> In Shiva, Vishnu, Brahma, he
> Has scorned the Holy Trinity.

Recalling this, she agreed, but added: "However, you must not come to dinner at a wrong place or time." "What is the right place and what is the right time?" he asked. "Being a newcomer, I am not *au courant*." And she replied: "When the king's body is mastered by wine, fatigue, or sleep, then you may quietly bite him on the feet. This is the right place and the right time." To these conditions he gave his assent.

In spite of this arrangement, the famished bungler, when the king had just dozed off in the early evening, bit him on the back. And the poor king, as if burned by a firebrand, as if stung by a scorpion, as if touched by a torch, bounded to his feet, scratched his back, and cried to a servant: "Rascal! Somebody bit me. You must hunt through this bed until you find the insect."

Now Leap heard the king's command and in terrified haste crept into a crevice in the bed. Then the king's servants entered, and following their master's orders, brought a lamp and made a minute inspection. As fate would have it, they came upon Creep as she crouched in the nap of the fabric, and killed her with her family.

"And that is why I say:

> With no stranger share your house, ...

and the rest of it. And another thing. My lord and king does wrong in neglecting the servants who are his by inheritance. For

> Whoever leaves his friends,
> Strange folk to cherish,
> Like foolish Fierce-Howl, will
> Untimely perish."

"How was that?" asked Rusty. And Victor told the story of

THE BLUE JACKAL

There was once a jackal named Fierce-Howl, who lived in a cave near the suburbs of a city. One day he was hunting for food, his throat pinched with hunger, and wandered into the city after nightfall. There the city dogs snapped at his limbs with their sharp-pointed teeth, and terrified his heart with their dreadful barking, so that he stumbled this way and that in his efforts to escape and happened into the house of a dyer. There he tumbled into a tremendous indigo vat, and all the dogs went home.

Presently the jackal—further life being predestined—managed to crawl out of the indigo vat and escaped into the forest. There all the thronging animals in his vicinity caught a glimpse of his body dyed with the juice of indigo, and crying out: "What is this creature enriched with that unprecedented color?" they fled, their eyes dancing with terror, and spread the report: "Oh, oh! Here is an exotic creature that has dropped from somewhere. Nobody knows what his conduct might be, or his energy. We are going to vamoose. For the proverb says:

> Where you do not know
> Conduct, stock, and pluck,
> 'Tis not wise to trust,
> If you wish for luck."

Now Fierce-Howl perceived their dismay, and called to them: "Come, come, you wild things! Why do you flee in terror at sight of me? For Indra, realizing that the forest creatures have no monarch, anointed me—my name is Fierce-Howl—as your king. Rest in safety within the cage formed by my resistless paws."

On hearing this, the lions, tigers, leopards, monkeys, rabbits, gazelles, jackals, and other species of wild life bowed humbly, saying: "Master, prescribe to us our duties." Thereupon he appointed the lion prime minister and the tiger lord of the bedchamber, while the leopard was made custodian of the king's betel, the elephant doorkeeper, and the monkey the bearer of the royal parasol. But to all the jackals, his own kindred, he administered a cuffing, and drove them away. Thus he enjoyed the kingly glory, while lions and others killed food-animals and laid them before him. These he divided and distributed to all after the manner of kings.

While time passed in this fashion, he was sitting one day in his court when he heard the sound made by a pack of jackals howling near by. At this his body thrilled, his eyes filled with tears of joy, he leaped to his feet, and began to howl in a piercing tone. When the lions and others heard this, they perceived that he was a jackal, and stood for a moment shamefaced and downcast, then they said: "Look! We have been deceived by this jackal. Let the fellow be killed." And when he heard this, he endeavored to flee, but was torn to bits by a tiger and died.

"And that is why I say:

> Whoever leaves his friends, ...

and the rest of it."

Then Rusty asked: "How am I to recognize that

he is treacherous? And what is his fighting technique?" And Victor answered: "Formerly he would come into the presence of my lord and king with limbs relaxed. If today he approaches timidly, in obvious readiness to thrust with his horns, then the king may understand that he has treachery in mind."

Hereupon Victor rose and visited Lively. To him, also, he showed himself sluggish, like one penetrated by discouragement. Therefore Lively said: "My good fellow, are you in spirits?" To which he replied: "How can a dependent be in spirits? For you know

> They see their wealth in others' power
> Who wait upon a king;
> They even fear to lose their lives:
> A doleful song they sing.

Again:

> With birth begin the sorrows which
> Forever after cling,
> The never ending train of woes
> In service of a king.
>
> Five deaths-in-life sage Vyasa notes
> With well-known epic swing:
> The poor man, sick man, exile, fool,
> And servant of a king.
>
> His food repels; he dare not say
> An independent thing;
> Though sleepless, he is not awake
> Who hangs upon a king.

The common phrase 'a dog's life' has
A most persuasive ring:
But dogs can do the things they like;
A slave obeys his king.

He must be chaste, sleep hard, grow thin,
And eat a meager dinner:
The servant lives as lives the saint,
Yet is not saint, but sinner.

He cannot do the things he would;
He serves another's mind;
He sells his body. How can such
A wretch contentment find?

According to the lesser distance,
A servant uses more persistence
In watching for his master's whim
And trembling at the sight of him:
And this because a fire, a king,
Are double name for single thing,
A burning thing that men can stand
Afar, but not too close at hand.

What flavor has a tidbit, though
It be as good as good,
Soft, dainty, melting in the mouth,
If bought by servitude?

To sum it all up:

What is my place? My time? My friends?
Expenditure or dividends?
And what am I? And what my power?
So must one ponder hour by hour."

After listening to this, Lively said, perceiving that Victor had a hidden purpose in mind: "Tell me, my good fellow, what you wish to imply." And Victor answered: "Well, you are my friend. I cannot help telling you what is to your profit. Here goes. The master, Rusty, is filled with wrath against you. And he said today: 'I will kill Lively and provide a feast for all who eat meat.' Of course, I fell into deep dejection on hearing this. Now you must do what the crisis demands."

To Lively this report was like the fall of a thunderbolt, and he fell into deep dejection. Yet as Victor's words were always plausible, he grew more and more troubled, fell into a panic, and said: "Yes, the proverb is right:

Women oft are tricked by scamps;
  Kings with rascals oft agree;
Toward the skinflints money drifts;
  Rain on mountains falls and sea.

Ah, me! Ah, me! What is this that has befallen me?

You serve your king most heedfully.
  Of course. Who could complain?
But enmity as your reward
  Is unexpected pain.

And again:

If one is angry, giving cause,
Remove it, and the wrath will pause:
But how may man propitiate
A mind that harbors causeless hate?

Who does not fear the scoundrel's art,
The causeless hate, the flinty heart?
For ever ready venom drips
Resistless from his serpent-lips.

The stupid king-swan pecks by night
At starshine, in the water bright,
Believing it a lotus white;

Then, fearing stars when shines the sun,
Avoids the lotus. Everyone
Who dreads a trap, will blessings shun.

Alas! What wrong have I done our master Rusty?"

"Comrade," said Victor, "kings love to injure without reason, and they seek out the vulnerable spot in an adversary." "True, too true," said Lively. "There is wisdom in the verse:

The serpent sandal-trees defiles;
In lotus-ponds lurk crocodiles;
The slanderer makes virtue vain:
No blessing lacks attendant pain.

No lotus decks the mountain height;
From scoundrels issues nothing right;
To saints no change of heart is known;
Rice never sprouts from barley sown.

Nobility's constraints
Are felt by gracious saints,
Who bear good deeds in mind
Forget the other kind.

"Yet, after all, the fault is mine, because I made advances to a false friend. As the story goes:

Harsh talk, untimely action,
  False friends—are worse than vain:
The swan in lilies sleeping,
  Was by the arrow slain."

"How was that?" asked Victor. And Lively told the story of

PASSION AND THE OWL

Within a certain forest was a broad expanse of lake. There lived a king-swan named Passion, who spent his days in a great variety of pastimes. One day death, fatal death, visited him in the person of an owl. And the swan said: "This is a lonely wood. Where do you come from?" The owl replied: "I came because I heard of your virtues. Furthermore,

In search of virtue roaming
  The wide world through,
No virtues being greater,
  I come to you.

That I must cling in friendship
  To you, is sure:
The impure turns, attaining
  The Ganges, pure.

And again:

The conch was bone that Vishnu's hand
  Has purified:
For contact with the righteous lends
  A noble pride."

After this address, the swan gave his assent, in the words: "My excellent friend, dwell with me as you like by this broad lake in this pleasant wood." So their time was spent in friendly diversions.

But one day the owl said: "I am going to my own home, which is called Lotus Grove. If you set any value on me and feel any affection, you must not fail to pay a visit as my guest." With these words he went home.

Now as time passed, the swan reflected: "I have grown old, living in this spot, and I do not know a single other region. So now I will go to visit my dear friend, the owl. There I shall find a brand-new recreation ground and new kinds of food, both hard and soft."

After these reflections, he went to visit the owl. At first he could not find him in Lotus Grove, and when, after a minute search, he discovered him, there was the poor creature crouching in an ugly hole, for he was blind in the daytime. But Passion called: "My dear fellow, come out! I am your dear friend the swan, come to pay you a visit."

And the owl replied: "I do not stir by day. You and I will meet when the sun has set." So the swan waited a long time, met the owl at night, and after giving the conventional information about his health, being wearied by his journey, he went to sleep on the spot.

Now it happened that a large commercial caravan had encamped at that very lake. At dawn the leader rose and had the signal of departure given by conch. This the owl answered with a loud, harsh hoot, then dived into a hole in the river-bank. But the swan did not stir. Now the evil omen so disturbed the leader's spirit that he gave orders to a certain archer who could aim by sound. This archer strung his powerful bow, drew an arrow as far as his ear, and killed the swan, who was resting near the owl's nest.

"And that is why I say:

Harsh talk, untimely action, ...

and the rest of it."

And Lively continued: "Why, our master Rusty was all honey at first, but at the last his purpose turns to poison. Ah, yes!

He compliments you to your face;
His whispered slanders never stop:
Avoid a friend like that. He is
A poison-jug with cream on top.

"Yes, I have learned by experience the truth of the well-known verse:

He lifts his hands to see you standing there;
His eyes grow moist; he offers half his chair;
He hugs you warmly to his eager breast;
In kindly talk and question finds no rest;
His skill is wondrous in deceptive tricks;
Honey without, within the poison sticks:
What play is this, what strange dramatic turns,
That every villain, like an actor, learns?

At first rogues' friendship glitters bright
With service, flattery, delight;
Thence, in its middle journey, shoot
Gay flowers of speech that fail to fruit;
Its final goal is treason, shame,
Disgust, and slanders that defame:
Alas! Who made the cursèd thing?
Its one foul purpose is to sting.

And again:

They bow abjectly; leap to greet
You with their speech seductive-sweet;
Pursue and hug you day by day;
Of deep devotion make display:
All praise your virtue. Never one
Finds time to *do* what should be done.

"Woe is me! How can I, a creature herbivorous, consort with this lion who devours raw flesh? There is wisdom in the saying:

Where wealth is very much the same,
And similar the family fame,
Marriage or friendship is secure;
But not between the rich and poor.

And there is a proverb:

The sun, already setting, shows
  His final flaming power,
And still the honey-thirsty bee
  Explores the lotus-flower,
Forgets that it will prove a trap
  That shuts at set of sun:
Ambition, thirsting for reward,
  Is blind to dangers run.

Abandoning the lotus-bloom
  With all its sweet content,
The jasmine's natural perfume
  And luxury of scent,
The water-bees seek toilsome food,
  On ichor-sipping bent:
So men reject the easy good,
  In rogues o'erconfident.

The bees that, too adventurous,
  A novel honey seek
In springtime ichor glistening on
  The elephant-monarch's cheek,
When, tossed by wind from flapping ears,
  They tumble to the ground,
Remember then what gentle sport
  In lotus-cups is found.

Yet, after all, virtues involve corresponding defects. For

The fruit-tree's branch by very wealth
  Of fruit is bended low;
The peacock's feathered pride compels
  A sluggish gait and slow;
The blooded horse that wins his race,
  Must like a cow be led:
The good in goodness often find
  An enemy to dread.

Where Jumna's waves roll blue
With sands of sapphire hue,
Black serpents have their lair;
And who would hunt them there,
But that a jewel's bright star
From each hood gleams afar?
By virtue rising, all
By that same virtue fall.

The man of virtue commonly
  Is hateful to the king,
While riches to the scamps and fools
  Habitually cling:
The ancient chant 'By virtue great
  Is man' has run to seed;
The world takes rare and little note
  Of any plucky deed.

Sad, shamefaced lions fail to rage,
Their spirit mastered by the cage;
And captive elephants' brows and pride
By drivers' goads are scarified;
Charms dull the cobras; hopeless woe
Lays scholars flat and soldiers low:
For Time, the mountebank, enjoys
A juggling bout with chosen toys.

The honey-greedy bee—poor fool!—
Deserts the flowering lotus-pool
Where danger is not found, to sip
The springtime ichor-rills that drip
From elephant foreheads; does not fear
The flapping of that monstrous ear:
So, by his nature, greedy man
Forgets the issue of his plan.

"Yes, by entering a vulgarian's sphere of power, I have certainly forfeited my life. As the proverb says:

All who live upon their wits,
  Many learnèd, too, are mean,
Do the wrong as quick as right:
  Illustration may be seen
In the well-known tale that features
Camel, crow, and other creatures."

"How was that?" asked Victor. And Lively told the story of

UGLY'S TRUST ABUSED

In a certain city lived a merchant named Ocean, who loaded a hundred camels with valuable cloth and set out in a certain direction. Now one of his camels, whose name was Ugly, was overburdened and fell limp, with every limb relaxed. Then the merchant divided the pack of cloth, loaded it on other camels, and because he found himself in a wild forest region where delay was impossible, he proceeded, leaving Ugly behind.

When the trader was gone, Ugly hobbled about and began to crop the grass. Thus in a very few days the poor fellow regained his strength.

In that forest lived a lion whose name was Haughty, who had as hangers-on a leopard, a crow, and a jackal. As they roamed the forest, they encountered the abandoned camel, and the lion said, after observing his fantastic and comical shape: "This is an exotic in our forest. Ask him what he is." So the crow informed himself of the facts and said: "This is what goes by the name of camel in the world." Thereupon the lion asked him: "My good friend, where did you come from?" And the camel gave precise details of his separation from the trader, so that the lion experienced compassion and guaranteed his personal security.

In this posture of affairs, the lion fought an elephant one day, received a thrust from a tusk, and had to keep his cave. And when five or six days had passed, they all found themselves in urgent distress from the failure of food. So the lion, observing how they drooped, said to them: "I am crippled by this wound and cannot supply you with the usual food.

You will just have to make an effort on your own account."

And they replied: "Why should we care to thrive, while our lord and king is in this state?" "Bravo!" said the lion. "You show the conduct and devotion of good servants. Round up some food-animal for me while I am in this condition." Then, when they made no answer, he said to them: "Come! Do not be bashful. Hunt up some creature. Even in my present condition I will convert it into food for you and myself."

So the four started to roam the woods. Since they found no food-animal, the crow and the jackal conferred together, and the jackal said: "Friend crow, why roam about? Here is Ugly, who trusts our king. Let us provide for our sustenance by killing him."

"A very good suggestion," said the crow. "But after all, the master guaranteed his personal security, and so cannot kill him."

"Quite so," said the jackal. "I will interview the master and make him think of killing Ugly. Stay right here until I go home and return with the master's answer." With this he hastened to the master.

When he found the lion, he said: "Master, we have roamed the entire forest, and are now too famished to stir a foot. Besides, the king is on a diet. So, if the king commands, one might fortify one's health today by means of Ugly's flesh."

When the lion had listened to this ruthless proposal, he cried out angrily: "Shame upon you, most degraded of sinners! The moment you repeat those words, I will strike you dead. Why, I guaranteed his personal security. How can I kill him with my own paw? You have heard the saying:

> The wise declare and understand
> No gift of cow or food or land
> To be among all gifts as grand
> As safety granted on demand."

"Master," replied the jackal, "if you kill him after guaranteeing his safety, then you are indeed blameworthy. If, however, of his own accord he devotedly offers his own life to his lord and king, then no blame attaches. So you may kill him on condition that he voluntarily destines himself to slaughter. Otherwise, pray eat one or another of the rest of us. For the king is on a diet, and if food fails, he will experience a change for the worse. In that case, what value have these lives of ours, which will no longer be spent in our master's service? If anything disagreeable happens to our gracious master, then we must follow him into the fire. For the proverb says:

> Save the chieftain of the clan,
>   Whatsoe'er the pain;
> Lose him, and the clan is lost:
>   Hubless spokes are vain."

After listening to this, Haughty said: "Very well. Do as you will."

With this message the jackal hastened to say to

the others: "Well, friends, the master is very low. The life is oozing from the tip of his nose. If he goes, who will be our protector in this forest? So, since starvation is driving him toward the other world, let us go and voluntarily offer our own bodies. Thus we shall pay the debt we owe our gracious master. And the proverb says:

> Servants, when disaster
> Comes upon their master,
> If alive and well,
> Tread the road to hell."

So they all went, their eyes brimming with tears, bowed low before Haughty, and sat down.

On seeing them, Haughty said: "My friends, did you catch any creature, or see any?" And the crow replied: "Master, though we roamed everywhere, we still did not catch any creature, nor see any. Master, pray eat me and support your life for a day. Thus the master will be replete, while I shall rise to heaven. For the saying goes:

> A servant who, in loyal love,
> Has yielded up his breath,
> Adorns a lofty seat in heaven,
> Secure from age and death."

On hearing this, the jackal said: "Your body is small. If he ate you, the master would scarcely prolong his life. Besides, there is a moral objection. For the verse tells us:

> Crows' flesh and such small leavings
> Are things to be passed by:

Why eat an evil somewhat
That does not satisfy?

"You have shown your loyalty, and have won a saintly reputation in both worlds. Now make way, while I address the master." So the jackal bowed respectfully and said: "Master, pray use my body to support your life today, thus conferring on me the best of earth and heaven. For the proverb says:

Since servants' lives on masters hang
In forfeit for their pay,
The master perpetrates no sin
In taking them away."

Hearing this, the leopard said: "Very praiseworthy, indeed, my friend. However, your body is rather small, too. Besides, he ought not to eat you, since you belong to the same unguipugnacious family. You know the proverb:

The prudent, though with life at stake,
Avoid forbidden food
(Too small at that)—from fear to lose
Both earth's and heaven's good.

Well, you have shown yourself a loyal servant. There is truth in the stanza:

That swarms of gentlemen delight
A monarch, is not strange,
Since, first and last and times between,
Their honor does not change.

Make way, then, so that I, too, may win the master's grace."

Thereupon the leopard bowed low and said:

"Master, pray prolong your life for a day at the cost of my life. Grant me an everlasting home in heaven, and spread my fame afar on earth. Pray show no hesitation. For the proverb says:

> A servant who, by loyal love,
> Has demonstrated worth,
> Attains a lasting home above
> And glory on the earth."

Hearing this, poor Ugly thought: "Well, they used the most elegant phrases. Yet the master did not kill a single one of them. So I, too, will make a speech befitting the occasion. I have no doubt that all three will contradict me."

Having come to this conclusion, he said: "Very admirable, friend leopard. But you too are unguipugnacious. How, then, can the master eat you? There is a proverb to fit the case:

> The mere imagining of wrongs
> To kinsmen done, confirms
> The loss of earth and heaven. Such rogues
> Turn into unclean worms.

Make way, then, so that I, too, may address the master."

So poor Ugly stood in the presence, bowed low and said: "Master, these you surely may not eat. Pray prolong your life by means of my life, so that I may win the best of earth and heaven. For the proverb says:

> No sacrificer and no saint
> Can ever rise as high

As do the simple servingfolk
Who for the master die."

Hereupon the lion gave the word, the leopard and the jackal tore his body, the crow pecked out his eyes, poor Ugly yielded up the ghost, and all the others ravenously devoured him.

"And that is why I say:

All who live upon their wits, ...

and the rest of it."

After telling the story, Lively continued, addressing Victor: "My dear fellow, this king, with his shabby advisers, brings no good to his dependents. Better have as king a vulture advised by swans than a swan advised by vultures. For from the vulture advisers many vices appear in their master, quite sufficient to bring ruin. Of the two, therefore, one should choose the former as king. But a king instigated by evil counsel is incapable of reflection. You know the saying:

Your jackal does not reassure;
Your crow's sharp bill offends:
You therefore see me up a tree—
I do not like your friends."

"How was that?" asked Victor. And Lively told the story of

THE LION AND THE CARPENTER

In a certain city lived a carpenter named Trustgod. It was his constant habit to carry his lunch and go with his wife into the forest, where he cut great anjana logs. Now in that forest lived a lion named Spotless, who had as hangers-on two carnivorous creatures, a jackal and a crow.

One day the lion was roaming the wood alone and encountered the carpenter. The carpenter for his part, on beholding that most alarming lion, whether considering himself already lost or perhaps with the ready wit to perceive that it is safer to face the powerful, advanced to meet the lion, bowed low, and said: "Come, friend, come! Today you must eat my own dinner which my wife—your brother's wife—has provided."

"My good fellow," said the lion, "being carnivorous, I do not live on rice. But in spite of that, I will have a taste, since I take a fancy to you. What kind of dainty have you got?"

When the lion had spoken, the carpenter stuffed him with all kinds of dainties—buns, muffins, chewers, and things, all flavored with sugar, butter, grape-juice, and spice. And to show his gratitude, the lion guaranteed his safety and granted unhindered passage through the forest. Then the carpenter said: "Comrade, you must come here every day, but please come alone. You must not bring anyone else to visit me." In this manner they spent their days in friendship. And the lion, since every day he received such hospitality, such a variety of goodies, gave up the practice of hunting.

Then the jackal and the crow, who lived on others' luck, went hungry, and they implored the lion. "Master," they said, "where do you go every day? And tell us why you come back so happy." "I don't go anywhere," said he. But when they urged the question with great deference, the lion said: "A friend of mine comes into this wood every day. His wife cooks the most delicious things, and I eat them every day, in order to show friendly feeling."

Then the jackal and the crow said: "We two will go there, will kill the carpenter, and have enough meat and blood to keep us fat for a long time." But the lion heard them and said: "Look here! I guaranteed his safety. How can I even imagine playing him such a scurvy trick? But I will get a delicious tidbit from him for you also." To this they agreed.

So the three started to find the carpenter. While they were still far off, the carpenter caught a glimpse of the lion and his seedy companions, and he thought: "This does not look prosperous to me." So he and his wife made haste to climb a tree.

Then the lion came up and said: "My good fellow, why did you climb a tree when you saw me? Why, I am your friend, the lion. My name is Spotless. Do not be alarmed." But the carpenter stayed where he was and said:

Your jackal does not reassure;
  Your crow's sharp bill offends:
You therefore see me up a tree—
  I do not like your friends.

"And that is why I say that a king with shabby advisers brings no good to his dependents."

After telling the story, Lively continued: "Somebody must have set Rusty against me. Besides:

Soft water's scars elide
The mighty mountain side,
  And leave it much diminished:
By those who have the trick
To make a whisper stick
  Man's gentleness is finished.

"Under these circumstances, what action is opportune? Indeed, there is nothing left save battle. For the proverb says:

By gifts, by self-denial,
By sacrificial trial,
  Some slowly win to heaven;
To him who yields his life
In glad, heroic strife,
  Quick entrance there is given.

And again:

The slain attains the sky,
  The victor joyful lives;
And heroes are content
  With these alternatives.

And once again:

Gay maidens, smart with gems and gold;
  The flyflap's royal toy;
Throne, horse, and elephant, and cash;
  The white umbrella, joy
And sign of monarchs—shun the coward,
  Are not for mamma's boy."

When he heard this, Victor thought: "The fellow has sharp horns and plenty of vigor. He might perhaps strike down the master, if fate decreed it. That would not do, either. And the proverb says:

> Even with heroes victory
> Whimsically may alight.
> Try three other methods first;
> Only *in extremis* fight.

So I will use my wits to turn his thoughts from fighting." And he said: "My dear fellow, this is not a good plan, because

> He loses fights who fights before
> His foeman's power is reckoned:
> The ocean and the plover fought,
> And ocean came out second."

"How was that?" asked Lively. And Victor told the story of

THE PLOVER WHO FOUGHT THE OCEAN

A plover and his wife once lived by the shore of the sea, the mighty sea that swarms with fish, crocodiles, turtles, sharks, porpoises, pearl oysters, shellfish, and other teeming life. The plover was called Sprawl, and his wife's name was Constance.

In due time she became pregnant and was ready to lay her eggs. So she said to her husband: "Please find a spot where I may lay my eggs." "Why," said he, "this home of ours, inherited from our ancestors, promises progress. Lay your eggs here." "Oh," said she, "don't mention this dreadful place. Here is the ocean near at hand. His tide might some day make a long reach and lick away my babies."

But the plover answered: "Sweetheart, he knows me, he knows Sprawl. Surely the great ocean cannot show such enmity to me. Did you never hear this?

What man is rash enough to take
The gleaming crest-jewel from a snake?
Or stirs the wrath of one so dread
His glance may strike his victim dead?

However summer heat distresses
In wild and treeless wildernesses,
Who, after all, would seek the shade
By some rogue elephant's body made?

And again:

When morning's chilly breezes blow
With whirling particles of snow,
What man with sense of value sure,
Employs for cold the water cure?

To visit Death what man desires,
So wakes the lion's sleeping fires,
Who, tired from slaying elephants,
Lies in a temporary trance?

Who dares to visit and defy
The death-god? Dares the fearless cry—
I challenge you to single strife;
If power be yours, pray take my life?

What son of man, with simple wit,
Defies the fire, and enters it—
The smokeless flame that terrifies,
Whose tongues by hundreds lick the skies?"

But even as he spoke, his wife laughed outright, since she knew the full measure of his capacity, and she said: "Very fine, indeed. There is plenty more where that came from. O king of birds,

> Your heavy boastings startle, shock,
> And make of you a laughingstock:
> One marvels if the rabbit plants
> A dung-pile like the elephant's.

How can you fail to appreciate your own strength and weakness? There is a saying:

> To know one's self is hard, to know
> Wise effort, effort vain;
> But accurate self-critics are
> Secure in times of strain.
>
> This much of effort brings success;
> I have the power; I can:
> So think, then act, and reap the fruit
> Of your judicious plan.

And there is sound sense in this:

> To take advice from kindly friends
> Be ever satisfied:
> The stupid turtle lost his grip
> Upon the stick, and died."

"How was that?" asked Sprawl. And Constance told the story of

SHELL-NECK, SLIM, AND GRIM

In a certain lake lived a turtle named Shell-Neck. He had as friends two ganders whose names were Slim and Grim. Now in the vicissitudes of time there came a twelve-year drought, which begot ideas of this nature in the two ganders: "This lake has gone dry. Let us seek another body of water. However, we must first say farewell to Shell-Neck, our dear and long-proved friend."

When they did so, the turtle said: "Why do you bid me farewell? I am a water-dweller, and here I should perish very quickly from the scant supply of water and from grief at loss of you. Therefore, if you feel any affection for me, please rescue me from the jaws of this death. Besides, as the water dries in this lake, you two suffer nothing beyond a restricted diet, while to me it means immediate death. Consider which is more serious, loss of food or loss of life."

But they replied: "We are unable to take you with us since you are a water-creature without wings." Yet the turtle continued: "There is a possible device. Bring a stick of wood." This they did, whereupon the turtle gripped the middle of the stick between his teeth, and said: "Now take firm hold with your bills, one on each side, fly up, and travel with even flight through the sky, until we discover another desirable body of water."

But they objected: "There is a hitch in this fine plan. If you happen to indulge in the smallest conversation, then you will lose your hold on the stick, will fall from a great height, and will be dashed to bits."

"Oh," said the turtle, "from this moment I take

a vow of silence, to last as long as we are in heaven." So they carried out the plan, but while the two ganders were painfully carrying the turtle over a neighboring city, the people below noticed the spectacle, and there arose a confused buzz of talk as they asked: "What is this cartlike object that two birds are carrying through the atmosphere?"

Hearing this, the doomed turtle was heedless enough to ask: "What are these people chattering about?" The moment he spoke, the poor simpleton lost his grip and fell to the ground. And persons who wanted meat cut him to bits in a moment with sharp knives.

"And that is why I say:

> To take advice from kindly friends, ...

and the rest of it." And Constance continued:

> Forethought and Readywit thrive;
> Fatalist can't keep alive.

"How was that?" asked Sprawl. And she told the story of

FORETHOUGHT, READYWIT, AND FATALIST

In a great lake lived three full-grown fishes, whose names were Forethought, Readywit, and Fatalist. Now one day the fish named Forethought overheard passers-by on the bank and fishermen saying: "There are plenty of fish in this pond. Tomorrow we go fishing."

On hearing this, Forethought reflected: "This looks bad. Tomorrow or the day after they will be sure to come here. I will take Readywit and Fatalist and move to another lake whose waters are not troubled." So he called them and put the question.

Thereupon Readywit said: "I have lived long in this lake and cannot move in such a hurry. If fishermen come here, then I will protect myself by some means devised for the occasion."

But poor, doomed Fatalist said: "There are sizable lakes elsewhere. Who knows whether they will come here or not? One should not abandon the lake of his birth merely because of such small gossip. And the proverb says:

> Since scamp and sneak and snake
> So often undertake
> A plan that does not thrive,
> The world wags on, alive.

Therefore I am determined not to go." And when Forethought realized that their minds were made up, he went to another body of water.

On the next day, when he had gone, the fishermen with their boys beset the inner pool, cast a net, and caught all the fish without exception. Under these circumstances Readywit, while still in the water, played dead. And since they thought: "This big fellow died without help," they drew him from the net and laid him on the bank, from which he wriggled back to safety in the water. But Fatalist stuck his nose into the meshes of the net, struggling until they pounded him repeatedly with clubs and so killed him.

"And that is why I say:

> Forethought and Readywit thrive;
> Fatalist can't keep alive."

"My dear," said the plover, "why do you think me like Fatalist?

> Horses, elephants, and iron,
>   Water, woman, man,
> Sticks and stones and clothes are built
>   On a different plan.

Feel no anxiety. Who can bring humiliation upon you while my arms protect you?"

So Constance laid her eggs, but the ocean, who had listened to the previous conversation, thought: "Well, well! There is sense in the saying:

> Of self-conceit all creatures show
>   An adequate supply:
> The plover lies with claws upstretched
>   To prop the falling sky.

I will just put his power to the test."

So the next day, when the two plovers had gone foraging, he made a long reach with his wave-hands and eagerly seized the eggs. Then when the hen-plover returned and found the nursery empty, she said to her husband: "See what has happened to poor me. The ocean seized my eggs today. I told you more than once that we should move, but you were stupid as Fatalist and would not go. Now I am so sad at the loss of my children that I have decided to burn myself."

"My dear," said the plover, "wait until you witness my power, until I dry up that rascally ocean with my bill." But she replied: "My dear husband, how can you fight the ocean? Furthermore,

> Gay simpletons who fight,
> Not estimating right
> The foe's power and their own,
> Like moths in flame atone."

"My dear," said the plover, "you should not say such things.

> The sun's new-risen beams
> Upon the mountains fall:
> Where glory is cognate,
> Age matters not at all.

With this bill I shall dry up the water to the last drop, and turn the sea into dry land." "Darling," said his wife, "with a bill that holds one drop how will you dry up the ocean, into which pour without ceasing the Ganges and the Indus, bearing the water of nine times nine hundred tributary streams? Why talk nonsense?" But the plover said:

> Success is rooted in the will;
> And I possess an iron-strong bill;
> Long days and nights before me lie:
> Why should not ocean's flood go dry?

The highest glory to attain
Asks enterprise and manly strain:
The sun must first to Libra climb
Before he routs the cloudy time.

"Well," said his wife, "if you feel that you must make war on the ocean, at least call other birds to your aid before you begin. For the proverb says:

A host where each is weak
  Brings victory to pass:
The elephant is bound
  By woven ropes of grass.

And again:

Woodpecker and sparrow
  With froggy and gnat,
Attacking *en masse*, laid
  The elephant flat."

"How was that?" asked Sprawl. And Constance told the story of

THE DUEL BETWEEN ELEPHANT AND SPARROW

In a dense bit of jungle lived a sparrow and his wife, who had built their nest on the branch of a tamal tree, and in course of time a family appeared.

Now one day a jungle elephant with the spring fever was distressed by the heat, and came beneath that tamal tree in search of shade. Blinded by his fever, he pulled with the tip of his trunk at the branch where the sparrows had their nest, and broke it. In the process the sparrows' eggs were crushed, though the parent-birds—further life being predestined—barely escaped death.

Then the hen-sparrow lamented, desolate with grief at the death of her chicks. And presently, hearing her lamentation, a woodpecker bird, a great friend of hers, came grieved at her grief, and said: "My dear friend, why lament in vain? For the Scripture says:

> For lost and dead and past
>   The wise have no laments:
> Between the wise and fools
>   Is just this difference.

And again:

> No life deserves lament;
>   Fools borrow trouble,
> Add sadness to the sad,
>   So make it double.

And yet again:

> Since kinsmen's sticky tears
>   Clog the departed,
> Bury them decently,
>   Tearless, whole-hearted."

"That is good doctrine," said the hen-sparrow, "but what of it? This elephant—curse his spring fever!—killed my babies. So if you are my friend, think of some plan to kill this big elephant. If that were done, I should feel less grief at the death of my children. You know the saying:

> While one brings comfort in distress,
>   Another jeers at pain;
> By paying both as they deserve,
>   A man is born again."

"Madam," said the woodpecker, "your remark is very true. For the proverb says:

> A friend in need is a friend indeed,
>   Although of different caste;
> The whole world is your eager friend
>   So long as riches last.

And again:

> A friend in need is a friend indeed;
> Fathers indeed are those who feed;
> True comrades they, and wives indeed,
> Whence trust and sweet content proceed.

"Now see what my wit can devise. But you must know that I, too, have a friend, a gnat called Lute-Buzz. I will return with her, so that this villainous beast of an elephant may be killed."

So he went with the hen-sparrow, found the gnat, and said: "Dear madam, this is my friend the hen-sparrow. She is mourning because a villainous elephant smashed her eggs. So you must lend your assistance while I work out a plan for killing him."

"My good friend," said the gnat, "there is only one possible answer. But I also have a very intimate friend, a frog named Cloud-Messenger. Let us do the right thing by calling him into consultation. For the proverb says:

> A wise companion find,
> Shrewd, learnèd, righteous, kind;
> For plans by him designed
> Are never undermined."

So all three went together and told Cloud-Messenger the entire story. And the frog said: "How feeble a thing is that wretched elephant when pitted against a great throng enraged! Gnat, you must go and buzz in his fevered ear, so that he may shut his eyes in delight at hearing your music. Then the woodpecker's bill will peck out his eyes. After that I will sit on the edge of a pit and croak. And he, being thirsty, will hear me, and will approach expecting to find a body of water. When he comes to the pit, he will fall in and perish."

When they carried out the plan, the fevered elephant shut his eyes in delight at the song of the gnat, was blinded by the woodpecker, wandered thirst-smitten at noonday, followed the croak of a frog, came to a great pit, fell in, and died.

"And that is why I say:

Woodpecker and sparrow, ...

and the rest of it."

"Very well," said the plover. "I will assemble my friends and dry up the ocean." With this in mind, he summoned all the birds and related his grief at the rape of his chicks. And they started to beat the ocean with their wings, as a means of bringing relief to his sorrow.

But one bird said: "Our desires will not be accomplished in this manner. Let us rather fill up the ocean with clods and dust." So they all brought what clods and dust they could carry in the hollow of their bills and started to fill up the ocean.

Then another bird said: "It is plain that we are not equal to a contest with mighty ocean. So I will tell you what is now timely. There is an old gander who lives beside a banyan tree, who will give us sound and practical advice. Let us go and ask him. For there is a saying:

> Take old folks' counsel (those are old
>   Who have experience)
> The captive wild-goose flock was freed
>   By one old gander's sense."

"How was that?" asked the birds. And the speaker told the story of

THE SHREWD OLD GANDER

In a part of a forest was a fig tree with massive branches. In it lived a flock of wild geese. At the root of this tree appeared a creeping vine of the species called *koshambi*. Thereupon the old gander said: "This vine that is climbing our fig tree bodes ill to us. By means of it, someone might perhaps climb up here some day and kill us. Take it away while it is still slender and readily cut." But the geese despised his counsel and did not cut the vine, so that in course of time it wound its way up the tree.

Now one day when the geese were out foraging, a hunter climbed the fig tree by following the spiral vine, laid a snare among the nests, and went home.

When the geese, after food and recreation, returned at nightfall, they were caught to the last one. Whereupon the old gander said: "Well, the disaster has taken place. You are caught, having brought it on yourselves by not heeding my advice. We are all lost now."

Then the geese said to him: "Sir, the thing having come to pass, what ought we to do now?" And the old fellow replied: "If you will take my advice, play dead when that hateful hunter comes. And when the hunter, inferring that we are dead, throws the last one to the ground, we then must all rise simultaneously, flying over his head."

At early dawn the hunter arrived, and when he looked them over, everyone seemed as good as dead. He therefore freed them from the snare with perfect assurance, and threw them all to the ground, one after the other. But when they saw him preparing to descend, they all followed the shrewd plan of the old gander and flew up simultaneously.

"And that is why I say:

> Take old folks' counsel, ...

and the rest of it."

When the story had been told, all the birds visited the old gander and related their grief at the rape of the chicks. Then the old gander said: "The king of us all is Garuda. Therefore, the timely course of action is this. You must all stir the feelings of Garuda by a chorus of wailing lamentation. In consequence, he will remove our sorrow." With this purpose they sought Garuda.

Now Garuda had just been summoned by blessèd Vishnu to take part in an impending battle between gods and demons. At just this moment the birds reported to their master, the king of the birds, what sorrow in the separation of loved ones had been wrought by the ocean when he seized the chicks. "O bird divine," they said, "while you gleam in royal radiance, we must live on what little is won by the labor of our bills. Because of our weak necessity of eating, the ocean has, in overbearing manner, carried away our young. Now there is a saying:

> The poor are in peculiar need
> Of being secret when they feed:
> The lion killed the ram who could
> Not check his appetite for food."

"How was that?" asked Garuda. And an old bird told the story of

THE LION AND THE RAM

In a part of a forest was a ram, separated from his flock. In the armor of his great fleece and horns, he roamed the wood, a tough customer.

Now one day a lion in that forest, who had a retinue of all kinds of animals, encountered him. At this unprecedented sight, since the wool so bristled in every direction as to conceal the body, the lion's heart was troubled and invaded by fear. "Surely, he is more powerful than I am," thought he. "That is why he wanders here so fearlessly." And the lion edged away.

But on a later day the lion saw the same ram cropping grass on the forest floor, and he thought: "What! The fellow nibbles grass! His strength must be in relation to his diet." So he made a quick spring and killed the ram.

"And that is why I say:

> The poor are in peculiar need
> Of being secret when they feed,

and the rest of it."

While they were thus conferring, Vishnu's messenger returned and said: "Garuda, Lord Vishnu sends orders that you repair at once to the celestial city." On hearing this, Garuda proudly said to him: "Messenger, what will the master do with so poor a servant as I am?"

"Garuda," said the messenger, "it may be that the blessèd one has spoken to you harshly. But why should you display pride toward the blessèd one?" And Garuda replied: "The ocean, the resting-place of the blessèd one, has stolen the eggs of the plover, who is my servant. If I do not chastise him, then I am not the servant of the blessèd one. Make this report to the master."

Now when Vishnu learned from the messenger's

lips that Garuda was feigning anger, he thought: "Ah, he is dreadfully angry. I will therefore go in person, will address him, and bring him back with all honor. For the proverb says:

> Shame no servant showing worth,
> Loyalty, and noble birth;
> Pet him ever like a son,
> If you wish your business done.

And again:

> Masters, fully satisfied,
> Pay by gratifying pride;
> Servants, for such honor's pay,
> Gladly throw their lives away."

Having reached this conclusion, he hastened to Garuda, who, beholding his master a visitor in his own house, modestly gazed on the ground, bowed low, and said: "O blessèd one, the ocean, made insolent by his service as your resting-place, has stolen—behold! has stolen the eggs of my servant, and thus brought shame upon me. From reverence for the blessèd one, I have delayed. But if nothing is done, I myself will this day reduce him to dry land. For the proverb says:

> A loyal servant dies, but shrinks
>   From doing deeds of such a kind
> As bring contempt from common men
>   And lower him in his master's mind."

To this the blessèd one replied: "O son of Vinata, your speech is justified. Because

> For servants' crimes the master should
> Be made to suffer, say the good,

> So long as he does not erase
> From service, cruel folk and base.

"Come, then, so that we may recover the eggs from ocean, may satisfy the plover, and then proceed to the celestial city on the gods' business." To this Garuda agreed, and the blessèd one reproached the ocean, then fitted the fire-arrow to his bow and said: "Villain, give the plover his eggs. Else, I will reduce you to dry land."

On hearing this, the ocean, while all his train shook with fright, tremblingly took the eggs and restored them to the plover, as the blessèd one directed.

"And that is why I say:

> He loses fights who fights before
> His foeman's power is reckoned, ...

and the rest of it."

Now when Lively understood the matter, he asked Victor: "Tell me, comrade. What is his fighting technique?" And Victor answered: "Formerly he would lie carelessly on a slab of stone, with limbs relaxed. If today his tail is drawn in at the very first, if his four paws are bunched and his ears pricked up, and if he is watching for you while you are still far off, then you may understand that he has treachery in mind."

Hereupon Victor visited Cheek, who asked: "What have you accomplished?" And he replied: "I have already set them at odds with each other."

"Have you really done it?" said Cheek. And Victor answered: "The outcome will show you." "Indeed," said Cheek, "it is not surprising. For the proverb says:

A well-devised estranging scheme
  The firmest prudence shocks,
As constant floods of water split
  The mountains' close-piled rocks."

Then Victor continued: "Having wrought an estrangement, a man should not fail to seek his own advantage in it. As the verse puts it:

The man who studies every book
And understands, yet does not look
To his advantage, learns in vain;
His books are merely mental strain."

"But in the final analysis," said Cheek, "there is no such thing as personal advantage. For

Since worms and filth and ashes cling,
The body is a loathsome thing;
What statecraft therefore may there be
In hurting it vicariously?"

"Ah," replied Victor, "you have no comprehension of the devious ways of statesmanship, the basic support of the profession of counselor. On this point there is a verse:

Let your speech like sugar be,
Steel your heart remorselessly;
Never draw a doubtful breath:
Pay for suffered wrongs with death.

And another thing. This Lively, even when killed, will provide us with nourishment. For you know,

The wise who wrongs another,
Pursuing selfish good,
Should keep his plans a secret,
As Smart did in the wood."

"How was that?" asked Cheek. And Victor told the story of

SMART, THE JACKAL

In a part of a forest lived a lion named Thunder-Fang, in company with three counselors, a wolf, a jackal, and a camel, whose names were Meat-Face, Smart, and Spike-Ear. One day he fought with a furious elephant whose sharp-pointed tusk so tore his body that he withdrew from the world.

Then, suffering from a seven-day fast, his body lean with hunger, he said to his famished advisers: "Round up some creature in the forest, so that, even in my present condition, I may provide needed nourishment for you." The moment he issued his orders, they roamed the wood, but found nothing.

Thereupon Smart reflected: "If Spike-Ear here were killed, then we should all be nourished for a few days. However, the master is kept from killing him by friendly feeling. In spite of that, my wit will put the master in a frame of mind to kill him. For, indeed,

All understanding may be won,
All things be slain, and all be done,
If mortals have sufficient wit;
For me, I make good use of it."

After these reflections, he said to Spike-Ear: "Friend Spike-Ear, the master lacks wholesome food, and is starving. If the master goes, our death is also a certain thing. So I have a suggestion for your benefit and the master's. Please pay attention." "My good fellow," said Spike-Ear, "make haste to inform me, so that I may unhesitatingly do as you say. Besides, one earns credit for a hundred good deeds by serving his master."

And Smart said: "My good fellow, give your own body at 100 per cent interest, so that you may receive a double body, and the master may prolong his life." On hearing this proposal, Spike-Ear said: "If that is possible, my friend, my body shall be so devoted. Tell the master that this thing should be done. I stipulate only that the Death-God be requested to guarantee the bargain."

Having made their decision, they all went to visit the lion, and Smart said: "O King, we did not find a thing today, and the blessèd sun is already near his setting." On hearing this, the lion fell into deep despondency. Then Smart continued: "O King, our friend Spike-Ear makes this proposal: 'If you call upon the Death-God to guarantee the bargain, and if you render it back with 100 per cent of interest, then I will give my body.' " "My good fellow," answered the lion, "yours is a beautiful act. Let it be as you say." On the basis of this pact, Spike-Ear was struck down by the lion's paw, his body was torn by the wolf and the jackal, and he died.

Then Smart reflected: "How can I get him all to

myself to eat?" With this thought in his mind, he noticed that the lion's body was smeared with blood, and he said: "Master, you must go to the river to bathe and worship the gods, while I stay here with Meat-Face to guard the food-supply." On hearing this, the lion went to the river.

When the lion was gone, Smart said to Meat-Face: "Friend Meat-Face, you are starving. You might eat some of this camel before the old master returns. I will make your apologies to the master." So Meat-Face took the hint, but had only taken a taste when Smart cried: "Drop it, Meat-Face. The master is coming."

Presently the lion returned, saw that the camel was minus a heart, and wrathfully roared: "Look here! Who turned this camel into leavings? I wish to kill him, too." Then Meat-Face peered into Smart's visage, as much as to say: "Come, now! Say something, so that he may calm down." But Smart laughed and said: "Come, come! You ate the camel's heart all by yourself. Why do you look at me?" And Meat-Face, hearing this, fled for his life, making for another country. But when the lion had pursued him a short distance, he turned back, thinking: "He, too, is unguipugnacious. I must not kill him."

At this moment, as fate would have it, there came that way a great camel caravan, heavily laden, making a tremendous jingling with the bells tied to the camels' necks. And when the lion heard the jingle of the bells, loud even in the distance, he said to the jackal: "My good fellow, find out what this horrible noise may be."

On receiving this commission, Smart advanced a little in the forest, then darted back, and cried in great excitement: "Run, master! Run, if you *can* run!"

"My good fellow," said the lion, "why terrify me so? Tell me what it is." And Smart cried: "Master, the Death-God is coming, and he is in a rage against you because you brought untimely death upon his camel, and had him guarantee the bargain. He intends to make you pay a thousand fold for his camel. He has immense pride in his camels. He also plans to make inquiries about the father and grandfathers of that one. He is coming. He is near at hand."

When the lion heard this, he, too, abandoned the dead camel and scampered for dear life. Whereupon Smart ate the camel bit by bit, so that the meat lasted a long time.

"And that is why I say:

> The wise who wrongs another,
> Pursuing selfish good, ...

and the rest of it."

Now when Victor was gone, Lively reflected: "What am I to do? Suppose I go elsewhere, then some other merciless creature will kill me, for this is a wild wood. Indeed, when the master is furious, it is not possible even to depart. For the proverb says:

Impunity comes not
By fleeing far away:
The long arms of the shrewd
Make careless sinners pay.

"My best course is to approach the lion. He might regard me as a suppliant, might even spare my life."

Having thus set his mind in order, he started very slowly, with troubled spirit, and when he perceived the lion in the posture foretold by Victor, he sank down at some little distance, thinking: "Ah, the unfathomable character of kings! As the proverb says:

'Tis a house with serpents crawling,
Wood with beasts of prey appalling,
Lotus-pond where blossoms smile
O'er the lurking crocodile,
Spot that sneaking rogues deface
With repeated slanders base—
Timid servant never learns
Whither kingly purpose turns."

Rusty for his part, perceiving the bull in the attitude predicted by Victor, made a sudden spring at him. And Lively, though his body was torn by sharp claws as formidable as thunderbolts, also scored the lion's belly with his horns, contrived to break away from him, and stood in fighting posture, ready to gore again.

At this point Cheek perceived that both of them, red as dhak trees in blossom, were intent on killing each other, and he said reproachfully to Victor: "You dunderhead! In setting these two at enmity, you have done a wicked deed. You have brought trouble and confusion into this entire forest, thus proving your ignorance of the true nature of statecraft. For the saying runs:

Those are counselors indeed,
Wise in statecraft, who succeed
In composing reckless strife
That, unhindered, threatens life:
Those on petty purpose bent,
Keen to visit punishment,
Quick in wrong and folly, bring
Risk to kingdom and to king.

Ah, poor fool!

Men of true discernment, first
  Try conciliation;
For the victories of peace
  Suffer no frustration.

Ah, poor simpleton! You seek the post of counselor, and are ignorant of the very name of conciliation. Your ambition is vain, since you love harsh measures. As the proverb puts it:

Lord Brahma bids the statesman try
  Conciliation first,
Postpone or shun (it can be done)
  Harsh deeds, of all deeds worst.

'Tis neither sun nor flashing gem
  Nor fiery spark,
'Tis peace, from bitter foemen's hearts
  That routs the dark.

And again:

Try peaceful means, not harsh, to make
   Your quarrel flit:
Take sugar, not cucumber, for
   A bilious fit.

And once again:

The doors that wit unlocks are three—
Peace, shrewd intrigue, and bribery;
The fourth device that brings success
In struggle, is plain manliness.

'Tis womanish, no doubt, to show
   Small strength, abundant sense;
But power is merely bestial, if
   Without intelligence.

Snake, lion, elephant, and fire,
   With water, wind, and sun,
Have power. From undirected power
   Is little profit won.

"Now if it was overweening pride in being the son of a counselor that has led you to outrage decency, the result will be merely your own ruin. As the proverb says:

What is learning whose attaining
Sees no passion wane, no reigning
   Love and self-control?
Does not make the mind a menial,
Finds in virtue no congenial
   Path and final goal?
Whose attaining is but straining
For a name, and never gaining
   Fame or peace of soul?

"Now in the treatises on the subject statesmanship is subsumed under five heads, to wit: proper inception; resources, human and material; determination of place and time; countermeasures for mischance; and successful accomplishment. At the present moment, the master finds himself in serious peril. So, if you have any such capacity, devise countermeasures for his mischance. For the wisdom of a counselor finds its test in the patching of friendship. Ah, you fool! That you cannot do, because you have a perverted mind. As the saying goes:

> No scamp can further others' work,
>   But can deprave it:
> The mole uproots the mulberry,
>   But cannot save it.

"After all, the fault is not yours, but rather the master's, who trusts your words, dull-witted as you are. And the proverb says:

> Educating sluggish wit
> Kills no pride but fosters it:
> In the sunlight others find
> Aid to vision; owls go blind.
>
> Education thrusts aside
> Man's fatuity and pride;
> If it foster them, who can
> Cure the educated man?
> Remedies are useless when
> Heaven's nectar poisons men."

And Cheek, beholding his master in pitiful plight, sank into deep dejection. "Dreadful," he cried, "dreadful is the penalty the master pays for taking evil counsel! Indeed, there is wisdom in the verse:

> Monarchs who adopt a plan
> From the mean and vicious man,
> Who refuse to tread the way
> That the prudent counsel—they
> Enter misadventure's cage
> Where the adversaries rage;
> Thence deliverance's gate
> Crowns an issue rugged, strait.

"Fool! Fool! All the world seeks the service of a master whose retinue is righteous. How, then, can such an evil counselor as you, who, like a beast, understand nothing but destruction—how can such a one enrich the master with righteous companions? For the proverb says:

> Monarchs, ill-advised, repel,
> Even though they purpose well:
> Sweet and placid waters smile,
> But beware the crocodile.

"Yet you, I suppose, seeking your own advantage, desire to have the king quite solitary. Ah, fool! Are you ignorant of the verse?

> Kings shine as social beings, not
> As solitaries;
> Whoever wish them lonely are
> Their adversaries.

And again:

> Draw benefit from comments harsh;
> No poison, this:
> In flattery see treason, not
> True nectar's bliss.

"And if you are grieved at seeing others happy and prosperous, that, too, is wicked. It is wrong to proceed thus when friends have fulfilled their nature. For

Those who seek, through treason, friends;
Seek, through humbug, righteous ends;
Property by wronging neighbors;
Learning's wealth by easy labors;
Woman's love by cruel pride—
These are fools, self-stultified.

Likewise:

The happiness of subjects makes
  The monarch gay and brave:
Nay, what would be the dancing sea
  With no gem-flashing wave?

"Furthermore, for one who has enjoyed the master's favor, modesty is peculiarly proper. As the verse puts it:

According to his favored state,
A servant's modest, humble gait
Is notably appropriate.

"Your character, however, is marked by levity. And the proverb says:

The great are firm, though battered, as before;
Great ocean is not fouled by caving shore:
For petty cause the fickle change and pass;
The gentlest breezes ruffle pliant grass.

"When all is said, it is the master's fault. For in pursuit of virtue, money, and love, he recklessly takes counsel with one like you—one who lives by the mere pretense of administrative competence, in total ignorance of the six expedients and the four devices for attaining success. Yes, there is wisdom in this:

> If kings are satisfied
> With servants at their side
> Who ply a wheedling tongue,
> Whose bows are never strung,
> Then kingly glory goes
> Embracing manlier foes.

"Indeed, there is much sense in the story which is summed up in the familiar verse:

> The counselor whose name was Strong
> Attained his dearest heart's desire:
> He won the favor of his king;
> He burned the naked monk with fire."

"How was that?" asked Victor. And Cheek told the story of

THE MONK WHO LEFT HIS BODY BEHIND

In the Koshala country is a city called Unassailable. In it ruled a king named Fine-Chariot, over whose footstool rippled rays of light from the diadems of uncounted vassal princes.

One day a forest ranger came with this report: "Master, all the forest kings have become turbulent, and in their midst is the forest chief named Vindhyaka. It is the king's affair to teach him modest manners." On hearing this report, the king summoned Counselor Strong, and despatched him with orders to chastise the forest chieftains.

Now in the absence of the counselor, a naked monk arrived in the city at the end of the hot season. He was master of the astronomical specialties, such as problems and etymologies, rising of the zodiacal signs, augury, ecliptic intersection, and the decanate; also stellar mansions divided into nine parts, twelve parts, thirty parts; the shadow of the gnomon, eclipses, and numerous other mysteries. With these the fellow in a few days won the entire population, as if he had bought and paid for them.

Finally, as the matter went from mouth to mouth, the king heard a report of its character, and had the curiosity to summon the monk to his palace. There he offered him a seat and asked: "Is it true, Professor, as they say, that you read the thoughts of others?" "That will be demonstrated in the sequel," replied the monk, and by discourses adapted to the occasion he brought the poor king to the extreme pitch of curiosity.

One day he failed to appear at the regular hour, but the following day, on entering the palace, he announced: "O King, I bring you the best of good tidings. At dawn today I flung this body aside within my cell, assumed a body fit for the world of the gods, and, inspired with the knowledge that all the immortals thought of me with longing, I went to heaven and have just returned. While there, I was requested by the gods to inquire in their name after the king's welfare."

When he heard this, the king said, his extreme curiosity begetting a feeling of amazement: "What, Professor! You go to heaven?" "O mighty King," replied the fellow, "I go to heaven every day." This the king believed—poor dullard!—so that he grew negligent of all royal business and all duties toward the ladies, concentrating his attention on the monk.

While matters were in this state, Strong entered the king's presence, after settling all disturbances in the forest domain. He found the master wholly indifferent to every one of his counselors, withdrawn in private conference with that naked monk, discussing what seemed to be some miraculous occurrence, his lotus-face ablossom. And on learning the facts, Strong bowed low and said: "Victory, O King! May the gods give you wit!"

Thereupon the king inquired concerning the counselor's health, and said: "Sir, do you know this professor?" To which the counselor replied: "How could there be ignorance of one who is lord and creator of a whole school of professors? Moreover, I have heard that this professor goes to heaven. Is it a fact?" "Everything that you have heard," answered the king, "is beyond the shadow of doubt."

Thereupon the monk said: "If this counselor feels any curiosity, he may see for himself." With this he entered his cell, barred the door from within, and waited there. After the lapse of a mere moment, the counselor spoke: "O King," he said, "how soon will he return?" And the king replied: "Why this impatience? You must know that he leaves his lifeless body within this cell, and returns with another, a heavenly body."

"If this is indeed the case," said Strong, "then bring a great quantity of firewood, so that I may set fire to this cell." "For what purpose?" asked the king. And the counselor continued: "So that, when this lifeless body has been burned, the gentleman may stand before the king in that other body which visits heaven. In this connection I will tell you the story of

THE GIRL WHO MARRIED A SNAKE

In Palace City lived a Brahman named Godly, whose childless wife wept bitterly when she saw the neighbors' youngsters. But one day the Brahman said: "Forget your sorrow, mother dear. See! When I was offering the sacrifice for birth of children, an invisible being said to me in the clearest words: 'Brahman, you shall have a son surpassing all mankind in beauty, character, and charm.' "

When she heard this, the wife felt her heart swell with supreme delight. "I only hope his promises come true," she said. Presently she conceived, and in course of time gave birth to a snake. When she saw him, she paid no attention to her companions, who all advised her to throw him away. Instead, she took him and bathed him, laid him with motherly tenderness in a large, clean box, and pampered him with milk, fresh butter, and other good things, so that before many days had passed, he grew to maturity.

But one day the Brahman's wife was watching the marriage festival of a neighbor's son, and the tears streamed down her face as she said to her husband: "I know that you despise me, because you do nothing about a marriage festival for my boy." "My good wife," answered he, "am I to go to the depths of the underworld and beseech Vasuki the serpent-king? Who else, you foolish woman, would give his own daughter to this snake?"

But when he had spoken, he was disturbed at seeing the utter woe in his wife's countenance. He therefore packed provisions for a long journey, and undertook foreign travel from love of his wife. In the course of some months he arrived at a spot called Kutkuta City in a distant land. There in the house of a kinsman whom he could visit with pleasure since each respected the other's character, he was hospitably received, was given a bath, food, and the like, and there he spent the night.

Now at dawn, when he paid his respects to his Brahman host and made ready to depart, the other asked him: "What was your purpose in coming hither? And where will your errand lead you?"

To this he replied: "I have come in search of a fit wife for my son." "In that case," said his host, "I have a very beautiful daughter, and my own person is yours to command. Pray take her for your son."

So the Brahman took the girl with her attendants and returned to his own place.

But when the people of the country beheld her incomparable opulence of beauty, her supreme loveliness and superhuman graces, their eyes popped out with pleasure, and they said to her attendants: "How can right-thinking persons bestow such a pearl of a girl upon a snake?" On hearing this, all her elderly relatives without exception were troubled at heart, and they said: "Let her be taken from this imp-ridden creature." But the girl said: "No more of this mockery! Remember the text:

> Do once, once only, these three things:
> Once spoken, stands the word of kings;
> The speech of saints has no miscarriage;
> A maid is given once in marriage.

And again:

> All fated happenings, derived
> From any former state,
> Must changeless stand: the very gods
> Endured poor Blossom's fate."

Whereupon they all asked in chorus: "Who was this Blossom person?" And the girl told the story of

POOR BLOSSOM

God Indra once had a parrot named Blossom. He enjoyed supreme beauty, loveliness, and various graces, while his intelligence was not blunted by his extensive scientific attainments.

One day he was resting on the palm of great

Indra's hand, his body thrilling with delight at that contact, and was reciting a variety of authoritative formulas, when he caught sight of Yama, lord of death, who had come to pay his respects at the time appointed. Seeing the god, the parrot edged away. And all the thronging immortals asked him: "Why did you move away, sir, upon beholding that personage?" "But," said the parrot, "he brings harm to all living creatures. Why not move away from him?"

Upon hearing this, they all desired to calm his fears, so said to Yama: "As a favor to us, you must please not kill this parrot." And Yama replied: "I do not know about that. It is Time who determines these matters."

They therefore took Blossom with them, paid a visit to Time, and made the same request. To which Time replied: "It is Death who is posted in these affairs. Pray speak to him."

But when they did so, the parrot died at the mere sight of Death. And they were all distressed at seeing the occurrence, so that they said to Yama: "What does this mean?" And Yama said: "It was simply fated that he should die at the mere sight of Death." With this reply they went back to heaven.

"And that is why I say:

All fated happenings, ...

and the rest of it. Furthermore, I do not wish my father reproached for double dealing on the part of his daughter." When she had said this, she married the snake, with the permission of her companions, and at once began devoted attendance upon him by offering milk to drink and performing other services.

One night the serpent issued from the generous chest which had been set for him in her chamber, and entered her bed. "Who is this?" she cried. "He has the form of a man." And thinking him a strange man, she started up, trembling in every limb, unlocked the door, and was about to dart away when she heard him say: "Stay, my dear wife. I am your husband." Then, in order to convince her, he reentered the body which he had left behind in the chest, issued from it again, and came to her.

When she beheld him flashing with lofty diadem, with earrings, bracelets, armbands, and rings, she fell at his feet, and then they sank into a glad embrace.

Now his father, the Brahman, rose betimes and discovered how matters stood. He therefore seized the serpent's skin that lay in the chest, and consumed it with fire, for he thought: "I do not want him to enter that again." And in the morning he and his wife, with the greatest possible joy, introduced to everybody as their own an extraordinarily handsome son, quite wrapped up in his love affair.

After Strong had related this parallel case to the king, he set fire to the cell that contained the naked monk.

"And that is why I say:

> The counselor whose name was Strong, ...

and the rest of it. Poor fool! Such men are true counselors, not creatures like you, who make a living by a mere pretense of administrative competence, though quite ignorant of the ways of statecraft. Your evil conduct demonstrates an inherited lack of executive capacity. Surely, your father before you was the same kind of person. For

> The character of sons
> The father e'er reflects:
> Who, from a screw-pine tree,
> An emblic fruit expects?

"While in men of learning and native dignity, an inner weakness is not detected even with the lapse of time. It remains hidden, unless of their own accord they cast dignity aside and display what is vulnerable in their minds. For

> Did not the silly peacock wheel
> In giddy dance at thunder's peal,
> What peering effort could reveal
> His nakedness?

"Since, then, you are a villain, good advice is thrown away upon you. As the saying goes:

> No knife prevails against a stone;
> Nor bends the unbending tree;
> No good advice from Needle-Face
> Helped indocility."

"How was that?" asked Victor. And Cheek told the story of

THE UNTEACHABLE MONKEY

In a part of a forest was a troop of monkeys who found a firefly one winter evening when they were dreadfully depressed. On examining the insect, they believed it to be fire, so lifted it with care, covered it with dry grass and leaves, thrust forward their arms, sides, stomachs, and chests, scratched themselves, and enjoyed imagining that they were warm. One of the arboreal creatures in particular, being especially chilly, blew repeatedly and with concentrated attention on the firefly.

Thereupon a bird named Needle-Face, driven by hostile fate to her own destruction, flew down from her tree and said to the monkey: "My dear sir, do not put yourself to unnecessary trouble. This is not fire. This is a firefly." He, however, did not heed her warning but blew again, nor did he stop when she tried more than once to check him. To cut a long story short, when she vexed him by coming close and shouting in his ear, he seized her and dashed her on a rock, crushing face, eyes, head, and neck so that she died.

"And that is why I say:

> No knife prevails against a stone; . . . .

and the rest of it. For, after all,

> Educating minds unfit
> Cannot rescue sluggish wit,
> Just as house-lamps wasted are,
> Set within a covered jar.

"Plainly, you are what is known as 'worse-born.' The technical explanation runs:

Sons of four divergent kinds
Are discerned by well-trained minds:
'Born,' and 'like-born,' 'better-born';
Lastly, 'worse-born' has their scorn.

'Born' the mother's image gives;
'Like-born' like the father lives;
'Better-born' more nobly acts;
'Worse-born' morally subtracts.

"Ah, there is wisdom in the saying:

By whom far-piercing wisdom or
Great wealth or power is won
To lift the family, in him
A mother has a son.

Again:

A merely striking beauty
Is not so hard to find;
A rarer gem is wisdom,
Far-reaching power of mind.

"Yes, there is sense in the story:

Right-Mind was one, and Wrong-Mind two;
I know the tale by heart:
The son in smoke made father choke
By being supersmart."

"How was that?" asked Victor. And Cheek told the story of

RIGHT-MIND AND WRONG-MIND

In a certain city lived two friends, sons of merchants, and their names were Right-Mind and

Wrong-Mind. These two traveled to another country far away in order to earn money. There the one named Right-Mind, as a consequence of favoring fortune, found a pot containing a thousand dinars, which had been hidden long before by a holy man. He debated the matter with Wrong-Mind, and they decided to go home, since their object was attained. So they returned together.

When they drew near their native city, Right-Mind said: "My good friend, a half of this falls to your share. Pray take it, so that, now that we are at home, we may cut a brilliant figure before our friends and those less friendly."

But Wrong-Mind, with a sneaking thought of his own advantage, said to the other: "My good friend, so long as we two hold this treasure in common, so long will our virtuous friendship suffer no interruption. Let us each take a hundred dinars, and go to our homes after burying the remainder. The decrease or increase of this treasure will serve as a test of our virtue."

Now Right-Mind, in the nobility of his nature, did not comprehend the hidden duplicity of his friend, and agreed to the proposal. Each then took a certain sum of money. They carefully hid the residue in the ground, and made their entrance into the city.

Before long, Wrong-Mind exhausted his preliminary portion because he practiced the vice of unwise expenditure and because his predetermined fate offered vulnerable points. He therefore made a second division with Right-Mind, each taking a second hundred. Within a year this, too, had slipped in the same way through Wrong-Mind's fingers. As a result, his thoughts took this form: "Suppose I divide another two hundred with him, then what is the good of the remainder, a paltry four hundred, even if I steal it? I think I prefer to steal a round six hundred." After this meditation, he went alone, removed the treasure, and leveled the ground.

A mere month later, he took the initiative, going to Right-Mind and saying: "My good friend, let us divide the rest of the money equally." So he and Right-Mind visited the spot and began to dig. When the excavation failed to reveal any treasure, that impudent Wrong-Mind first of all smote his own head with the empty pot, then shouted: "What became of that good lucre? Surely, Right-Mind, you must have stolen it. Give me my half. If you don't, I will bring you into court."

"Be silent, villain!" said the other. "My name is Right-Mind. Such thefts are not in my line. You know the verse:

> A man right-minded sees but trash,
> Mere clods of earth, in others' cash;
> A mother in his neighbor's wife;
> In all that lives, his own dear life."

So together they carried their dispute to court and related the theft of the money. And when the magistrates learned the facts, they decreed an ordeal for each. But Wrong-Mind said: "Come! This judgment is not proper. For the legal dictum runs:

> Best evidence is written word;
> Next, witnesses who saw and heard;
> Then only let ordeals prevail
> When witnesses completely fail.

In the present case, I have a witness, the goddess of the wood. She will reveal to you which one of us is guilty, which not guilty. And they replied: "You are quite right, sir. For there is a further saying:

> To meanest witnesses, ordeals
> Should never be preferred;
> Of course much less, if you possess
> A forest goddess' word.

Now we also feel a great interest in the case. You two must accompany us tomorrow morning to that part of the forest." With this they accepted bail from each and sent them home.

Then Wrong-Mind went home and asked his father's help. "Father dear," said he, "the dinars are in my hand. They only require one little word from you. This very night I am going to hide you out of sight in a hole in the mimosa tree that grows near the spot where I dug out the treasure before. In the morning you must be my witness in the presence of the magistrates."

"Oh, my son," said the father, "we are both lost.

This is no kind of a scheme. There is wisdom in the old story:

> The good and bad of given schemes
> Wise thought must first reveal:
> The stupid heron saw his chicks
> Provide a mungoose meal."

"How was that?" asked Wrong-Mind. And his father told the story of

A REMEDY WORSE THAN THE DISEASE

A flock of herons once had their nests on a fig tree in a part of a forest. In a hole in the tree lived a black snake who made a practice of eating the heron chicks before their wings sprouted.

At last one heron, in utter woe at seeing the young ones eaten by a snake, went to the shore of the pond, shed a flood of tears, and stood with downcast face. And a crab who noticed him in this attitude, said: "Uncle, why are you so tearful today?" "My good friend," said the heron, "what am I to do? Fate is against me. My babies and the youngsters belonging to my relatives have been eaten by a snake that lives in a hole in the fig tree. Grieved at their grief, I weep. Tell me, is there any possible device for killing him?"

On hearing this, the crab reflected: "After all, he is a natural-born enemy of my race. I will give him such advice—a kind of true lie—that other herons may also perish. For the proverb says:

> Let your speech like butter be;
> Steel your heart remorselessly:

Stir an enemy to action
That destroys him with his faction."

And he said aloud: "Uncle, conditions being as they are, scatter bits of fish all the way from the mungoose burrow to the snake's hole. The mungoose will follow that trail and will destroy the villainous snake."

When this had been done, the mungoose followed the bits of fish, killed the villainous snake, and also ate at his leisure all the herons who made their home in the tree.

"And that is why I say:

The good and bad of given schemes, ...

and the rest of it."

But Wrong-Mind disdained the paternal warning, and during the night he hid his father out of sight in the hole in the tree. When morning came, the scamp took a bath, put on clean garments, and followed Right-Mind and the magistrates to the mimosa tree, where he cried in piercing tones:

"Earth, heaven, and death, the feeling mind,
Sun, moon, and water, fire and wind,
Both twilights, justice, day and night
Discern man's conduct, wrong or right.

O blessèd goddess of the wood, which of us two is the thief? Speak."

Then Wrong-Mind's father spoke from his hole in the mimosa: "Gentlemen, Right-Mind took that money." And when all the king's men heard this statement, their eyes blossomed with astonishment, and they searched their minds to discover the appropriate legal penalty for stealing money, in order to visit it on Right-Mind.

Meanwhile Right-Mind heaped inflammable matter about the hole in the mimosa and set fire to it. As the mimosa burned, Wrong-Mind's father issued from the hole with a pitiful wail, his body scorched and his eyes popping out. And they all asked: "Why, sir! What does this mean?"

"It is all Wrong-Mind's doing," he replied. Whereupon the king's men hanged Wrong-Mind to a branch of the mimosa, while they commended Right-Mind and caused him satisfaction by conferring upon him the king's favor and other things.

"And that is why I say:

Right-mind was one, and Wrong-mind two, ...

and the rest of it."

After telling the story, Cheek continued: "Poor fool! By your oversubtle wisdom you have burned your own family. Yes, there is wisdom in the saying:

Rivers find their ending
  In the salty sea;
Household peace, as soon as
  Women disagree;
Secrets end that do not
  Every traitor shun;
Families are ended
  In a wicked son.

"Besides, who can trust a creature, whether human or not, that has two tongues in a single mouth? As the proverb says:

Mouths of snake and scamp
Bear a savage stamp;
Rough and ruthless still,
Only good for ill:
Where the tongue is double,
You may look for trouble.

"Consequently, your conduct makes me fearful for my own person. For

I would not trust a rascal;
His ways I understand:
The petted, pampered serpent
Will bite the feeding hand.

Again:

A fire will burn, though kindled
In fragrant sandalwood:
A rascal is a rascal,
Although his birth is good.

"After all, this is the very nature of rascals. As the proverb says:

Each self-advertising traitor,
Skilful as calumniator,
Fate condemns to ruin all
Who within his clutches fall.

Oh, any tongue in human mouth
That lends itself to slander's cant
Yet does not split a hundred times,
Is surely made of adamant.

Oh, may no evil e'er befall
The lion-man who loves his kind,
Who practices a silent vow
When others' faults are in his mind.

"Ah, one must use great circumspection in making acquaintances. As the proverb says:

With the shrewd and upright man
Seek a friendship rare;
Exercise with shrewd and false
Superheedful care;
Pity for the upright fool
Find within your heart;
If a man be fool and false,
Shun him from the start.

"Yes, your efforts have tended to the destruction not only of your own family, but, toward the last, of the master too. Since you reduce your own master to this state, other persons mean no more to you than withered grass. As the saying goes:

Where mice eat balance-beams of iron
A thousand *pals* in weight,
A hawk might steal an elephant;
A boy is trifling freight."

"How was that?" asked Victor. And Cheek told the story of

THE MICE THAT ATE IRON

In a certain town lived a merchant named Naduk, who lost his money and determined to travel abroad. For

The meanest of mankind is he
Who, having lost his money, can

Inhabit lands or towns where once
He spent it like a gentleman.

And again:

The neighbor gossips blame
His poverty as shame
Who long was wont to play
Among them, proud and gay.

In his house was an iron balance-beam inherited from his ancestors, and it weighed a thousand *pals*. This he put in pawn with Merchant Lakshman before he departed for foreign countries.

Now after he had long traveled wherever business led him through foreign lands, he returned to his native city and said to Merchant Lakshman: "Friend Lakshman, return my deposit, the balance-beam." And Lakshman said: "Friend Naduk, your balance-beam has been eaten by mice."

To this Naduk replied: "Lakshman, you are in no way to blame, if it has been eaten by mice. Such is life. Nothing in the universe has any permanence. However, I am going to the river for a bath. Please send your boy Money-God with me, to carry my bathing things."

Since Lakshman was conscience-stricken at his own theft, he said to his son Money-God: "My dear boy, let me introduce Uncle Naduk, who is going to the river to bathe. You must go with him and carry his bathing things." Ah, there is too much truth in the saying:

> There is no purely loving deed
> Without a pinch of fear or greed
> Or service of a selfish need.

And again:

> Wherever there is fond attention
> That does not seek a service pension,
> Was there no timid apprehension?

So Lakshman's son took the bathing things and delightedly accompanied Naduk to the river. After Naduk had taken his bath, he thrust Lakshman's son Money-God into a mountain cave, blocked the entrance with a great rock, and returned to Lakshman's house. And when Lakshman said: "Friend Naduk, tell me what has become of my son Money-God who went with you," Naduk answered: "My good Lakshman, a hawk carried him off from the river-bank."

"Oh, Naduk!" cried Lakshman. "You liar! How could a hawk possibly carry off a big boy like Money-God?" "But, Lakshman," retorted Naduk, "the mice could eat a balance-beam made of iron. Give me my balance-beam, if you want your son."

Finally, they carried their dispute to the palace gate, where Lakshman cried in a piercing tone: "Help! Help! A ghastly deed! This Naduk person has carried off my son—his name is Money-God."

Thereupon the magistrates said to Naduk: "Sir, restore the boy to Lakshman." But Naduk pleaded: "What am I to do? Before my eyes a hawk carried him from the river-bank." "Come, Naduk!" said they, "you are not telling the truth. How can a hawk carry off a fifteen-year-old boy?" Then Naduk laughed outright and said: "Gentlemen, listen to my words.

> Where mice eat balance-beams of iron
> A thousand *pals* in weight,
> A hawk might steal an elephant;
> A boy is trifling freight."

"How was that?" they asked, and Naduk told them the story of the balance-beam. At this they laughed and caused the restoration of balance-beam and boy to the respective owners.

"And that is why I say:

> Where mice eat balance-beams of iron, ...

and the rest of it." And Cheek continued: "Dunderhead! You have done this because you could not cheerfully see Rusty's favor bestowed on Lively. Yes, yes, there is wisdom in the saying:

> Cowards reproach the hero here on earth;
> Base-born rascals blame the man of birth;
> Misers, him who gives whate'er he can;
> Misfit lovers blame the ladies' man;
> Rogues, the righteous; cripples blame the straight;
> Those unlucky blame the fortunate;
> Last, the scholar—'tis the wretched rule—
> Listens to reproaches from the fool.

Again:

> Learnèd men from fools have hate;
> Rich, from those less fortunate;

Men of virtue, from the vicious;
Wives, from creatures meretricious.

Yet, after all:

Wise men, even, carry through
What their nature bids them do:
Nature ever will direct;
What can punishment effect?

"Instruction has value only for him who grasps what has been said once. But you are like a stone—brainless, immovable. Why waste effort to instruct you? More than that, O fool! it is a mistake even to live beside you. A disaster might some day befall me from mere association with you. As the proverb says:

To live beside a dunderhead
  In house or village, town or nation,
Is evil pure and simple, though
  One may escape all litigation.

Better plunge in sea or fire,
  Hell or deepest pit,
Than associate with one
  Quite devoid of wit.

With the bad or good consort,
  Vice or virtue clings;
Just as when the breezes in
  Distant wanderings
Carry odors foul or sweet
  On their restless wings.

"Indeed, there is wisdom in the old story:

Two birds were we. I and the other
One father had; we had one mother.

But I was taught by hermits, while
Beef-eaters gave him training vile.
Beef-eaters' speech, O King, he heard;
I listened to the hermits' word.
Our education, good and bad,
The obvious consequences had."

"How was that?" asked Victor. And Cheek told the story of

THE RESULTS OF EDUCATION

On a part of a mountain a hen-parrot brought two chicks into the world. These chicks were caught by a hunter when the mother had left the nest to search for food. One of them—since fate decreed it—contrived to escape, while the other was kept in a cage and taught to speak. Meanwhile, the first chick encountered a wandering holy man, who caught him, took him to his own hermitage, and gave him kindly care.

While time was passing in this manner, a certain king, whose horse ran away and separated him from his guard, came to that part of the forest where the hunters lived. The moment he perceived the king's approach, the parrot straightway began to chuckle from his cage: "Come, come, my masters! Here comes somebody riding a horse. Bind him, bind him! Kill him, kill him!" And when the king heard the parrot's words, he quickly spurred his horse in another direction.

Now when the king came to another wood far

away, he saw a hermitage of holy men, and in it a parrot who addressed him from a cage: "Enter, O King, and find repose. Taste our cool water and our sweet fruit. Come, hermits! Pay him honor. Give him water to wash his feet in the cool shade of this tree."

When he heard this, the king's eyes blossomed wide, and he wonderingly pondered what it might mean. And he said to the parrot: "In another part of the forest I met another parrot who looked like you, but who had a cruel disposition. 'Bind him, bind him!' he cried; 'kill him, kill him!' " And the parrot replied to the king by giving a precise relation of the course of his life.

"And that is why I say:

> Our education, good and bad,
> The obvious consequences had.

Thus mere association with you is an evil. As the proverb says:

> To foes of sense, not foolish friends,
> 'Tis wiser far to cling:
> The robber for his victims died;
> The monkey killed the king."

"How was that?" asked Victor. And Cheek told two stories, called

THE SENSIBLE ENEMY

There was once a prince who made friends with a merchant's son and the son of a man of learning.

Every day the three found entertainment in various diversions, flirtations, and pastimes in public squares, parks, and gardens. Every day the prince showed his aversion to the science of archery, to equitation and elephant-riding, to driving and hunting. At last, when his father one day gave him a wigging, telling him that he showed no aptitude for kingly pursuits, he disclosed to his two friends the injury inflicted on his self-esteem.

And they rejoined: "Our fathers, too, are continually talking nonsense when we show our aversion to their business. This tribulation, however, we have not noticed for many days because of the pleasure we took in your friendship. But now that we see you also grieved with the same grief, we are grieved exceedingly."

Thereupon the prince said: "It would be unmanly to remain here after being insulted. Let us depart together, all grieved with the same grief, and go somewhere else. For

> The truly self-respecting man
> Discovers what he is, and can,
> Deserves, and dares, and understands
> By traveling in foreign lands."

So much being determined, they considered where it was advisable to go. And the merchant's son said: "You know that no desire is anywhere attained without money. Let us therefore go to Climbing Mountain, where we may find precious gems and enjoy every heart's desire." The truth of this presentation they all recognized, so started for Climbing Mountain.

There, as fate decreed, each of them found a priceless, magnificent gem, whereupon they debated as follows: "How are we to guard these gems when we leave this spot by a forest trail thick with peril?" Then the son of the man of learning said: "You know I am the son of a counselor, and I have consequently thought out an appropriate plan, namely, that we swallow our gems and carry them in our stomachs. Thus we shall not be an object of interest to merchants, highwaymen, and other such people."

Having adopted this plan, each inserted his gem in a mouthful of food at dinner time, and swallowed it. But while they were doing so, a fellow who was resting unperceived on the mountain slope, observed them and reflected: "Look here! I, too, have tramped Climbing Mountain for many days, searching for gems. But I had no luck. I found nothing. So I will travel with them and wherever they grow weary and go to sleep, I will cut their stomachs open and take all three gems."

With this in mind, he came down the slope and overtook them, saying: "Good masters, I cannot pierce the frightful forest alone and reach my home. Let me join your caravan and travel with you." To this they assented, for they desired the increase of friendliness, and the four continued their journey.

Now in that forest, near the trail, was a Bhil village, nestling in a rugged bit of jungle. As the travelers passed through its outskirts, an old bird in a cage began to sing—this bird belonging to a numerous aviary kept as pets in the hut of the village chief.

This chief understood the meaning that all kinds of birds express in their song. He therefore comprehended the old bird's intention, and cried with great delight to his men: "Listen to what this bird tells us. He says that there are precious gems in the possession of yonder travelers on the trail, and that we ought to stop them. Catch them, and bring them here."

When the robbers had done so, the chief stripped the travelers with his own hand, but found nothing. So he set them free to resume their journey, clad in loincloths only. But the bird sang the same story, so that the village chief had them brought back, and freed them only after a most particular and minute inspection.

Once more they started, but when the bird impatiently screamed the same song, the chief recalled them once more and questioned them, saying: "I have tested this bird time and again, and he never tells a lie. Now he says there are gems in your possession. Where are they?" And they replied: "If there are gems in our possession, how did your most careful search fail to reveal them?"

But the chief retorted: "If this bird says the thing

over and over, the gems are certainly there, in your stomachs. It is now evening. At dawn I am determined to cut your stomachs open for gems." After this scolding, he had them thrust into a dungeon.

Then the captive thief reflected: "In the morning, when their stomachs are cut open and the chief finds such splendid gems, the greedy villain will be quite certain to slash my belly too. So my death is a certainty, whatever happens. What am I to do? Well, the proverb says:

> When that last hour arrives, that none,
> However shrewd, may miss,
> A noble spirit serves his kind,
> And death itself is bliss.

It is best, then, to offer my own stomach first to the knife, saving the very men I had planned to kill. For when my stomach is cut open first of all and that villain finds nothing, grub as he may, then he will cease to suspect the existence of gems and, heartless though he be, will yet have mercy enough to renounce the cutting of the stomachs of those others. Thus, by giving them life and wealth I shall gain the glory of a generous deed in this world, and a rebirth in purity hereafter. This is, so to speak, a wise man's death, though I did not seek the opportunity." And so the night passed.

At dawn the village chief was preparing to cut open their stomachs when the thief clasped his hands and humbly entreated him. "I cannot," he said, "behold the cutting of the stomachs of these my brothers. Pray be gracious, and cut my stomach first."

To this the chief mercifully agreed, but he found no sign of a gem in the stomach, cut as he would. Thereupon he penitently cried: "Woe, woe is me! Swelling with greed at the mere interpretation of a bird's song, I have done a ghastly deed. I infer that no more gems will be found in the other stomachs than in this." The three were therefore set free uninjured, and hastening through the forest, they reached a civilized spot.

"And that is why I say:

> The robber for his victims died.

Better the sensible enemy than

THE FOOLISH FRIEND

In this spot they sold all three gems, the merchant's son serving as their agent. The considerable capital thus obtained he laid before the prince, who, having appointed the son of the man of learning his prime minister, planned to seize the kingdom of the monarch of that country, and made the merchant's son his secretary of the treasury. He then, by offering double pay, assembled an army of picked elephants, horse, and infantry, began hostilities with a prime minister intelligent in the six expedients, killed the king in battle, seized his kingdom, and himself became king. Next he delegated all burdensome administrative functions to his two friends and consulted his ease in a life of graceful luxury.

After a time, as he dallied now and then in the ladies' apartments, he made a pet and constant companion of a monkey from the stable near by. For it is a well-known fact that kings take naturally to parrots, partridges, pigeons, rams, monkeys, and such creatures. In course of time the monkey, regaled with a variety of dainties from the royal hand, grew to be a big fellow, and became an object of respect to the entire court. The king, indeed, felt such confidence in the monkey and such affection that he made him his personal sword-bearer.

Now the king had near his palace a pleasure-grove made charming by clumps of trees of various species. When springtime came, he perceived how delightful was this grove, since it advertised the glory of Love in the humming of swarms of bees, and was fragrant with the perfumes of crowding blossoms. He therefore entered it with his queen in a passion of love, and all his human retinue were left behind at the entrance.

After a period of delighted wandering and gazing, the king grew weary and said to the monkey: "I shall rest and sleep a moment in this arbor. You must keep careful watch to prevent anyone from disturbing me." With this he went to sleep.

Presently a bee, drawn by the fragrance of flowers, of musk, and other perfumes, hovered over him and alighted on his head. On seeing this, the monkey angrily thought: "What! Under my very eyes this wretched creature looks upon the king!" And he undertook to drive him away.

But when the bee, for all his efforts, continued to approach the king, the monkey went blind with rage, drew his sword, and fetched a blow at the bee—a blow that split the king's head.

And the queen, who was sleeping beside him, started up in terror, screaming when she beheld the incomprehensible fact: "You fool! You monkey! The king trusted you. How could you do it?"

Then the monkey told what had happened, after which everybody, by common consent, scolded him and shunned him.

"So there is reason in saying that one should not make friends with a fool, inasmuch as the monkey killed the king. Indeed, that is why I say:

> To foes of sense, not foolish friends,
> 'Tis wiser far to cling:
> The robber for his victims died;
> The monkey killed the king."

And Cheek continued:

> "Where *your* sort have the final word,
> By whom friends' enmities are stirred,
> Whose wisdom lies in tricky traps,
> All efforts end in sad mishaps.

And again:

> The saint, however deep his need,
> Still shuns the guilt of evil deed;

Still does the deeds that bring no shame
To honorable name and fame.

Again:

The wise in need still does the deed
  That keeps his honor bright:
The shell a peacock ate and dropped,
  Remains a pearly white.

And the proverb says:

Wrong is wrong; the wise man never
  Wrong as right will treat:
None would drink, however thirsty,
  Water in the street.

To sum it all up:

Do the right, the right, the right,
  Till the breath of death;
Shun the wrong, although the right
  Lead to death of breath."

Hereupon, being a tortuous-minded creature to whom a sermon advocating such moral standards was sheer poison, Victor slunk away.

At this moment Rusty and Lively, their minds blinded by rage, renewed the battle. But when Rusty had killed Lively, his wrath subsided into pity at the memory of past affection. He wiped his weeping eyes with a blood-smeared paw and penitently said: "Ah, me! It was very wrong. Lively was almost my second life. In killing him, I have only hurt myself. For the proverb says:

When bits are lost of royal land
Or servants true who understand,

The servants' loss is deadly pain;
Lost lands are quickly won again."

But Victor, the impudent, perceiving that Rusty was mastered by irresolution, slowly crept near and said: "Master, what conduct is this—to show yourself irresolute after slaying a rival? For the saying runs:

None leaves a father, brother, son,
  Or bosom-friend alive
Who treasonably threatens him,
  If he desires to thrive.

Likewise:

A king compassionate,
A careless magistrate,
A wilful wife, a friend
Whose thoughts to treason tend,
A guzzling Brahman, or
A sulky servitor,
With all who do not know
Their business—let them go.

Go however far to find
  Honest joy;
Learn from any who is wise,
  Though a boy;
Give your life, the altruist's
  Bliss to win;
Cut your very arm away,
  If it sin.

"And the morality of kings has nothing in common with that of ordinary men. As the proverb says:

To ruling monarchs let no trace
  Of common nature cling;

For what is vice in other men,
  Is virtue in a king.

And once more:

Kings' policy is fickle, like
  A woman of the town:
For now it hoards its money up,
  Now flings it careless down;
'Tis rough and flattering by turns;
  'Tis kind, and cruel too;
Exacting much and giving much,
  At once 'tis false and true."

Hereupon Cheek, since Victor did not return, drew near, sat down beside the lion, and said to Victor: "Sir, you know nothing of the business of administration, since the stirring of strife means the destruction of those who had enjoyed mutual friendship. It is not the practice of genuine counselors, when objects of ambition are attainable through conciliation, bribery, or intrigue, to advise the master to fight his own servant, so bringing him into deadly danger. As the proverb says:

The god of wealth, the god of war,
  The god of water, and
The god of fire have planned to win,
  Then lost the fights they planned;
For victory is not a thing
  That men or gods command.

And besides:

No wisdom lies in fighting, since
  It is the fools who fight;

The wise discover in wise books
  What course is wise and right,
And wise books in the course that is
  Not violent, delight.

"Therefore a counselor should under no circumstances advise his master to fight. And there is another wise saying:

Where the palace harbors servants
  Kindly, modest, pure,
Death to enemies, and deaf to
  Avarice's lure,
Foes may struggle, but the royal
  Honor is secure.

Therefore

Speak the truth, though harsh it be:
Blarney is true enmity.

And again:

Where royal servants, asked or not,
  Indulge in pleasant lies
That lead the royal mind astray,
  The royal glory dies.

"Furthermore, counselors should be consulted severally by the master, who should thereupon make his own decision concerning the advice given by each, as tending to the king's loss or profit. For it happens at times that even an established fact seems otherwise to a wandering judgment. As the proverb says:

The firefly seems a fire, the sky looks flat;
Yet sky and fly are neither this nor that.

And again:

> The true seem often false, the false seem true;
> Appearances deceive, so think it through.

"Consequently, a master should not implicitly rely on the advice of a servant who lacks the administrative sense, inasmuch as rascally servants, for their personal profit, present matters to the master in a false light, and with bewildering eloquence. Hence, a master should undertake a matter only after full reflection. As the proverb says:

> Let fit and friendly counsel first,
> And more than once, be heard;
> Then ponder on the plan proposed
> From first to final word;
> Then act, and harvest fame and wealth,
> Avoiding the absurd.

"Finally, let no master suffer his mind to be twitched aside by others' counsel. Let him always be mindful of the differences in men, let him fully consider the ultimate issue, whether favorable or the reverse, of various counsels, answers, and times of action. Let him *be* the master, a wise master, ever cognizant of the multiform complexities of duty."

Here ends Book I, called "The Loss of Friends." The first verse runs:

> The forest lion and the bull
> Were linked in friendship, growing, full;
> A jackal then estranged the friends
> For greedy and malicious ends.

BOOK II

THE WINNING OF FRIENDS

BOOK II

THE WINNING OF FRIENDS

Here, then, begins Book II, called "The Winning of Friends." The first verse runs:

> The mouse and turtle, deer and crow,
> Had first-rate sense and learning; so,
> Though money failed and means were few,
> They quickly put their purpose through.

"How was that?" asked the princes. And Vishnusharman told the following story.

In the southern country is a city called Maidens' Delight. Not far away was a very lofty banyan tree with mighty trunk and branches, which gave refuge to all creatures. As the verse puts it:

> Blest be the tree whose every part
> Brings joy to many a creature's heart—
> Its green roof shelters birds in rows,
> While deer beneath its shadow doze;
> Its flowers are sipped by tranquil bees,
> And insects throng its cavities,
> While monkeys in familiar mirth
> Embrace its trunk. That tree has worth;
> But others merely cumber earth.

In the tree lived a crow named Swift. One morning he started toward the city in search of food. But he saw a hunter who lived in the neighborhood and who was already near the tree, approaching to trap birds. He was hideous in person, flat of hand and foot, bare to the calf of the leg, dreadfully ugly of complexion, had bloodshot eyes, was accompanied by dogs, wore his hair in a knot, carried snare and club in his hand—why spin it out? He seemed a second god of destruction, noose in hand; the incarnation of evil; the heart of unrighteousness; the teacher of every sin; the bosom friend of death.

When Swift saw him, he was disturbed in spirit and reflected: "What does he mean to do, the sinner? To hurt me? Or has he some other purpose?" And he clung to the hunter's heels, being filled with curiosity.

Now the hunter picked a spot, spread a snare, scattered grain, and hid not far away. But the birds who lived there were held in check by Swift's counsel, regarded the rice-grains as deadly poison, and did not peep.

At this juncture a dove-king named Gay-Neck, with hundreds of dove retainers, was wandering in search of food, and spied the rice-grains from afar. In spite of dissuasion from Swift, he greedily sought to eat them and alighted in the great snare. The moment he did so, he and his retainers were caught in the meshes. Nor should he be blamed. It happened through hostile fate. As the saying goes:

> How did Ravan fail to feel
> That 'tis wrong, a wife to steal?

How did Rama fail to see
Golden deer could never be?
How Yudhishthir fail to know
Gambling brings a train of woe?
Clutching evil dims the sense,
Darkening intelligence.

And again:

When once the mind is gripped by fate,
The judgment even of the great,
In mortal meshes fettered, wends
To unintended, crooked ends.

So the hunter gleefully lifted his club and ran forward. Then Gay-Neck and his retainers, seeing him advancing, were distressed by their disastrous position in the snare. But the king, with much presence of mind, said to the doves: "Have no fear, my friends. For

Provided judgment does not fail,
  Whatever the distress,
Men reach the farther shore of woe,
  And rest in happiness.

We must all agree in purpose, must fly up in unison, and carry the snare away. This is not possible without united action. For death befalls those of disunited purpose. As the saying goes:

Bharunda birds will teach you why
The disunited surely die:
For, single-bellied, double-necked,
They took a diet incorrect."

"How was that?" asked the doves. And Gay-Neck told the story of

THE BHARUNDA BIRDS

By a certain lake in the world lived birds called "bharunda birds." They had one belly and two necks apiece.

While one of these birds was sauntering about, his first neck found some nectar. Then the second said: "Give me half." And when the first refused, the second neck angrily picked up poison somewhere and ate it. As they had one belly, they died.

"And that is why I say:

> Bharunda birds will teach you why, ...

and the rest of it. Thus union is strength."

When the doves heard this, being eager to live, they united their efforts to carry the snare away, flew just an arrow-shot into the air, formed a canopy in the sky, and proceeded without fear.

When the hunter saw the snare carried away by birds, he looked up in amazement, thinking: "This is unprecedented." And he recited a stanza:

> So long as they agree, they may
> Carry the fatal snare away;
> But they will quickly disagree,
> And then those birds belong to me.

With this in mind, he started to pursue. And when Gay-Neck perceived the savage pursuer and recognized his purpose, with judgment unconfused, he started to fly over regions rough with hills and trees.

And Swift in turn, astonished both by Gay-Neck's prudent conduct and the hunter's cruel purpose, repeatedly shifted his glance, looking now up, now down, forgot his concern for food, and followed the flock of doves with keenest interest. For he was thinking: "What will this noble soul do next? And what this villain?" At last the hunter, observing that the flock of doves was protected by the roughness of the paths, turned back in disappointment, saying:

"What shall not be, will never be;
What shall be, follows painlessly;
The thing your fingers grasp, will flit,
If fate has predetermined it.

And again:

If fate be hostile, even gains
Acquired no man can hold;
They go, and take his other wealth,
Like hoards of magic gold.

"For, to say nothing of getting birds to eat, I have actually lost the snare which was my means of supporting the family."

Now when Gay-Neck saw that the hunter had turned back hopeless, he said to the doves: "See! We may travel quietly. The villainous hunter has turned back. This being so, our best plan is to fly to the city Maidens' Delight. For in its northeastern quarter dwells a mouse named Gold, a dear friend of mine. He will cut our bonds in a hurry. He is quite competent to set us free from our trouble."

So they all did as he said, for they were eager to find the mouse named Gold. And when they reached the hole which he had converted into a fortress, they alighted. Now previously

The mouse, in social ethics skilled,
Saw danger coming. Then
He built and was residing in
A hundred-gated den.

This being so, Gold was alarmed at the whir of birds' wings, darted along one path in his fortress-den until just beyond reach of a cat's paw, and remained on the *qui vive*, wondering what it meant. But Gay-Neck took his stand at a gate of the den, and said: "My dear Gold, pray hasten to me. See what a plight I am in."

Thereupon Gold, still within his fortress, said: "My good sir, who are you? What is your errand? And of what nature is your misfortune? Please inform me." And Gay-Neck answered: "Why, my name is Gay-Neck. I am king of the doves, and a friend of yours. Hasten to me." At this the mouse felt a quiver in his body and a thrill in his soul. He hastened forth, saying:

If daily to his home
The friends who love him come,
And coming, bring delight
To eyes that kindle bright,
A man has found the whole
Of life within his soul.

Then, observing that Gay-Neck and his retainers were caught in a snare, he sadly said: "My good friend, what is this, and whence? Tell me."

"My good friend," answered Gay-Neck, "why do you ask me? For you know it well. As the proverb says:

Whence, what, by whom, how long, when, where,
  And how deserved is good or ill,
Thence, that, by him, so long, then, there,
  And so it comes. Fate has its will.

And again:

The peacock seems the world to view
From thousand eyes that mock the hue
  Of some bright water-lily;
When fear of death beclouds his mind,
His conduct is of one born blind;
  He sinks disheartened, silly.

A hundred leagues and twenty-five
  The vulture spies his meat,
But—fate decreeing—fails to see
  The snare before his feet.

And again:

Snake, bird, and elephant are caged;
  The moon and sun go through eclipse;
The wise are poor: all this I see,
  And think how dreadfully fate grips.

And once again:

The birds that in the sky securely soar,
  Endure calamities;
While fish are plucked by men from ocean's floor
  In far, unsounded seas:

Why speak of virtue here or moral harm?
What stance could help or mar?
'Tis Time that stretches forth a fatal arm,
And seizes from afar."

When Gay-neck had spoken thus, Gold began to cut his bonds, but Gay-Neck checked him, saying: "My good friend, this is wrong. Please do not cut my bonds first, but my followers'." Now Gold grew angry at this and said: "Come now! You are mistaken. For servants follow the master." "No, no, my good friend," said Gay-Neck. "All these poor creatures left others to take service with me. Shall I fail to show them this petty honor? You know the proverb:

The king who offers honor to
His followers beyond their due,
Has servants glad who never quail,
Not even should his money fail.

And again:

Through trust, the root of happy power,
A creature wins to kingship's flower;
While lions, born to kingship, must
As tyrants govern, lacking trust.

"Besides, after cutting my bonds, you might perhaps get a toothache. Or that villainous hunter might return. In that case, I should surely plunge to hell. As the proverb says:

A king who is content to know
That loyal servants suffer woe,
Will later go to hell, but first
Will see his earthly projects burst."

"Yes," said Gold, "I am well aware of this royal duty. It was to test you that I said what I did. Now I will cut the bonds of all, and you will have in them a numerous retinue. For the proverb says:

> The king who mercifully grants
> Due share in all good circumstance
> To serving-folk, may fitly rise
> The triple world to supervise."

After making these observations, Gold cut the bonds of all, then said to Gay-Neck: "Now, my friend, you are free to go home." So Gay-Neck went home with his retinue. Yes, there is wisdom in the saying:

> Because a man can gain his ends,
> Though difficult, with aid of friends,
> Get friends, and feel those friends to be
> Integral with prosperity.

Now Swift, who had followed the whole matter of Gay-Neck's capture and release, was filled with astonishment, and he thought: "What intelligence has this Gold! What capacity! What an ingenious fortress! It would therefore be wise for me also to make friends with Gold. Even though I am of a suspicious temperament, confiding in nobody, even if I am too clever to be overreached by anybody, even so I should win a friend. For the proverb says:

> Even the self-sufficient should
> Get friends, and seek a greater good:
> The ocean fears no diminution,
> Yet waits Arcturus' contribution."

After these reflections, he flew down from his tree, approached the gate of the den, and called out—for he had previously heard the name of Gold: "Gold, my dear sir, pray come out."

And Gold, hearing this, reflected: "Is this perhaps some other dove who, still somewhat entangled, is addressing me?" And he said: "Who are you, sir?" "I am a crow," was the answer. "My name is Swift."

On hearing this, Gold hugged a far corner and said: "My very dear sir, please leave this neighborhood." "But," replied the crow, "I have come to see you on weighty business. Please grant me an interview."

"I see no advantage in making your acquaintance," said Gold. "But," said the crow, "I feel great confidence in you—the result of seeing how Gay-Neck was relieved of bonds through your exertions. I too may possibly be caught some day and find deliverance through you. Please enter into friendship with me."

"Sir," answered Gold, "you eat, and I am food. How can I feel friendship for you? You have heard the saying:

> The dull think inequalities
>   In strength no fatal blocks
> To friendship. True—but they *are* dull,
>   And public laughingstocks.

Please begone."

"Look!" said the crow. "Here I perch at the gate of your den. If you do not make friends with me, I shall starve to death." "But," said Gold, "how can I make friends with you, with an enemy? For the proverb says:

> Make no truce, however snug,
> With foemen dire:
> Water, even boiling hot,
> Will quench a fire."

"Why," said the crow, "you do not even know me by sight. Why should there be strife? Why say a thing so little to the purpose?"

"Sir," said Gold, "strife is of two kinds, natural and incidental. Now you are in natural strife with me. And the saying goes:

> By incidental means one ends
> An incidental strife,
> And quickly. Nature's kind endures
> Until the loss of life."

"Sir," said the crow, "I should like to learn the characteristic quality of each kind." "Well," said the mouse, "incidental strife springs from a specific cause, and can therefore be removed by rendering an appropriate service. But strife rooted in nature never disappears. Thus there is enduring strife between mungoose and snake—herbivorous creatures and those armed with claws—water and fire—gods and devils—dogs and cats—rival wives—lions and elephants—hunter and deer—crow and owl—scholar and numskull—wife and harlot—saint and sinner. In these cases, nobody belonging to anybody has been killed by anybody, yet they fight to the death."

"But this is senseless," said the crow. "Listen to me.

For cause a man becomes a friend;
For cause grows hostile. So
The prudent make a friend of him,
And never make a foe."

"But," said Gold, "what commerce can there be between you and me? Listen to the kernel of social ethics:

Whoever trusts a faithless friend
And twice in him believes,
Lays hold on death as certainly
As when a mule conceives.

And again:

A lion took the life of Panini,
Grammar's most famous name;
A tusker madly crushed sage Jaimini
Of metaphysic fame;
And Pingal, metric's boast, was slaughtered by
A seaside crocodile—
What sense for scholarly attainments high
Have beasts besotted, vile?"

"True enough," said the crow. "But listen to this:

The beasts and birds as friends are won
For cause; plain folks, for service done;
And silly souls, for greed or fright—
But good men are your friends at sight.

And again:

Like pots of clay, the wicked friend
Is quick to smash and hard to mend:
Like pots of gold the righteous flash,
As quick to mend, as hard to smash.

And yet again:

Each segment of a sugar-cane
  Beyond the tip, is sweeter;
The friendship of the good is so—
  The other kind grows bitter.

Now I assure you that I am upright. Besides, I will reassure you by taking oaths."

But Gold replied: "I have no confidence in your oaths. There is a saying:

Though a foe be bound by oaths,
  Trust him none the more:
Indra struck the demon down,
  Spite of oaths galore.

And again:

Even gods must try to lull
  Foes with measures mild:
Indra, soothing Diti first,
  Smote her unborn child.

Through a narrow crevice slip
  Enemies who gloat,
Bringing slow destruction, like
  Water in a boat.

If, relying on their means,
  Men confide in foes,
Or in wives whose love is lost,
  Life abruptly goes."

To this Swift found no rejoinder, and he thought: "What an eminent intelligence he has in the field of social ethics! Yet for that very reason I crave his friendship." And he said:

"True friendship, sir, is an affair
Of seven words, the wise declare;
I've forced you, then, to be a friend—
So hear my pleading to the end.

Now grant me your friendship. If you refuse, I shall starve where I stand."

And Gold reflected: "He is not unintelligent. His speech proves it.

None lacking shrewdness flatter well;
None but a lover plays the swell;
No saints are found in judgment seats;
No clear, straightforward speaker cheats.

So I must certainly grant him my friendship."

Having made up his mind to this, he said to the crow: "My dear sir, you have won my confidence. But it was necessary first to test your intelligence. Now I lay my head in your lap." With this he started to come forth, but when scarcely halfway out, he stopped again. And Swift said: "Do you cherish even yet some reason for mistrusting me? I see you do not leave your fortress."

"I have no fear of you," said Gold, "for I have examined your mind. But if I gave my confidence, I might perhaps meet death through other friends of yours." Then the crow spoke:

Friends purchased at the price of death
To other friends and true,
One should avoid, like worthless corn
Where finest rice-plants grew.

Hearing this, Gold hastened forth, and there was a civil greeting on both sides. After a moment Swift said to Gold: "I will not keep you longer outdoors. I am in search of food." With this he left his friend and flew into thick jungle where he found a wild buffalo that a tiger had killed. Of this he ate his fill, then returned to Gold, carrying a lump of meat red as a dhak-blossom. And he cried: "Come out, my dear Gold! Come out! Enjoy this meat that I have brought."

Now Gold, with sedulous forethought, had constructed a great heap of corn and rice for his friend's use. And he said: "My dear friend, pray enjoy this rice which I have provided to the best of my ability." So each was highly pleased with the other, and they ate in order to manifest kindly feeling. This, indeed, is the seed of friendship. As the verse puts it:

Six things are done by friends:
  To take, and give again;
To listen, and to talk;
  To dine, to entertain.

No friendship ever comes
  Without some kindly deed:
The very gods respond
  To gifts they have decreed.

As soon as presents cease,
  So soon does friendship die:
The calf deserts the cow
  Whose udder has gone dry.

So, to make a long story short:

The mouse and crow became
  Such friends as never fail,
Enduring, hard to split
  As flesh and finger nail.

Indeed, the mouse was so captivated by the crow's attentions that he grew confident to the point of feeling quite at home between his wings.

Now one day the crow appeared with tears filling his eyes, and sobs choked him as he said: "My very dear Gold, I have grown dissatisfied with this country. I intend to travel." "My dear friend," said Gold, "what cause have you for discontent?"

"Listen, my friend," said the crow. "There has been a dreadful drought in this country, so that all the city people, driven by famine, not only cease to give the birds a few mere crumbs, but actually set bird-traps in every house. To be sure, I have not been caught, for further life is appointed me. Yet this is why I shed tears—for I think of foreign travel. This is why I plan to visit another land." "Then tell me where you plan to go," said Gold. And Swift replied:

"In the far south is a great lake in the heart of the jungle. There lives a turtle named Slow, a bosom friend of mine, dearer even than you are. He will give me bits of fish, a digestible diet. In his society I shall be happy, enjoying the delight of conversation spiced with wit. Besides, I cannot behold such slaughter of birds. For the proverb says:

Blest are they who do not see
Death upon the family,
Friend in trouble, stolen wife,
Ruin of the nation's life."

"Considering the circumstances," said Gold, "I will accompany you. I, too, have a great sorrow." "Of what nature?" asked Swift. "Oh," said Gold, "it is a long story. When we get there, I will tell you in detail."

"But," said the crow, "I travel in the air, you on the ground. How will you accompany me?" And Gold answered: "If you feel concern for the preservation of my life, mount me on your back and carry me very gently."

At this the crow was delighted and said: "If that is possible, then I am blest indeed. There is none more blest than I. Let it be done. For I know the eight flights, Full-Flight and the rest. Thus I shall carry you in comfort."

"My friend," said Gold, "I should like to know the flights by name." And the crow recited:

Full-Flight, Part-Flight, and the Rise,
Great-Flight, and the Curve likewise,
Horizontal, Downward-Flight;
Number eight is called the Light.

After listening to this, Gold mounted the crow, who set off at Full-Flight. And very gently he brought his friend to the lake.

Thereupon Slow saw a mouse riding a crow, and wondering who he might be, plopped into the water—

for he was a judge of occasions. And Swift, after depositing Gold in a hole in a tree on the bank, perched on the tip of a twig and called in a piercing tone: "Friend Slow! Come here! I am your crow friend. After long absence I have come, my heart filled with longing. Come, embrace me. For the saying runs:

> Bring sandalwood or camphor? No!
> Nor even flakes of cooling snow;
> All are not worth the sixteenth part
> Of rest upon a friendly heart."

When he heard this, Slow made a narrow inspection, then, with a quiver of delight and with eyes swimming in joyful tears, he hurriedly scrambled from the water, saying: "I did not know you. I am much to blame. Forgive me." And when Swift flew down from the tree, he embraced him.

So the two, after exchanging embraces, thrilled with delight, and sitting beneath the tree told each other their adventures during the long separation. Gold also, with a bow to Slow, sat down there. And Slow, spying him, said to Swift: "Tell me, who is this mouse? And why did you mount him, your natural food, on your back and bring him hither?"

And Swift replied: "Ah, he is a mouse named Gold, a friend of mine, almost my second life. To make a short story of it:

> His virtues, like the streams of rain
> Or stars that dot the sky
> Or like the grains of dust on earth
> All numbering defy;

Yes, mathematics fails to count
His lofty virtues through;
Yet he, in deep dejection sunk,
Has come to visit you."

"And what," said Slow, "is the cause of his gloom?" "That," said the crow, "I asked him yonder. But he put me off, saying: 'It is a long story. I will tell you when we get there.' Now, my very dear Gold, pray tell us both the cause of your gloom."

And Gold told the story of

GOLD'S GLOOM

In the southern country is a city called Maidens' Delight, and in the neighborhood a shrine to Shiva. In a cell near by lived a hermit named Crop-Ear. During his begging hour he would fill his alms-bowl with dainties from the city, eatables jellified, melting in the mouth, toothsome, flavored with sugar, treacle, and pomegranate. Then, returning to his cell, he satisfied himself according to the ordinance, hid what food was left in the alms-bowl, and hung it on a peg, keeping it for the servants' breakfast. On this food I subsisted with my companions. And so the time passed.

Since I nibbled his food, however carefully he hid it, the hermit was disgusted, and in fear of me he moved it from place to place, always hanging it higher. Even so I got at it easily enough and ate it.

Now one day a guest arrived, a holy man named Wide-Bottom. And Crop-Ear welcomed him, paid him due respect, and relieved his fatigue. At night they lay on the same couch and started to relate pious tales. But Crop-Ear's thoughts were so preoccupied with mice that he kept striking the alms-bowl with a frazzled bamboo and returned an absent-minded answer to Wide-Bottom as he told a pious tale.

Then the guest grew extremely angry and said: "Come, Crop-Ear! I perceive that your friendship is dead. For you do not talk with me whole-heartedly. So, night though it be, I shall leave your cell and go elsewhere. For there is a saying:

> 'Come! Enter! News from town?
> A chair! You look run down!
> Welcome! Why have you slighted
> Our home so long? Dee-lighted!'
> Such kindly words as these
> May set the mind at ease,
> And friends be glad to go
> Where they are greeted so.

And again:

> Wherever hosts look vaguely round
> Or fix their glances on the ground,
> The guests who visit such a place
> Are hornless, yet of bovine race.
>
> You should not visit any home
> From which no gentle greetings come,
> Which fails in eager promptitude,
> With gossip touching bad and good.

"But this you do not understand, having forgotten friendship through pride in the ownership of one mere cell. So that you seem to dwell here, but in reality you have earned a place in hell. For the proverb says:

> A certain course for hell to steer,
> Become a chaplain for a year;
> Or try more expeditious ways—
> Become an abbot for three days.

Poor fool! You take pride in what should cause contrition."

When he heard this, Crop-Ear was terrified and said: "Do not speak thus, holy sir. There is no friend nearer my heart than you. Pray hear the reason of my inattention. There is a villainous mouse that jumps and climbs to my alms-bowl, however high I hang it, and he eats my leavings. Thus the servants get no recompense, and refuse to tidy up. So to frighten the mouse, I strike the alms-bowl repeatedly with my bamboo. This is the whole story. But I should add that the villain has such cleverness in jumping as to put cats, monkeys, and other creatures to the blush."

Then Wide-Bottom said: "But have you found the mouse-hole anywhere?" "Holy sir," said Crop-Ear, "I have not." "Surely," said the other, "his hole is over his hoard. Beyond question, the fragrance from his hoard makes him spry. For

> The smell of wealth is quite enough
> To wake a creature's sterner stuff;
> And wealth's enjoyment, even more,
> With virtuous giving from his store.

And again:

'Tis certain Mother Shandilee
If bargaining in sesame—
Her hulled grains for the unhulled kind—
Has some good reason in her mind."

"How was that?" asked Crop-Ear. And Wide-Bottom told the story of

MOTHER SHANDILEE'S BARGAIN

At one time I asked a certain Brahman in a certain town for shelter during the rainy season, and this he gave me. So there I lived, occupied with pious duties.

One day I woke betimes, and listening to a conversation between my host and his wife, I heard the Brahman say: "My dear, tomorrow will be the winter solstice, an extremely profitable season. So I will go to another village in search of donations. And you, in honor of the sun, should give some Brahman food to the extent of your ability."

But his wife snapped at him harshly, saying: "Who would give food to a poor Brahman like you? Are you not ashamed to talk like that? And besides:

Since first I put my hand in yours,
I haven't had a thing:
I've never tasted stylish food;
Don't mention gem or ring."

At this the Brahman was terrified and he stammered: "My dear, my dear, you should not say such things. You have heard the saying:

You have a mouthful only? Give
  A half to feed the needy:
Will any ever own the wealth
  For which his soul is greedy?

And again:

The poor man can but give a mite;
  Yet his reward is such—
The Scriptures tell us—as is his,
  From riches giving much.

The cloud gives only water, yet
The whole world treats him as a pet:
But none can bear the sun, who stands
With rays that look like outstretched hands.

"Bearing this in mind, even the poor should give to the right person at the right time—though the gift seems beneath contempt. For

Great faith, a gift appropriate,
  Fit time, a fit recipient,
An understanding heart—and gifts
  Are blest beyond all measurement.

And some quote this:

Indulge in no excessive greed
(A little helps in time of need)
But one, by greed excessive led,
Perceived a topknot on his head."

"How was that?" asked the wife. And the Brahman told the story of

SELF-DEFEATING FORETHOUGHT

There was once a hillman in a certain place who set out to increase his sins by hunting. As he walked along, he met a boar that resembled the top of Sooty Mountain. Straightway he drew an arrow as far as his ear, and recited this verse:

> The fitted shaft and bow-string's tension
> He sees, and shows no apprehension;
> The psychological conclusion
> Is: Death has prompted this intrusion.

Then with a sharp arrow he shot the boar, who in turn angrily tore the hillman's stomach with a pointed fang that shone like the crescent moon, so that the man fell dead. The boar also, after killing the hunter, died in torment from the arrow-wound.

At this point a starving jackal reached the spot in his aimless wanderings. When he spied a boar and a hunter, both dead, he gleefully thought: "Fate is kind to me, providing this unlooked-for store of food. There is wisdom in the verse:

> The fruit of actions good or bad
> In each preceding state,
> Without a further effort, comes
> Upon us, brought by fate.

And again:

> Each deed from every time and place
> And age, as consequence
> Brings good or evil in exact
> And fitting recompense.

"Now I will eat in such a way as to have sustenance for many days. I will begin with the sinew wrapped round the bow-tip. I will hold it in my paws and eat very slowly. For the saying goes:

Consumption of a treasure earned
  Should very slowly follow,
As wise men sip elixir down,
  Not bolt it at a swallow."

After these reflections, he took into his mouth the sinew with its end hanging from the bow. And when the gut snapped, the bow-tip pierced the roof of his mouth and came out like a topknot. And the jackal perished from the pain of it.

"And that is why I say:

Indulge in no excessive greed, ...

and the rest of it."

Then the Brahman continued: "My dear, did you never hear this?

These five are fixed for every man
  Before he leaves the womb:
His length of days, his fate, his wealth,
  His learning, and his tomb."

After this preachment, the wife said: "Well, I believe I have a bit of sesame grain in the house. I will grind it into flour and feed a Brahman." And her husband, having received her promise, went off to another village.

Then the wife softened the sesame grains in hot water, hulled them, placed them in the hot sun, and returned to her chores in the house. In this state of affairs a dog made water in the dish of grain, and she thought when she saw it: "Dear me! See how shrewd fate is, when it has turned against you. Even these poor sesame grains it has made unfit to eat. Well, I will take them to some neighbor's house, and make an exchange, unhulled for hulled. For anybody will bargain on those terms." So she put her grain in a basket and went from house to house, saying: "Who cares to exchange sesame unhulled for sesame hulled?"

Now she happened to enter with her grain a house which I had entered to beg alms, and she made her offer there. The housewife was delighted and took the hulled grain in exchange for unhulled. Later, her husband came home and asked: "My dear, what does this mean?" And she told him: "I made a bargain, hulled sesame for unhulled."

Over this he pondered, then said: "To whom did this grain belong?" And his son Kamandaki told him: "To Mother Shandilee." Then he said: "My dear wife, she is mighty shrewd at a bargain. You had better throw this sesame away.

'Tis certain Mother Shandilee,
If bargaining in sesame—
Her hulled grains for the unhulled kind—
Has some good reason in her mind."

"So," said Wide-Bottom, "he surely derives this vigor in jumping from the smell of his hoard." And he continued: "Do you know his manner of attack?" "Yes, holy sir, I do," answered Crop-Ear. "He comes not alone, but with a school of mice."

"Well now," said Wide-bottom, "is there any digging tool about?" "Indeed there is," said Crop-Ear. "Here is a handy pickaxe, solid iron." "In that case," said the guest, "you and I must wake early, so as to follow their tracks together, while the footprints still dirty the floor."

Now when I heard the villain's speech fall like a thunderbolt, I thought: "Ah, this spells ruin for me. For his words imply something more. Just as he has marked my hoard, so he will surely discover my fortress, also. Of this his implied meaning convinces me. For the proverb says:

> Shrewd characters at sight
> Can estimate aright
> Their man, as some are deft
> To gauge an ounce by heft.

And again:

> The budding fancy first betrays
> The character that strives
> For birth as recompense of good
> Or ill in former lives:
> No marking tail has grown, yet when
> You see the beggar pick
> His mincing steps about the pond,
> You cry: 'A peacock chick!' "

So I was terrified, deserted the beaten track to my fortress, and with my followers started on another track.

Then a prodigious cat met us, and seeing the whole pack before him, pounced into our midst. And the mice who survived the slaughter scolded me for picking a bad trail, and sought shelter in the old fortress, drenching the floor with blood. Yes, there is wisdom in the old story:

> A deer there was that burst his bonds;
> He flung the trap aside;
> He violently broke apart
> The hobbling snare that tied;
>
> From woods uncouth with tufted flames
> Around him bristling, fled;
> The hunters' arrows left behind;
> To seeming safety sped;
>
> Into a well at last he tumbles:
> On hostile fate all effort stumbles.

Then I departed, alone. The others—poor dolts! plunged into the old fortress. Thereupon the holy man, perceiving that the floor was smeared with drops of blood, followed the trail to the fortress, and began to ply the pickaxe. As he dug, he came upon the hoard over which I had lived so long, and the smell of which used to guide me back to the fortress.

Then Wide-Bottom was filled with glee and said: "Now, Crop-ear, sleep in peace. It was the smell of this that enabled the mouse to wake you." So they took the hoard and turned to the cell.

Now when I returned to the spot, I could not bear to look at the sad, disturbing sight. And I reflected: "Ah, what shall I do? Where shall I go? How may I win peace of mind?" In such reflections the day dragged drearily away.

Still, when the sun had laid his thousand beams to

rest, I went with my companions to the same cell, though I was troubled and lacking in vigor. And when Crop-Ear heard the patter of our pack, time and again he started to strike the alms-bowl with his frazzled bamboo.

Then his guest said: "My friend, why not go peacefully to sleep at last?" "Holy sir," he replied, "I am sure that villainous mouse has come with his followers. I do this from fear of him."

But Wide-Bottom laughed and said: "Have no fear, my friend. His jumping energy is gone with his property. This rule applies to all creatures without exception. As the saying goes:

> The man has constant vigor? Dares
> On others' backs to mount?
> Speaks in a self-sufficient tone?
> He has a bank account."

This angered me so that I made a desperate jump for the alms-bowl, but missed and fell to the floor. And my enemy saw me and said to Crop-Ear: "Look, my friend! It is quite wonderful. You could put it into poetry:

> The wealthy men are men of force;
> And they are scholars all, of course:
> The mouse who lost his wealthy store,
> Is now a mouse and nothing more.

And there is point in this:

> A fangless snake; an elephant
> Without an ichor-store;

A man who lacks a cash account—
Are names and nothing more."

When I heard this, I reflected: "Alas! It is true, though it is my enemy who says it. For today I have not the power to jump a mere finger's breadth. A curse upon a fellow's life without money! As the saying goes:

After money has departed,
If the wit is frail,
Then, like rills in summer weather,
Undertakings fail.

Forest sesame, crow-barley,
Men who have no cash,
Owning names but lacking substance,
Are accounted trash.

Beggars have, no doubt, their virtues,
Yet they do not flash:
As the world has need of sunlight,
Virtues ask for cash.

Beggars-born less keenly suffer
Than the men who crash
From a life of comfort to a
Deficit of cash.

Like the flabby breasts of widows,
Hopes and wishes rash
Helpless fall upon the bosom,
When there is no cash.

The sun that stuns the eyes that shun,
In vain he strains to see:
The light so bright is wrapped in night
By veils of poverty."

With this broken-spirited lamentation I saw my own hoard of wealth converted into a pillow for my enemy, and at dawn I crept into my fortress—a failure.

Then my attendants retired and gossiped together. "Look here!" said they, "the fellow has no power to fill our bellies. Those who ride his back get nothing but buffets—from cats, for example. Why pay him reverence? For the proverb says:

> A king from whom no bounties come,
> But only buffets fall,
> Had better be avoided, and
> By soldiers first of all."

Such remarks I heard on the trail. And since, when I returned to the fortress, not one of my followers accompanied me (for I was penniless) I began to ponder deeply.

"A curse, a curse on a life of poverty! There is sound sense in the verse:

> Even relatives are sure
> Scornfully to treat the poor;
> Pride is docked, and virtue's moon
> Loses luster, waning soon;
> Friends that were, disgusted fly;
> Sorrows breed and multiply;
> Comes the imputation then
> Of the sins of other men.

> When man is crushed by poverty
> And stricken down by fate,
> His best of friends become his foes,
> And tried affection, hate.

And again:

Empty is the childless home;
  Hearts that lack a friendship sure;
Wide horizons, to the fool;
  All is empty to the poor.

And once again:

His passions are entire; his name,
Keen wit, and speech are just the same;
The man's the same. No! See him change!
Cash fails. The life is out! Ah, strange!

"Yet what have folk like me to do with money? Folk whose final fate is such as this? Positively my best course, now that property is gone, is to withdraw to the forest. As the proverb says:

Pride builds a proper house;
  Never be humble:
Spurn cars of heaven, where
  Pride takes a tumble.

Failure may dog the step;
  Pride stands erect,
Stoops not to widest wealth
  Tainted, abject."

And I continued my reflections: "Yes, the curse of beggary is dreadful as death. For

Gutted by the forest fire,
  Stands in sterile soil a tree,
Gnarled, and riddled by the worms—
  Better that than beggar be.

And as for beggary:

It is the shrine of wretchedness,
  The dwelling-place of tears,

The thief of mind, the soil of doubts,
  The treasury of fears,

Concreted meanness, home of woe,
  And haughty honor's knell,
A form of death—to self-esteem
  No different from hell.

And again:

A beggar is a man of shame,
Who bids farewell to honor's name;
From this, humiliations grow,
Then melancholy's gloomy woe;
But gloom with sadness dims the sense,
And sad men lack intelligence;
Now death is folly's certain fruit—
Thus, money's lack is evil's root.

And once again:

Thrust your hands between the jaws
  Of an angry snake;
Slumber in the house of Death;
  Poisoned liquor take;
Dash yourself to pieces down
  Himalaya's side:
Do not feast on riches wrung
  From a villain's pride.

To sum it up:

Feed your body to the flames,
  Friend, if you are needy;
Do not cringe to beg a dole
  From the selfish-greedy.

Better roam in forest wilds
  With the beasts of prey
Than, by whimpering for gifts,
  Baseness to betray.

"This being the case, what possible course shall I adopt to keep alive? How about robbery? That too is damnable, for it means appropriating what belongs to others. As the verse puts it:

Better let your tongue be tied
Than to know that you have lied;
Better to be impotent
Than adulterously bent;
Better die than take delight
In the petty pricks of spite;
Better beg as monk than feel
That you live by what you steal.

Well, then, shall I live on charity? That, too, is damnable, my friends, damnable. That too is a second gate of death. As the saying goes:

Parasite, or exiled scamp,
Invalid, or homeless tramp—
Life is death for these. The best
Would be death. For death is rest.

"Then I must at any cost recover the very treasure that Wide-bottom has stolen. For I saw my money-bag converted into a pillow for those two villains. I must regain my property, and if I die in the attempt, it will be better than this. For

If cowards who see themselves despoiled
Too tamely feel the sting,
Their fathers in the world beyond
Will spurn their offering."

After reaching this conclusion, I went there at night and gnawed a hole in the bag after he had gone to sleep. Thereupon that dreadful holy man awoke and struck me on the head with the frazzled bamboo. Yet somehow I escaped death—predestination, you see. As the old rhyme puts it:

> What's duly his, a man receives;
> This law not even God can break;
> My heart is not surprised, nor grieves;
> For what is mine, no strangers take.

"How was that?" asked the crow and the turtle. And Gold told the story of

MISTER DULY

In a certain city lived a merchant named Ocean. His son picked up a book at a sale for a hundred rupees. In this book was the line:

> What's duly his, a man receives.

Now Ocean saw it and asked his son: "My boy, what did you give for this book?" "A hundred rupees," said the son. "Simpleton!" said Ocean, "if you pay a hundred rupees for a book with one line of poetry written in it, how do you calculate to make money? From this day you are not at home in my house." After this wigging, he showed him the door.

This melancholy rebuff drove the young man to another country far away, where he came to a city and stopped there. After some days a native asked him: "Whence are you, sir? What might your name be?" And he replied:

> "What's duly his, a man receives."

To a second inquirer he gave the same reply. Then on all who questioned him, he bestowed his stereotyped answer. This is how he came by his nickname of Mister Duly.

Now a princess named Moonlight, who was in the first flush of youth and beauty, stood one day with a girl friend, looking out over the city. At that spot a prince, extraordinarily handsome and charming, chanced to come—it was fate's doing—within her range of vision. The moment she saw him, she was smitten by the arrows of Love, and said to her friend: "Dear girl, you must make an effort to bring us together this very day."

So the friend went straight to him and said: "Moonlight sent me to you. She sends you this message: 'The sight of you has reduced me to the last extremity of love. If you do not hasten to me, I shall die, nothing less.' "

On hearing this, he said: "If I cannot avoid the trip, please tell me how to get into the house." And the friend said: "When night comes, you must climb up a stout strap that will be hanging from an upper story of the palace." And he replied: "If you have it all settled, I will do my part." With this understanding the girl returned to Moonlight.

But when night came, the prince thought it over:

> "A Brahman-slayer, so they say,
> Is he who tries to house
> With teacher's child, or wife of friend,
> Or royal servant's spouse.

And again:

> A deed that brings dishonor,
> Whereby a man must fall,
> That causes disadvantage,
> Don't do it—that is all."

So after full reflection he did not go to her. But Mister Duly was roaming through the night and spied a strap hanging down the wall of a fine stucco house. Out of curiosity mingled with bravado he took hold and climbed.

Now the princess, being perfectly confident that he was the right man, treated him with high consideration, giving him a bath, a meal, a drink, fine garments, and the like. Then she went to bed with him, and her limbs thrilled with joy at touching him. But she said: "I fell in love with you at first sight, and have given you my person. I shall never have another husband, even mentally. Why don't you realize this and talk to me?" And he replied:

> "What's duly his, a man receives."

When she heard this, her heart stopped beating, and she sent him down the strap in a hurry. So he made for a tumble-down temple and went to sleep. Presently a policeman who had an appointment with a woman of easy virtue arrived there and found him asleep. As the policeman wished to hush the matter up, he said: "Who are you?" and the other answered:

> "What's duly his, a man receives."

When he heard this, the policeman said: "This temple is deserted. Go and sleep in my bed." And he agreed, but made a blunder, lying down in the wrong bed. In that bed lay the policeman's daughter, a big girl named Naughty, beautiful and young. She had made a date with a man she loved, and when she saw Mister Duly, she thought: "Here is my sweetheart." So, her blunder due to the pitchy darkness of the night, she rose, gave herself in marriage by the ceremony used in heaven, then lay with him in bed, her lotus-eyes and lily-face ablossom. But she said: "Even yet you do not talk nicely with me. Why not?" And he replied:

"What's duly his, a man receives."

On hearing this, she thought: "This is what one gets for being careless." So she gave him a sorrowful scolding and sent him packing.

As he walked along a business street, there approached a bridegroom named Fine-Fame. He came from another district and marched with a great whanging of tom-toms. So Mister Duly joined the procession. Since the happy moment was near at hand, the bride, a merchant's daughter, was standing at the door of her father's house near the highway. She stood on a raised step under an awning provided for the occasion, and displayed her wedding finery.

At this moment an elephant reached the spot, running amuck. He had killed his driver, had got beyond control, and the crowd was in a hubbub, everyone scared out of his wits. When the bridegroom's parade caught a glimpse of him, they ran—the bridegroom, too—and started for the horizon.

In this crisis Mister Duly perceived the girl, all alone, her eyes dancing with terror, and with the words: "Don't worry. I will save you," manfully reassured her, put his right arm around her, and with enormous *sang-froid* gave the elephant a cruel scolding. And the elephant—it was fate's doing—actually went away.

Presently Fine-Fame appeared with friends and relatives, too late for the wedding; for another man was holding his bride's hand. At the sight of his rival, he said: "Come, father-in-law! This is hardly respectable. You promised your daughter to me, then gave her to another man." "Sir," said the father-in-law, "I was frightened by the elephant, and I ran too. I came back with you gentlemen, and do not know what has been going on."

Then he turned and questioned his daughter: "My darling girl, what you have been doing is scarcely the thing. Tell me what this business means." And she replied: "This man saved me from deadly peril. So long as I live, no man but him shall hold my hand."

When the story got abroad, dawn had come. And as a great crowd gathered in the early morning, the princess heard the story of events and came to the spot. The policeman's daughter also, hearing what passed from lip to lip, visited the place. And the king in turn, learning of the gathering of a great crowd, arrived in person, and said to Mister Duly: "Speak without apprehension. What sort of business is this?" And Mister Duly said:

"What's duly his, a man receives."

Then the princess remembered, and she said:

"This law not even God can break."

Then the policeman's daughter said:

"My heart is not surprised, nor grieves."

And hearing all this, the merchant's daughter said:

"For what is mine, no strangers take."

Then the king promised immunity to one and all, arrived at the truth by piecing their narratives together, and ended by respectfully giving Mister Duly his own daughter, together with a thousand villages. Then he bethought himself that he had no son, so he anointed Mister Duly crown prince. And the crown prince, together with his family, lived happily; for means of enjoyment were provided in great variety.

"And that is why I say:

What's duly his, a man receives, ...

and the rest of it." And Gold continued:

"After these reflections, I recovered from my money-madness. For there is much wisdom in this:

Not rank, but character, is birth;
It is not eyes, but wits, that see;

True learning 'tis, to cease from wrong;
  Contentment is prosperity.

And again:

Yes, all prosperities are his,
  Whose heart is filled with mirth:
The feet in leather sandals shod,
  Travel a leather earth.

A hundred leagues is naught to him
  Whose vehicle is greed:
To clasp the wealth that fingers touch
  Contentment has no need.

Since Vishnu, universal lord,
  Through thee a dwarf was made,
O manhood's solvent, Greed divine,
  To thee be homage paid.

No feat is hard for thee, O Greed,
  Dishonor's wedded dame,
Who, for the men of kindest heart,
  Preparest draughts of shame.

What man should never bear, I bore;
  I spoke and, speaking, lied;
I waited at the stranger's door:
  O Greed, be satisfied!

And again:

I've drunk foul water; slept forlorn
On gathered bits of broken thorn;
I've lost my love, I've begged for alms,
Enduring heart- and belly-qualms;
I've crossed the sea; I've walked afar;
I've treasured half a shattered jar:
Of further labors is there need?
Quick, damn you! Give your orders, Greed!

No poor man's evidence is heard,
Though logic link it word to word:
While wealthy babble passes muster
Though crammed with harshness, vice, and bluster.

The wealthy, though of meanest birth,
Are much respected on the earth:
The poor whose lineage is prized
Like clearest moonlight, are despised.

The wealthy are, however old,
Rejuvenated by their gold:
If money has departed, then
The youngest lads are aged men.

Since brother, son, and wife, and friend
Desert when cash is at an end,
Returning when the cash rolls in,
'Tis cash that is our next of kin.

"At the moment when, with such thoughts in my mind, I went to my quarters, our friend Swift came to me and suggested a journey hither. So here I am. I have come with him to visit you. Thus I have related to you the cause of my gloom.

"Well, there is this to be said:

The world—gods, elephants, and men,
  Deer, devils, snakes—
Before the noonday hour is spent,
  Its dinner takes.

When hour and appetite arrive,
  There should suffice
For world-wide conqueror or slave
  A bowl of rice.

For this, what man of sense would do
  Base deeds perverse,
Whose consequences drag him down
  From bad to worse?"

When he had listened to this, Slow began to offer consolation. "My dear fellow," said he, "you must not lose heart at leaving your country. Intelligent as you are, why feel disturbed without occasion? Consider the saying:

The merely learnèd is a fool;
The wise man uses action's tool:
For no remembered drug can cure
The sick by name alone, 'tis sure.

To brave and wise what land is strange,
Or native? Whatsoever change
Befall, he makes the land his own
By strength of valiant arm alone:
The lion's whim is jungle law
By strength of tooth and tail and claw;
He slaughters elephants for food,
And slakes his servants' thirst with blood.

"Therefore, my dear fellow, we must always be energetic. Where will money feel at home, or pleasures? You know the saying:

As frogs will find a drinking-hole,
  Or birds a brimming lake,
So friends and money seek a man
  Whose vigor does not break.

From another point of view:

The goddess Fortune seeks as home
  The brave and friendly man,

The grateful, righteous soul who does
  Each moment what he can,
Who regulates a sturdy life
  Upon an active plan.

Or, put it this way:

The brave, wise, hopeful, and persistent,
From tricks, freaks, meanness equidistant—
    If such there be,
    And Fortune flee,
The joke on Fortune falls, insistent.

While, on the other hand:

If man be fatalist and slacker,
Irresolute and *sang-froid* lacker,
Him Fortune—as a bouncing miss
Her aged lover—hates to kiss.

Abysmal learning does not aid
To virtue those who are afraid:
As men with lamps no sooner find
Lost objects, if those men are blind.

The prince becomes a beggar;
  By weak are slayers slain;
The beggar ceases begging;
  When fate revolves again.

"Nor must you, in view of the aphorism,

Since teeth and nails and men and hair,
If out of place, are ugly there

draw the coward's conclusion:

Let no man leave his native place.

"For to the competent there is no distinction between native and foreign land. You must have heard the saying:

Brave, learnèd, fair,
  Where'er they roam,
Without delay
  Are quite at home.

The shrewdly valiant on the earth
Will always master money's worth;
Not those of godlike scholarship—
'Tis certain—if they lose their grip.

"Today, no doubt, your purse is light. For all that, you are not in the position of the commonplace fellow, for you have sense and vigor. And the proverb says:

Let sturdy resolution guide,
And poor men touch the peak of pride;
Let money fold in its embrace
The mean, they sink to lowly place:
The lion's majesty derives
From nature, rich because he strives
To crown his feats with nobler feats.
What golden-collared dog competes?

And again:

Some men compacted of self-rigor
With valor, enterprise, and vigor
Indifferently view the muddle
Of ocean and the petty puddle;
As at some wretched ant-hill, frown
At Himalaya's highest crown:
To these, not those who wait and see,
Comes Fortune, tripping eagerly.

And once more:

Mount Meru is not very high,
  Hell is not very low,

The sea not shoreless, if a man
  Abounding vigor show.

For, after all:

Why, wealthy, puff with pride?
Why, poor, in gloom subside?
Since, like a stricken ball,
Men's fortunes rise and fall.

In any case, remember that youth and wealth are unstable as water-bubbles. As the saying goes:

With shadows of the passing cloud,
  New grain, and knavish friends,
With women's love, and youth, and wealth,
  Enjoyment quickly ends.

This being so, if an intelligent man catches slippery money, let him make it fruitful, by giving it away or enjoying it. As the proverb tells us:

The coin that cost a hundred toils,
  That men are wont to cherish
Beyond their life, will, if it be
  Not given to others, perish.

And again:

Bestow, or use your wealth for pleasure;
If not, you hoard another's treasure:
As in your home, your lovely girl
Awaits a stranger—*his* dear pearl.

And once again:

The miser for another hoards
  His bags of needless money:
The bees laboriously pack,
  But others taste the honey.

In any event, fate has the last word. As the proverb puts it:

> In weapon-bristling battle or at home,
> In flaming fire, wild cave, or monstrous sea,
> Among thanatophidian fangs elate,
> The to-be is, is not the not-to-be.

Now you are healthy and enjoy peace of mind. This is the supreme possession. As the saying goes:

> The lord of seven continents,
> Beset by crawling greed,
> Is but a beggar; he who lives
> Content, is rich indeed.

Besides, on this earth

> No treasure equals charity;
> Content is perfect wealth;
> No gem compares with character;
> No wish fulfilled, with health.

Nor must you think: 'How can I survive, having lost my possessions?' For money passes away, man's character abides. There is a proverb to fit the case:

> The noble man, indeed, may fall
> To earth—like an elastic ball;
> The coward who drops is down to stay,
> Is flattened like a ball of clay.

But why bore you? Here is the nub of duty. Certain men are born to enjoy the pleasures that money brings, certain others are born money's guardians. There is a verse about it:

> Your wealth will flee,
> If fate decree,

Though it was fairly earned:
So silly Soft,
When perched aloft
In that great forest, learned."

"How was that?" asked Gold. And Slow told the story of

SOFT, THE WEAVER

In a certain town lived a weaver. His name was Soft, and he spent his time making garments dyed in various patterns, fit for such people as princes. But for all his labors, he could not collect a bit of money beyond food and clothes. Yet he saw other weavers, who made coarse fabrics, rolling in wealth, and he said to his wife: "Look at these fellows, my dear. They make coarse stuff, but they earn heaps of money. This city does not offer me a decent living. I am going to move."

"Oh, my dear," said his wife, "it is a mistake to say that money comes to those who travel. There is a proverb:

What shall not be, will never be;
What shall be, follows painlessly:
The thing your fingers grasp, will flit,
If fate has predetermined it.

And again:

A calf can find its mother cow
Among a thousand kine:
So good or evil done, returns
And whispers: 'I am thine.'

And once again:

> As shade and sunlight interbreed,
> So twined are Doer and his Deed.

So stay here and mind your business."

"You are mistaken, my dear," said he. "No deed comes to fruition without effort. There is a proverb:

> You cannot clap a single hand;
> Nor, effortless, do what you planned.

And again:

> Although, at meal-time, fate provide
> A richly loaded plate,
> No food will reach the mouth, unless
> The hand co-operate.

And once again:

> Through work, not wishes, every plan
> Its full fruition reaps:
> No deer walk down the lion's throat
> So long as lion sleeps.

And one last quotation:

> Suppose he gave the best he had,
> Yet no fruition came,
> 'Twas fate that blocked his efforts, not
> The man who was to blame.

I must go to another country." So he went to Growing City, stayed three years, and started home with savings of three hundred gold-pieces.

In mid-journey, he found himself in a great forest when the blessèd sun went to rest. So, forethoughtful for his safety, he climbed upon a stout branch of a banyan tree and dozed. In the middle of the night, as he slept, he saw two human figures whose eyes were bloodshot with fury, and heard them abusing each other.

The first of them was saying: "Come now, Doer! You know you have, in every possible way, prevented this fellow Soft from getting any capital beyond food and clothes. So you have no right ever to let him have any. Why did you give him three hundred gold-pieces?"

"Now, Deed!" said the other, "I am constrained to give the enterprising a reward in proportion to their enterprise. The final consequence is your affair. Take it from him yourself." On hearing this, Soft awoke and looked for his bag of gold.

When he found it empty, he thought: "Oh, dear! It was so much trouble to earn the money, and it went in a flash. I have had my work for nothing. I haven't a thing. How can I look my wife in the face, or my friends?" So he made up his mind to return to Growing City. There he earned five hundred gold-pieces in just one single year, and started home again by a different road.

When the sun went down, he came upon the very same banyan tree, and he thought: "Oh, oh, oh! What is fate up to—damn the brute! Here is that same fiendish old banyan tree once more." But he dozed off on a branch, and saw the same two figures.

One of them was saying: "Doer, why did you give

this fellow Soft five hundred gold-pieces? Don't you know that he doesn't get a thing beyond food and clothes?"

"Friend Deed," said the other, "I am constrained to give to the enterprising. The final consequence is your affair. So why blame me?"

When poor Soft heard this, he looked for his bag and found it empty. This plunged him into the depths of gloom, and he thought: "Oh, dear! What good is life to me if I lose my money? I will just hang myself from this banyan tree and say goodbye to life."

Having made up his mind, he wove a rope of spear-grass, adjusted it as a noose to his neck, climbed out a branch, fastened it, and was about to let himself drop, when one of the figures appeared in the sky and said: "Do not be so rash, Friend Soft. I am the person who takes your money, who does not allow you one cowrie beyond food and clothes. Now go home. But, that you may not have seen me without result, ask your heart's desire."

"In that case," said Soft, "give me plenty of money." "My good fellow," said the other, "what will you do with money which you cannot enjoy or give away? For you are to have no use of it beyond food and clothes."

But Soft replied: "Even if I get no use of it, still I want it. You know the proverb:

> The man of capital,
> Though ugly and base-born,

Is honored by the world
For charity forlorn.

And again:

Loose they are, yet tight;
Fall, or stick, my dear?
I have watched them now
Till the fifteenth year."

"How was that?" asked the figure. And Soft told the story of

HANG-BALL AND GREEDY

In a certain town lived a bull named Hang-Ball. From excess of male vigor he abandoned the herd, tore the river-banks with his horns, browsed at will on emerald-tipped grasses, and went wild in the forest.

In that forest lived a jackal named Greedy. One day he sprawled at ease with his wife on a sandy river-bank. At that moment the bull Hang-Ball came down to the same stretch of sand for a drink. And the she-jackal said to her husband when she saw the hanging testicles: "Look, my dear! See how two lumps of flesh hang from that bull. They will fall in a moment, or a few hours at most. So you must follow him, please."

"My dear," said the jackal, "nobody knows. Perhaps they will fall some day, perhaps not. Why send me on a fool's errand? I would rather stay here with you and eat the mice that come to water. They follow this trail. And if I should follow him, somebody else would come here and occupy the spot. Better not do it. You know the proverb:

> If any leave a certain thing,
> For things uncertain wandering,
> The sure that was, is sure no more;
> What is not sure, was lost before."

"Come," said she, "you are a coward, satisfied with any little thing. You are quite wrong. We always ought to be energetic, a man especially. There is a saying:

> Depend on energetic might,
> And banish indolence's blight,
> Let enterprise and prudence kiss—
> All luck is yours—it cannot miss.

And again:

> Let none, content with fate's negation,
> Sink into lazy self-prostration:
> No oil of sesame, unless
> The seeds of sesame you press.

"And as for your saying: 'Perhaps they will fall, perhaps not,' that, too, is wrong. Remember the proverb:

> Mere bulk is naught. The resolute
>   Have honor sure:
> God brings the plover water. Who
>   Dare call him poor?

"Besides, I am dreadfully tired of mouse-flesh, and these two lumps of meat are plainly on the point of falling. You must not refuse me."

So when he had listened to this, he left the spot

where mice were to be caught and followed Hang-Ball. Well, there is wisdom in the saying:

Only while he does not hear
Woman's whisper in his ear,
Goading him against his will,
Is a man his master still.

And again:

In action, should-not is as should,
In motion, cannot is as can,
In eating, ought-not is as ought,
When woman's whispers drive a man.

So he spent much time wandering with his wife after the bull. But they did not fall. At last in the fifteenth year, in utter gloom he said to his wife:

"Loose they are, yet tight;
Fall, or stick, my dear?
I have watched them now
Till the fifteenth year.

Let us draw the conclusion that they will not fall in the future either, and return to the old mouse-trail."

"And that is why I say:

Loose they are, yet tight, ...

and the rest of it.

"Now anybody as rich as that becomes an object of desire. So give me plenty of money."

"If things stand so," said the figure, "go once more to Growing City. There dwell two sons of merchants; their names are Penny-Hide and Penny-Fling. When you have observed their conduct, you may ask for yourself the nature of one or the other." With this he vanished, and Soft returned to Growing City, his mind in a maze.

At evening twilight, he wearily inquired for Penny-Hide's residence, learned with some trouble where it was, and called there. In spite of scoldings from the wife, the children, and others, he made his way into the courtyard and sat down. Then at dinner-time he received food but no kind word, and went to sleep there.

During the night he saw the same two human figures holding council. One of them was saying: "Come now, Doer! Why are you making extra expense for this fellow Penny-Hide, in providing Soft with a meal?"

And the second replied: "Friend Deed, it is no fault of mine. I am constrained to attend to acquisition and expenditure. But their final consequence is your affair." Now when the poor fellow awoke, he had to fast because Penny-Hide was in the second day of a cholera attack.

So Soft left that house and went to Penny-Fling's, who showed him much honor, greeting him cordially and providing food, garments, and the like. In his house Soft rested in a comfortable bed, and in the night he saw the same two figures taking counsel together. One of them was saying: "Come now, Doer! This fellow Penny-Fling is at no little expense today, entertaining Soft. So how will he pay that debt? He has drawn everything from the bank." "Friend Deed," said the second, "I had to do it. The final consequence is your affair." Now at dawn a policeman came with money, a favor from the king, and gave it all to Penny-Fling.

When he saw this, Soft thought: "This Penny-Fling person, even without any capital, is a better kind of thing than that scaly old Penny-Hide. The proverb is right:

> The Scriptures' fruit is pious homes;
> Right conduct, that of learnèd tomes;
> Wives fructify in joy and son;
> And money's fruit is gifts and fun.

"So may the blessèd Lord of All make me a person whose money goes in gifts and fun. I see no good in Penny-Hiding."

So the Lord of All took him at his word, making him that kind of person.

"And that is why I say:

> Your wealth will flee,
> If fate decree, ...

and the rest of it. Therefore, my dear friend Gold, recognize the facts and feel no uneasiness in the department of finance. You know the proverb:

> A lofty soul, in days of power,
> Is tender as a lotus-flower;
> But, meeting misadventure's shock,
> Grows hard as Himalayan rock.

And again:

> The goal desiderating powers at strain,
> Is reached by listless sleepers with no pain:
> Though panting life go struggling ceaselessly,
> The to-be is, is not the not-to-be.

And once again:

> Why think and think without relief?
> Why weight the mind with aimless grief?
> All finds fulfilment, soon or late,
> If written on the brow by fate.

Or put it this way:

> From distant island, central sea,
>   Or far horizon's brink,
> Fate brings and links its wilful whims,
>   Before a man can wink.

Or this way:

> Fate links the unlinked, unlinks links;
> It links the things that no man thinks.
>
> All life, unwilling, faces its
>   Unbidden doom—
> Some ill, no doubt, but blessings, too—
>   Why sink in gloom?

And yet again:

> Courageous, cultivated minds
>   Their fate would supervise;
> But linked causation masters them,
>   And makes it otherwise.
>
> And He who made the parrots green,
>   But made the king-swans white,
> And peacocks particolored, He
>   Will order us aright.

There is great wisdom in the old story:

> Within a basket tucked away
> In slow starvation's grim decay,
> A broken-hearted serpent lay.
>
> But see the cheerful mouse that gnaws
> A hole, and tumbles in his jaws
> At night—new hope's unbidden cause!
>
> Now see the serpent, sleek with meat,
> Who hastens through the hole, to beat
> From quarters cramped, a glad retreat!
>
> So fuss and worry will not do;
> For fate is somehow muddling through
> To good or bad for me and you.

"Adopt this point of view, and give some attention to ultimate salvation. There is a verse about that, too:

> Let some small rite—vow, fasting, self-control—
> Be daily practiced with a quiet soul;
> For fate chips daily from our days to be,
> Though panting life go struggling ceaselessly.

"This being so, contentment is always wise:

> Contentment's nectar-draught supplies
> The quiet joy that satisfies;
> How can the money-maddened know
> That joy in bustlings to and fro?

And once again:

> No penance like forbearance;
> No pleasure like content;
> No friend like gifts; no virtue
> Like hearts on mercy bent.

"But why bore you with a sermon? In this place you are at home. Pray divest yourself of disturbing worries, and spend your time in friendship with me."

Now when Swift had listened to these observations of Slow, set off as they were with the inner truth of numerous authoritative works, his face blossomed, his heart was satisfied, and he said: "Slow, my dear fellow, you are good. Your virtue is something to rely on. For in the act of offering this comfort to Gold, you have brought perfect satisfaction to my heart. As the proverb puts it:

> They taste the best of bliss, are good,
> And find life's truest ends,
> Who, glad and gladdening, rejoice
> In love, with loving friends.

And again:

> The richest man is penniless,
> A living naught, a vain distress,
> If greed, true wealth destroying, bends
> His soul to lack the charm of friends.

"Now by means of this first-class advice you have rescued our poor friend, sunk in the sea of wretchedness. After all, it is quite in the nature of things:

> The good forever save the good,
> When dull misfortunes clog:
> For only elephants can drag
> Their comrades from the bog.

And again:

> No man deserves the praise of men,
> Nor meets the vow of virtue, when

The poor or suppliant from him go
Averted, sunk in hopeless woe.

Yes, there is wisdom in this:

What manhood is there, making not
  The sad, secure?
What wealth is that, availing not
  To aid the poor?
What sort of act, performed without
  Good consequence?
What kind of life, that glory feels
  To be offense?"

While they were conversing thus, a deer named Spot arrived, panting with thirst and quivering for fear of hunters' arrows. On seeing him approach, Swift flew into a tree, Gold crept into a grass-clump, and Slow sought an asylum in the water. But Spot stood near the bank, trembling for his safety.

Then Swift flew into the air, inspected the terrain for the distance of a league, then settled on his tree again, and called to Slow: "Slow, my dear fellow, come out, come out! No evil threatens you here. I have inspected the forest minutely. There is only this deer who has come to the lake for water." Thereupon all three gathered as before.

Then, out of friendly feeling toward a guest, Slow said to the deer: "My good fellow, drink and bathe. Our water is of excellent quality, and cool." And Spot thought, after meditating on this invitation: "Not the slightest danger threatens me from these. And this because a turtle has no capacity for mischief when out of water, while mouse and crow feed only on what is dead. So I will make one of their company." And he joined them.

Then Slow bade him welcome and did the honors, saying: "I trust your circumstances are happy. Pray tell us how you happened into this neck of the woods." And Spot replied: "I am weary of a life without love. I have been hard pressed on every side by mounted grooms and dogs and hunters. But fear lent speed, I left them all behind, and came here to drink. Now I am desirous of your friendship."

Upon hearing this, Slow said: "We are little of body. It is unnatural for you to make friends with us. One should make friends with those capable of returning favors." But Spot rejoined:

"Better with the learnèd dwell,
Even though it be in hell
Than with vulgar spirits roam
Palaces that gods call home.

"And since you know that one little of body may be of no little consequence, why these self-depreciatory remarks? Yet after all, such speech is becoming to the excellent. I therefore insist that you make friends with me today. There is a good old saying:

Make friends, make friends, however strong
Or weak they be:
Recall the captive elephants
That mice set free."

"How was that?" asked Slow. And Spot told the story of

THE MICE THAT SET ELEPHANTS FREE

There was once a region where people, houses, and temples had fallen into decay. So the mice, who were old settlers there, occupied the chinks in the floors of stately dwellings with sons, grandsons (both in the male and female line), and further descendants as they were born, until their holes formed a dense tangle. They found uncommon happiness in a variety of festivals, dramatic performances (with plots of their own invention), wedding-feasts, eating-parties, drinking-bouts, and similar diversions. And so the time passed.

But into this scene burst an elephant-king, whose retinue numbered thousands. He, with his herd, had started for the lake upon information that there was water there. As he marched through the mouse community, he crushed faces, eyes, heads, and necks of such mice as he encountered.

Then the survivors held a convention. "We are being killed," they said, "by these lumbering elephants—curse them! If they come this way again, there will not be mice enough for seed. Besides:

> An elephant will kill you, if
> He touch; a serpent if he sniff;
> King's laughter has a deadly sting;
> A rascal kills by honoring.

Therefore let us devise a remedy effective in this crisis."

When they had done so, a certain number went to the lake, bowed before the elephant-king, and said respectfully: "O King, not far from here is our community, inherited from a long line of ancestors. There we have prospered through a long succession of sons and grandsons. Now you gentlemen, while coming here to water, have destroyed us by the thousand. Furthermore, if you travel that way again, there will not be enough of us for seed. If then you feel compassion toward us, pray travel another path. Consider the fact that even creatures of our size will some day prove of some service."

And the elephant-king turned over in his mind what he had heard, decided that the statement of the mice was entirely logical, and granted their request.

Now in the course of time a certain king commanded his elephant-trappers to trap elephants. And they constructed a so-called water-trap, caught the king with his herd, three days later dragged him out with a great tackle made of ropes and things, and tied him to stout trees in that very bit of forest.

When the trappers had gone, the elephant-king reflected thus: "In what manner, or through whose assistance, shall I be delivered?" Then it occurred to him: "We have no means of deliverance except those mice."

So the king sent the mice an exact description of

his disastrous position in the trap through one of his personal retinue, an elephant-cow who had not ventured into the trap, and who had previous information of the mouse community.

When the mice learned the matter, they gathered by the thousand, eager to return the favor shown them, and visited the elephant herd. And seeing king and herd fettered, they gnawed the guy-ropes where they stood, then swarmed up the branches, and by cutting the ropes aloft, set their friends free.

"And that is why I say:

Make friends, make friends, however strong, ...

and the rest of it."

When Slow had listened to this, he said: "Be it even so, my dear fellow. Have no fear. In this place you are at home. Pray dismiss anxieties and behave as in your own dwelling." So they all took food and recreation at such hours as suited each, met at the noon hour in the shade of crowding trees beside the broad lake, and spent their time in reciprocated friendship, discussing a variety of masterly works on religion, economics, and similar subjects. And this seems quite natural:

For men of sense, good poetry
And science will suffice:
The time of dunderheads is spent
In squabbling, sleep, and vice.

And again:

A thrill
Will fill
  The wisest heart,
When flow
Bons mots
  Composed with art,
Though fe-
Males be
  Removed apart.

Now one day Spot failed to appear at the regular hour. And the others, missing him, alarmed also by an evil omen that appeared at that moment, drew the conclusion that he was in trouble, and could not keep up their spirits. Then Slow and Gold said to Swift: "Dear fellow, we two are prevented by locomotive limitations from hunting for our dear friend. We beg you, therefore, to hunt about and learn whether the poor fellow is eaten by a lion, or singed by forest fire, or fallen into the power of hunters and such creatures. There is a saying:

One quickly fears for loved ones who
  In pleasure-gardens play:
What, then, if they in forests grim
  And peril-bristling stay?

By all means go, search out precise news concerning Spot, and return quickly."

On hearing this, Swift flew a little distance to the edge of a swamp, and finding Spot caught in a stout trap braced with pegs of acacia-wood, he sorrowfully said: "My dear friend, how did you fall into this distress?" "My friend," said Spot, "there is no time for delay. Listen to me.

When life is near an end,
The presence of a friend
Brings happiness, allying
The living with the dying.

Oh, pardon any expressions of friendly impatience I may have used in our discussions. Likewise, say to Gold and Slow in my name:

If any ugly word
Was willy-nilly heard,
I pray you both, forgive—
Let only friendship live."

On hearing this, Swift replied: "Feel no fear, my dear fellow, while you have friends like us. I will return with all speed, bringing Gold to cut your bonds."

Thereupon, with his heart in a flutter, he found Slow and Gold, explained the nature of Spot's captivity, then returned to Spot, carrying Gold in his beak. Gold, for his part, on seeing the plight of his friend, sorrowfully said: "My dear fellow, you always had a wary mind and a shrewd eye. How, then, did you fall into this dreadful captivity?"

And Spot rejoined: "Why ask, my friend? Fate, you know, does what it will. As the saying goes:

What mortal flies
(However wise)
When billows rise
To fatal size
On seas of woe?

In dead of night,
Or broad daylight,
Grim fate may smite;
Ah, who can fight
  An unseen foe?

You, my saintly friend, are familiar with the caprices of constraining destiny. Therefore be quick. Cut my bonds before the pitiless hunter comes."

"Have no fear," said Gold, "while I am at your side. In my heart, however, is great sorrow, which I beg you to remove by telling your story. You are guided by an eye of wisdom. How did you fall into this captivity?"

"Well," said Spot, "if you insist on knowing, listen, and learn how I have been made captive a second time, having once before suffered the woes of captivity."

"Tell me," said Gold, "how once before you suffered the woes of captivity. I am eager to learn the full detail." And Spot told the story of

SPOT'S CAPTIVITY

Long ago, when I was six months old, I used to gambol in front of all the rest, as a youngster does. Out of sheer spirits I would run far ahead, then wait for the herd. Now we deer have two gaits, called the Jump-Up and the Straightaway. Of these I knew the Straightaway, but not the Jump-Up.

While amusing myself one day, I lost touch with the herd. At this I was dreadfully worried, gazed about the horizon to learn where they might be, and discovered them ahead. Now they had avoided a snare by means of the Jump-Up; they stood in a body ahead of me, and waited, all looking at me. But I, ignorant of the Jump-Up, was caught in the hunter's snare.

While I was trying to drag it toward the herd, the hunter bound all my limbs and I fell to the ground, head foremost. And the herd of deer vanished, seeing no hope of saving me.

When the hunter came up, he did not put me to death, for pity softened his heart at the thought: "He is a fawn, fit only for a pet." Instead, he carefully took me home and gave me as a plaything to a prince, who showed his delight at seeing me by giving the hunter a generous reward.

The prince treated me kindly, providing ointments, massage, baths, food, perfumes, and salves, while my meals were appropriate and palatable. But as I was passed from hand to hand by the curious women and princes at court, I was seriously inconvenienced by petting and scratching, which did not spare neck, eye, front hoof, hind hoof, or ear. Finally, one day in the rainy season, as the prince reclined on a couch, I observed the lightning, listened to the thunder, and, my heart wistful for my fondly remembered herd, I recited:

When shall I follow on the herd
Of coursing deer again?

When brace myself against the wind
That whistles by? Ah, when?

"Who said that?" cried the prince, and looked about him, terrified. When he saw me, he thought: "No man said it, but a deer. It is a prodigy. I am undone," and like one possessed by a devil, he tottered from the house, his garments in disarray.

Thinking himself ridden by a demon, he tempted the sorcerers and magicians with a great reward, saying: "If any free me from this torment, I will pay him no small honor."

Meanwhile, overhasty individuals were striking me with sticks, bricks, and cudgels, but—further life being predestined—I was rescued by a certain holy man who said: "Why kill the poor beast?" Furthermore, he penetrated the cause of my malady, and respectfully said to the prince: "Dear sir, in the rainy season he wistfully remembered his native herd, and therefore recited:

When shall I follow on the herd
Of coursing deer again?
When brace myself against the wind
That whistles by? Ah, when?"

On hearing this, the prince was cured of his feverish malady, returned to his normal state, and said to his men: "Douse the poor deer's head in plenty of water, and set him free in the forest he came from." And they did so.

"Thus, though having suffered a previous captivity, I am caught again through constraining destiny."

At this moment Slow joined them. For his heart was so full of love for his friend that he had followed, leaving grass, shrubs, and spear-grass crushed behind him. At sight of him, they were more distressed than ever, and Gold became their spokesman. "My dear fellow," said he, "you have done wrong in leaving your fortress to come here, since you are not able to save yourself from the hunter, while on us he cannot lay hands. For when the bonds are cut and the hunter stands near, Spot will bound away and disappear, Swift will fly into a tree, while I, being a little fellow, will find some chink to slide into. But what will you do, when within his reach?"

To this Slow listened, but he said: "Oh, do not blame me, you of all people. For

> The loss of love and loss of wealth
>   Who could endure
> But for restoratives of health
>   In friendship sure?

And again:

> The days when meetings do not fail
>   With wise and good
> Are lovely clearings on the trail
>   Through life's wild wood.

> The heart finds rest in telling things
>   (When troubles toss)

To honest wife, or friend who clings,
  Or kindly boss.

Ah, my dear fellow,

The wistful glances wander,
The wits, bewildered, ponder
In good men separated,
Whose love is unabated.

And more than that:

Better lose your life than friends;
Life returns when this life ends,
Not the sympathy that blends."

At this moment the hunter arrived, bow and arrow in hand. Under his very eyes Gold cut the bonds and slipped into the before-mentioned chink. Swift flew into the air and was gone. Spot darted away.

Now when the hunter saw that the deer's bonds had been cut, he was filled with amazement and said: "Under no circumstances do deer cut their own bonds. It was through fate that a deer has done it." Then he spied a turtle on most improbable terrain, and with mixed feelings he said: "Even if the deer, with fate's help, cut his bonds and escaped, still I've got this turtle. As the saying goes:

Nothing comes, of all that walks,
  All that flies to heaven,
All that courses o'er the earth,
  If it be not given."

After this meditation, the hunter cut spear-grass with his knife, wove a stout rope, tied the turtle's feet tightly together, fastened the rope to his bow-tip, and started home. But when Gold saw his friend borne away, he sorrowfully said: "Ah, me! Ah, me!

No sooner sorrow's ocean-shore
I reach in safety, than once more
A bitter sorrow is my lot:
Misfortunes crowd the weakest spot.

Fresh blows are dreadful on a wound;
Food fails, and hunger-pangs abound;
Woes come, old enmities grow hot:
Misfortunes crowd the weakest spot.

One walks at ease on level ground
  Till one begins to stumble;
Let stumbling start, and every step
  Is apt to bring a tumble.

And besides:

'Tis hard to find in life
A friend, a bow, a wife,
Strong, supple to endure,
In stock and sinew pure,
In time of danger sure.

False friends are common. Yes, but where
True nature links a friendly pair,
The blessing is as rich as rare.

To bitter ends
You trust true friends,
Not wife nor mother,
Not son nor brother.

No long experience alloys
True friendship's sweet and supple joys;

> No evil men can steal the treasure;
> 'Tis death, death only, sets a measure.

"Ah, what is this fate that smites me ceaselessly? First came the loss of property; then humiliations from my own people, the result of poverty; because of gloom thereat, exile; and now fate prepares for me the loss of a friend. As the proverb says:

> In truth, I do not grieve though riches flee;
> Some lucky chance will bring them back to me:
> 'Tis this that hurts me—lacking riches' stay,
> The best of friends relax and fall away.

And again:

> Fate's artful linkage since my birth
> Of evil deeds and deeds of worth
> Pursues me on this present earth
>
> Till states of mind that play and sway
> And change and range from day to day,
> Seem lives that strive and pass away.

Ah, there is only too much wisdom in this:

> The body, born, is near its doom;
> And riches are the source of gloom;
> All meetings end in partings: yes,
> The world is all one brittleness.

"Ah, me! Ah, me! The loss of my friend is death to me. What care I even for my own people? As the saying goes:

> A foe of woe and pain and fear,
> A cup of trust and feelings dear,
> A pearl—who made it? Who could blend
> Six letters in that name of friend?

Oh, friendly meetings!

O joy to which the righteous cling,
Machine that answers love's sole string,
Pure happiness in every breath,
Cut short by one stern exile—Death!

And once again:

Pleasant riches; friendship's course
  In familiar ruts;
Enmities of men of sense—
  Death abruptly cuts.

And one last word:

If birth and death did not exist
Nor age nor fear of loved ones missed,
If all were not so quick to perish,
Whose life were not a thing to cherish?"

While Gold recited these grief-stricken sentences, Spot and Swift joined him and united their lamentations with his. And Gold said to them: "So long as our dear Slow is within sight, so long we have a chance to save him. Leave us, Spot. You must slip past the hunter unobserved, drop to earth somewhere near water, and pretend to be dead. Swift, you must spread your claws in the cagework of Spot's horns, and pretend to peck out his eyes. Then that dreadful beast of a hunter, in the greedy belief that he has found a dead deer, will certainly wish to seize him, will throw the turtle on the ground, and hurry up. When his back is turned, I for my part will in a mere twinkling set Slow free to seek refuge in the water near by, his natural fortress. I myself will slide into a grass-clump. You, furthermore, must plan a second escape when the beast of a hunter is upon you." So they put this plan into practice.

Now when the hunter saw a deer as good as dead beside the water, and noticed that a crow was pecking at him, he joyfully threw the turtle on the ground, and ran for a club. As soon as Spot could tell from the tramp of feet that the hunter was close upon him, with a supreme burst of speed he swept into dense forest. Swift flew into a tree. The turtle, his fettering cord cut by Gold, scrambled to shelter in the water. Gold slipped into a grass-clump.

To the hunter it seemed a conjurer's trick. "What does it mean?" he cried in his disappointment. Then he returned to the spot where he had left the turtle, and saw the cord cut in a hundred pieces no longer than a finger's breadth. Then he perceived that the turtle had vanished like a magician, and anticipated danger for his own person. With troubled heart he made all speed out of the wood for home, casting anxious glances at the horizon.

Meanwhile the four friends, free of all injury, came together, expressed their mutual affection, took a new lease on life, and lived happily. And so

> If beasts enjoy so great a prize
> Of friendship, why should wonder rise
> In men, who are so very wise?

Here ends Book II, called "The Winning of Friends." The first verse runs:

> The deer and turtle, mouse and crow
> Had first-rate sense and learning; so,
> Though money failed and means were few,
> They quickly put their purpose through.

BOOK III

CROWS AND OWLS

BOOK III

CROWS AND OWLS

Here, then, begins Book III, called "Crows and Owls," which treats of peace, war, and so forth. The first verse runs:

> Reconciled although he be,
> Never trust an enemy.
> For the cave of owls was burned,
> When the crows with fire returned.

"How was that?" asked the princes, and Vishnusharman told the following story.

In the southern country is a city called Earth-Base. Near it stands a great banyan tree with countless branches. And in the tree dwelt a crow-king named Cloudy with a countless retinue of crows. There he made his habitation and spent his time.

Now a rival king, a great owl named Foe-Crusher, had his fortress and his habitation in a mountain cave, and he had an unnumbered retinue of owls. This owl-king cherished a grudge, so that whenever he met a crow in his airings, he killed him and passed on. In this way his constant aggression gradually spread rings of dead crows about the banyan tree. Nor is this surprising. For the proverb says:

If you permit disease or foe
To march unheeded, you may know
That death awaits you, sure if slow.

Now one day Cloudy summoned all his counselors and said: "Gentlemen, as you are aware, our enemy is arrogant, energetic, and a judge of occasions. He always comes at nightfall to work havoc in our ranks. How, then, can we counter-attack? For we do not see at night, and in the daytime we cannot discover his fortress. Otherwise, we might go there and strike a blow. What course, then, shall we adopt? There are six possibilities—peace, war, change of base, entrenchment, alliances, and duplicity."

And they replied: "Your Majesty does well to put this question. For the saying goes:

Good counselors should tell their king,
Unasked, a profitable thing;
  If asked, they should advise.
While flatterers who shun the true
(Which in the end is wholesome, too)
  Are foemen in disguise.

Therefore it is now proper to confer in secret session."

Then Cloudy started to consult severally his five ancestral counselors, whose names were Live-Again, Live-Well, Live-Along, Live-On, and Live-Long. And first of all he questioned Live-Again: "My worthy sir, what is your opinion under the circumstances?" And Live-Again replied: "O King, one should not make war with a powerful enemy. And this one is powerful and knows when to strike. Therefore make peace with him. For the saying goes:

> Bow your head before the great,
> Lifting it when times beseem,
> And prosperity will flow
> Ever onward, like a stream.

And again:

> Make your peace with powerful foes
> Who are rich and good and wise,
> Who are seasoned conquerors,
> In whose home no discords rise.
>
> Make your peace with wicked men,
> If your life endangered be;
> Life, itself first made secure,
> Gives the realm security.

And again:

> Make your peace with him whose wont
> 'Tis to conquer in a fight;
> Other foes will bend their necks
> To you, fearful of his might.
>
> Even with equals make your peace;
> Victory is often given
> Whimsically; take no risks—
> Says the current saw in heaven.
>
> Even with equals victory
> Whimsically may alight.
> Try three other methods first;
> Only *in extremis* fight.

And yet again:

> See! The bully to whose soul
> Power is all, and peace is not,

Clashing with an equal foe,
  Crumbles like an earthen pot.

Land and friends and gold at most
  Have been won when battles cease;
If but one of these should fail,
  It is best to live in peace.

When a lion digs for moles
  Hiding in their pebbly house,
He is apt to break his nails,
  And at best he gets a mouse.

Therefore, where no prize is won
  And a healthy fight is sure,
Never stir a quarrel, but
  Whatsoe'er the cost, endure.

By a stronger foe assailed,
  Bend as bends the river reed;
Do not strike, as serpents do,
  If you wish your luck to speed.

Imitators of the reed
  Slowly win to glory's peak;
But the luckless serpent-men
  Only earn the death they seek.

Shrink like turtles in their shells,
  Taking blows if need there be;
Raise your head from time to time
  Like the black snake, warily.

To sum it up:

Never struggle with the strong
  (If you wish to know my mind)
Who has ever seen a cloud
  Baffle the opposing wind?"

Having heard this view, the king said to Live-Well: "My worthy sir, I desire to hear your opinion also." And Live-Well said: "O King, I disagree. Inasmuch as the enemy is cruel, greedy, and unprincipled, you should most certainly not make peace with him. For the proverb says:

> With foes unprincipled and false
> 'Tis vain to seek accommodation:
> Agreements bind them not; and soon
> They show a wicked transformation.

Therefore you should, in my judgment, fight with him. You know the saying:

> 'Tis easy to uproot a foe
> Contemning fighters, never steady,
> Cruel and greedy, slothful, false,
> Foolish and fearful and unready.

"But more than this—we have been humiliated by him. Therefore, if you propose peace, he will be angry and will employ violence again. There is a saying:

> The truculence of fevered foes
> By gentle measures is abetted:
> What wise physician tries a douche?
> He knows that fever should be sweated.

> Conciliation simply makes
> A foeman's indignation splutter,
> Like drops of water sprinkled on
> A briskly boiling pan of butter.

Besides, the previous speaker's point about the strength of the enemy is not decisive.

The smaller often slays the great
By showing energy and vigor:
The lion kills the elephant,
And rules with unrestricted rigor.

And more than that:

Foes indestructible by might
Are slain through some deceptive gesture,
As Bhima strangled Kichaka,
Approaching him in woman's vesture.

And yet again:

When kings are merciless as death,
All foes are quick to knuckle under;
Quick, too, to kill the kings who fall
Into compassion's fatal blunder.

And he whose sun of glory sets
Before the glory of another
Is born in vain; he wastes for naught
The youthful vigor of his mother.

For Regal Splendor, unbesmeared
With foemen's blood as rich cosmetic,
Though dear, is insufficient for
Ambitions truly energetic.

And in a kingdom unbedewed
With foemen's blood in slaughter gory,
And hostile women's falling tears,
The king enjoys no living glory."

Having heard this view, the king put the question to Live-Along: "My worthy sir, pray express your opinion also." And Live-Along said: "O King, the enemy is vicious and powerful and unscrupulous.

Therefore you should make neither peace nor war with him. Only a change of base can be recommended. For the saying goes:

With vicious foemen, proud of power,
  From hindering scruples free,
Adopt a change of base, not peace
  Nor war, for victory.

Now change of base is known to be
  No single thing, but twin—
Retreat, to save imperiled life;
  Invasion, planned to win.

A warlike and ambitious king
  May choose 'twixt April and
November—other months are barred—
  To invade the hostile land.

For storming-parties—so the books
  Prescribe—all times are fair,
If hostile forces show distress,
  And lay some weakness bare.

A king should put his realm in charge
  Of heroes strong and fit;
Then pounce upon the hostile land,
  When spies have peopled it.

The case in hand requires, O King,
  The base-change called Retreat,
Nor peace nor war; the foe is vile,
  And very hard to beat.

"Furthermore, a recessive movement is made, says the science of ethics, with due regard to cause and effect. The point is thus expressed in poetry:

When rams draw back, their butting fiercer stings;
The crouching king of beasts more deadly springs:
So wise dissemblers, holding vengeance sure,
In dumb communion with their hearts, endure.

And once again:

A king, abandoning his realm
  To foes of fighting worth,
Preserves his life, as Fight-Firm did,
  And later rules the earth.

And so, to sum it up:

The weak who, struggling with the strong,
  Are not too proud to fight,
Bring great rejoicing to their foes,
  And on their kinsmen, blight.

"Therefore, since you are engaged with a powerful foe, there is occasion for a change of base. It is no time for peace or war."

When he had listened to this view, the king said to Live-On: "My worthy sir, pray express your opinion also." And Live-On said: "O King, I disapprove of peace, war, and change of base, all three of them; and particularly change of base. For

A crocodile at home
  Can beat an elephant;
But if he goes abroad,
  A dog can make him pant.

And again:

When stronger foes attack,
  Close in your fortress stay;
But sally to relieve
  Your friends, and save the day.

If, panic-struck, you flee
  When foes are at the door,
And leave the land to them,
  You ne'er will see it more.

One man, entrenched, can hold
  A hundred foes at bay
(Strong foes at that), therefore
  In your entrenchment stay.

Therefore provide your fort
  With shaft and gun; adorn
It well with moat and wall,
  And store abundant corn.

Stand ever firm within,
  Resolved to do or die:
So, living, earn renown;
  Or dead, the starry sky.

And there is a further consideration:

The union of the weak
  A powerful bully stumps:
The hostile blizzard spares
  The shrubs that grow in clumps.

And single trees, though huge
  And posted for defense,
May be uprooted by
  The stout wind's violence.

While groves of trees, where each
  Receives and gives defense,
Unitedly defy
  The wind's fierce violence.

Just so, one man alone,
However brave he be,
Is scorned by foes, who soon
Proceed to injury."

Having listened to this view likewise, the king said to Live-Long: "My worthy sir, pray express your opinion also." And Live-Long said: "O King, from among the six possibilities, I recommend alliance. Pray adopt that. For the saying goes:

Though deft and brilliant, what good end
Can you attain without a friend?
The fire that seems immortal will
Die when the fanning wind is still.

"Therefore you should stay at home and seek some competent ally, to make a counterweight against the enemy. But if you leave home and travel, no one will give you so much as a friendly word. For the proverb says:

The wind is friend to forest-fire
And causes it to flame the higher;
The same wind blows a candle out.
Who cares what poor folk are about?

"Nor is it even essential that the ally be powerful; the alliance even of feeble folk makes for defense. You know the saying:

However weak, a bamboo stem
From others takes, and gives to them
Strength to resist uprooting: so
Weak kings unite against a foe.

"And how much more so, if you have alliance with the truly great! For the poet says:

Who is there whom a friendly state
With great folk does not elevate?
The raindrop, hiding in a curl
Of lotus-petal, shines like pearl.

"Thus, O King, there is no counterweight to your enemy save in alliance. Therefore let an alliance be concluded. Such is my opinion."

After these opinions had been given, Cloudy bowed low before an ancient, farsighted counselor of his race. This was a crow who had persevered to the last page of every textbook of social ethics, and his name was Live-Strong. "Father," said the king, "I had a secret purpose in questioning the others in your very presence; namely, that you might listen to everything, and instruct me as to what is fitting. Pray instruct me in the appropriate course of action."

And Live-Strong said: "My son, all that these have proposed is drawn from the textbooks of social ethics, and all is highly proper, each course in its own good time. But the present hour demands duplicity. You have heard the saying:

You must regard with like distrust
Both peace and warlike measures; must
Seek through duplicity your goal,
With powerful foes of evil soul.

"In this way those who themselves trust nobody and have a single eye to self-interest can win the trust of an enemy and easily destroy him. For the saying goes:

Shrewd enemies will cause a foe
Whom they would ruin, first to grow:
The flow of mucus by molasses
Is first increased, but later passes.

And again:

To foe, to false friend, to female
(Particularly her for sale)
The man so simple as to give
Straightforward conduct, does not live.

Proceed in pure straightforwardness
With Brahmans, with the gods no less,
With teachers, with yourself; but treat
All other creatures to deceit.

A hermit mastering his soul
May see life simple, see it whole;
Not those who thirst for carnal things,
Nor, most particularly, kings.

And so:

Strong through duplicity, you will
Preserve your habitation still;
For death will prove a friend in need,
To crush a foe possessed by greed.

"Furthermore, if a vulnerable point appears in him, you will destroy him by being aware of it."

But Cloudy said: "Father, I do not know his residence. So how shall I become aware of a vulnerable point?"

And Live-Strong replied: "My son, through spies I will reveal not only his dwelling, but also his vulnerable point. For

Cows see a thing by sense of smell;
While Scripture serves the Brahman well;
The king perceives by means of spies:
And other creatures use their eyes.

And in this connection there is another saying:

The king, well served by spies, who knows
The functionaries of his foes,
Who knows his retinue no less,
Is never plunged in deep distress."

Then Cloudy said: "Father, what are these functionaries? What is their number? And of what character are secret-service men? Pray tell me all."

And Live-Strong replied: "On these points the sage Narada gave the following information when questioned by King Fight-Firm. In the hostile camp are eighteen functionaries; in one's own, fifteen. Their conduct is discovered by assigning to each three secret-service men, by whose efforts both friends and enemies are kept in good control. The facts are put in a bit of doggerel:

The foe has eighteen functionaries;
  And you have five and ten:
Give each, as unknown secretaries,
  Three secret-service men.

"The term 'functionary' implies a delegated task. If this be shamefully performed, it ruins the king; if admirably, it brings him high success.

"Now for details. The functionaries in the hostile camp are—the counselor, the chaplain, the commander-in-chief, the crown prince, the concierge, the superintendent of the gyneceum, the adviser, the tax-collector, the introducer, the master of ceremonies, the director of the stables, the treasurer, the minister for elephants, the assessor, the war-minister, the minister for fortifications, the favorite, the forester, and so forth. By sowing intrigue among these the enemy is subdued. In one's own camp the functionaries are—the queen, the queen-mother, the chamberlain, the florist, the lord of the bedchamber, the chief of the secret service, the star-gazer, the court physician, the purveyor of water, the purveyor of spices, the professor, the life-guard, the quartermaster, the bearer of the royal umbrella, and the geisha. It is by way of these that ruin befalls one's own party. As the saying goes:

> Professor, star-scout, and physician
> Find flaws within your home position:
> The madman and snake-charmer know
> Points vulnerable in the foe."

"Father," said Cloudy, "what is the origin of the deadly feud between crows and owls?"

And Live-Strong answered: "Listen. I will tell you

HOW THE BIRDS PICKED A KING

Once upon a time the bird-clans gathered for consultation. There were swans and cranes and nightingales; there were peacocks, plovers, and owls; there were doves and pigeons and partridges; there were bluejays, vultures, skylarks; there were demoiselles and cuckoos and woodpeckers and many others.

And they said: "We have in Garuda a king, to be sure. But he is ever intent on serving holy Vishnu, and pays no heed to us. What is the good of a sham king? He does not defend us when we are in genuine distress—when we are caught in traps, for instance. There is a saying:

> Only one, but anyone
> Is my king, when all is done—
> Only one who will restore
> Health and joy I felt before:
> Anyone, but only one—
> For the moon a single sun.

"Any other is king only in name. As the poet says:

> Let him calm the panting breath
>   Of his people, quivering
> Under blows; or he is Death
>   Masquerading as a king.

And again:

> These six should every man avoid
>   Like leaky ships at sea—
> A dull professor; and a priest
>   Without theology;
>
> A king who does not give defense;
>   A wife whose tongue can slash;
> A cowboy hankering for town;
>   A barber after cash.

We must therefore pitch upon someone else as king of the birds."

Thereupon, observing that the owl had a venerable appearance, they all said: "Let this owl be our king. And let a plentiful supply be provided of all substances prescribed for the anointing of a king."

Straightway water was brought from various holy streams; a bouquet of one hundred and eight roots was provided, including the one marked with a wheel and the yellow-stemmed lotus; and the lion-throne was set in place. Moreover, there was drawn on the ground a relief map of the seven continents, oceans, and mountains. A tiger-skin was spread. Golden jars were filled with five twigs, blossoms and grains; oblations were prepared; the most eminent bards chanted poetry. Furthermore, Brahmans, skilled in reciting the four Vedas, also chanted, while maidens sang songs, sweet holiday songs being their specialty. In the forefront was prepared a vessel of consecrated rice set off with white mustard, parched grain, rice-grains, yellow pigment, wreaths of flowers, conch-shells, and so forth. The materials for lustration ceremonies were provided, and holiday drums rumbled. In the midst of a consecrated spot strewn with potash stood the lion-throne, adorned by the person of the owl as he waited the anointing.

At that moment a crow came into the assembly from nobody knew where, announcing his entrance with a raucous caw. And he thought: "Well, well! What means this gathering of all the birds, and this great festival?"

But when the birds saw him, they whispered together: "He is the shrewdest of the birds, they say.

So let us have a speech from him, too. For the proverb says:

Of men, the barber smartest is;
  The jackal, of the beasts;
The crow is cleverest of birds;
  The White-Robe, of the priests.

And besides:

Concerted counsels of the wise,
  If heedfully thought through,
Will never founder, being sound
  From every point of view."

So the birds said to the crow: "You know, the birds have no king. They have therefore decided unanimously to anoint this owl as their supreme monarch. Please express your opinion also. You come in the nick of time."

Then the crow laughed and said: "Gentlemen, this is foolish. When you have eminent swans, peacocks, nightingales, partridges, sheldrakes, pigeons, cranes, and others, why anoint this ugly-faced fellow who is blind in the daytime? It seems wrong to me. For

Big hooked nose, and eyes asquint,
Ugly face without a hint
Of tenderness or beauty in 't.
Good-natured, it is fierce to see;
If he were mad, what might it be?

And furthermore:

Ugly, cruel, full of spleen,
Every word he speaks is mean;

If you make the owl your king,
You will fail in everything.

Besides, when Garuda is your king, what is this fellow good for? Suppose he has virtue, still a second king is not a good idea when you already have one. For the saying runs:

A single king of lordly sway
Is good; but more than one will slay,
Like plural suns on Judgment Day.

Why, the very name of your genuine king keeps others from taking liberties. As the proverb puts it:

Mere mention of a lordly monarch's name
To mean men, straightway saves from loss and shame.

And there is a saying:

The feigning of a great commission
Immensely betters your condition:
Feigning a message from the moon,
The rabbits dwelt in comfort soon."

"How was that?" asked the birds. And the crow told

HOW THE RABBIT FOOLED THE ELEPHANT

In a part of a forest lived an elephant-king named Four-Tusk, who had a numerous retinue of elephants. His time was spent in protecting the herd.

Now once there came a twelve-year drought, so that tanks, ponds, swamps, and lakes went dry. Then all the elephants said to the lord of the herd: "O King, our little ones are so tortured by thirst that some are like to die, and some are dead. Pray devise a method of removing thirst." So he sent in eight directions elephants fleet as the wind to search for water.

Now those who went east found beside a path near a hermitage a lake named Lake of the Moon. It was beautiful with swans, herons, ospreys, ducks, sheldrakes, cranes, and water-creatures. It was embowered in flowering sprays of branches drooping under the weight of various blossoms. Both banks were embellished with trees. It had beaches made lovely by sheets of foam born of the splashing of transparent waves that danced in the breeze and broke on the shore. Its water was perfumed by the ichor-juice that oozed from elephant-temples washed clean of bees; for these flew up when the lordly creatures plunged. It was ever screened from the heat of the sun by hundreds of parasols in the shape of the countless leaves of trees on its banks. It gave forth deep-toned music from uncounted waves that turned aside on meeting the plump legs, hips, and bosoms of mountain maidens diving. It was brimming with crystal water, and beautified with thickets of water-lilies in full bloom. Why describe it? It was a segment of paradise.

When they saw this, they hastened back to report to the elephant-king.

So Four-Tusk, on hearing their report, traveled with them by easy stages to the Lake of the Moon. And finding a gentle slope all around the lake, the elephants plunged in, thereby crushing the heads, necks, fore-paws and hind-paws of thousands of rabbits who long before had made their home on the banks. Now after drinking and bathing, the elephant-king with his followers departed to his own portion of the jungle.

Then the rabbits who were left alive held an emergency convention. "What are we to do now?" said they. "Those fellows—curse their tracks!—will come here every day. Let some plan be framed at once to prevent their return."

Thereupon a rabbit named Victory, perceiving their terror and their utter woe at the crushing of sons, wives, and relatives, said compassionately: "Have no fear. They shall not return. I promise it. For my guardian angel has granted me this grace."

And hearing this, the rabbit-king, whose name was Block-Snout, said to Victory: "Dear friend, this is beyond peradventure. For

> Good Victory knows every fact
> The textbooks teach; knows how to act
> In every place and time. Where he
> Is sent, there comes prosperity.

And again:

> Speak for pleasure, speak with measure,
> Speak with grammar's richest treasure,
> Not too much, and with reflection—
> Deeds will follow words' direction.

The elephants, sir, making acquaintance with your ripe wisdom, will become aware of my majesty, wisdom, and energy, though I am not present. For the proverb says:

> I learn if foreign kings be fools or no
> By their dispatches or their nuncio.

And there is a saying:

> The envoy binds; he loosens what is bound;
> Through him success in war, if found, is found.

And if you go, it is as if I went myself. Because, if you

> Speak what lies in your commission,
> Speak with careful composition,
> Grammar and good ethics seeking,
> 'Tis as if myself were speaking.

And again:

> This is, in brief, the envoy's care:
> An argument to fit the facts
> And sound results, so far as speech
> May be translated into acts.

"Depart then, dear friend. And may the office of envoy prove a second guardian angel to you."

So Victory departed and espied the elephant-king in the act of returning to the lake. He was surrounded by thousands of lordly elephants, whose ears, like flowering branches, were swaying in a dignified dance. His body was dappled with masses of pollen from his couch made of twigs from the tips of branches of flowering cassia trees; so that he seemed a laden cloud with many clinging lightning-flashes. His trumpeting was as deep toned and awe inspiring as the clash of countless thunderbolts from which in the rainy season piercing flashes gleam. He had the glossy beauty of leaves in a bed of pure blue lotuses. His twisting trunk had the charm of a perfect snake. His presence was that of an elephant of heaven. His two tusks, shapely, smooth, and full, had the color of honey. Around his entire visage rose a charming hum from swarms of bees drawn by the fragrant perfume of the ichor-juice that issued from his temples.

And Victory reflected: "It is impossible for folk like me to come too near. Because, as the proverb puts it:

> An elephant will kill you if
> He touch; a serpent if he sniff;
> King's laughter has a deadly sting;
> A rascal kills by honoring.

I must by all odds seek impregnable terrain before introducing myself."

After these reflections, he climbed upon a tall and jagged rock-pile before saying: "Is it well with you, lord of the two-tusked breed?" And the elephant king, hearing this, peered narrowly about, and said "Who are you, sir?" "I am an envoy," said the rabbit. "In whose service?" asked the elephant, and the envoy answered: "In the service of the blessèd Moon." "State your business," said the elephant-king, and the rabbit stated it thus.

"You are aware, sir, that no injury may be done an envoy in the discharge of his function. For all kings, without exception, use envoys as their mouthpieces. Indeed, there is a proverb:

> Though swords be out and kinsmen fall in strife,
> The king still spares the harsh-tongued envoy's life.

"Therefore by command of the Moon I say to you: 'Why, O mortal, why have you used violence upon others, with no true reckoning of your own power or your foe's? For the Scripture says:

> All those who madly march to deeds,
>   Not reckoning who are masters,
> Themselves or powerful enemies,
>   Are asking for disasters.

"'Now you have sinfully violated the Lake of the Moon, known afar by my sacred name. And there you have slain rabbits who are under my special protection, who are of the race of that rabbit-king cherished in my bosom. This is iniquitous. Nay, one would think you the only creature in the world who does not know the rabbit in the moon. But what is gained by much speaking? Desist from such actions, or great disaster will befall you at my hands. But if from this hour you desist, great distinction will be yours; for your body will be nourished by my moonlight, and with your companions you shall pursue your happy, carefree fancies in this forest. In the alternative case, my light shall be withheld, your body will be scorched by summer heat, and you with your companions will perish.'"

On hearing this, the elephant-king felt his heart

stagger, and after long reflection he said: "It is true, sir. I have sinned against the blessèd Moon. Who am I that I should longer contend with him? Pray point out to me, and quickly, the way that I must travel to win the blessèd Moon's forgiveness."

The rabbit said: "Come, sir, alone. I will point it out." So he went by night to the Lake of the Moon, and showed him the moon reflected in the water. There was the brilliant, quivering disk, of lustrous loveliness, surrounded by planets, the Seven Sages, and hosts of stars, all dancing in the reflection of heaven's broad expanse. And its circle was complete, with the full complement of digits.

Seeing this, the elephant said: "I purify myself and worship the deity," and he dropped upon the water a trunk that two men's arms might have encircled. Thereby he disturbed the water, the moon's disk danced to and fro as if mounted on a whirling wheel, and he saw a thousand moons.

Then Victory started back in great agitation, and said to the elephant-king: "Woe, woe to you, O King! You have doubly enraged the Moon." The elephant said: "For what reason is the blessèd Moon angry with me?"

"Because," said Victory, "you have touched this water." So the elephant-king, with drooping ears, bowed his head to the very earth in deep obeisance, in order to win forgiveness from the blessèd Moon. And he spoke again to Victory: "My worthy sir, in all other manners, also, beseech for me the forgiveness of the blessèd Moon. I shall never return here." And with these words he went to his own place.

"And that is why I say:

> The feigning of a great commission, ...

and the rest of it.

"But worse remains behind. The owl is a seedy rascal, with a wicked soul. He could never protect subjects. Or rather, to say nothing of protection, you may anticipate actual danger from him. You know the stanza:

> A seedy umpire is not very
> Pleasing to either adversary:
> Rabbit and partridge teach you that—
> They died, confiding in the cat."

"How was that? Tell us about it," said the birds, and the crow told the story of

THE CAT'S JUDGMENT

At one time I was myself living in a certain tree. And beneath the same tree dwelt another bird, a partridge. So by virtue of our near neighborhood there sprang up between us a firm friendship. Every day after taking our meals and airings we spent the evening hours in a round of amusements, such as repeating witty sayings, telling tales from the old story-books, solving puzzles and conundrums, or exchanging presents.

One day the partridge went foraging with other birds to a spot where the rice was ripe and abundant, and he did not return at nightfall. Of course, I missed him greatly and I thought: "Alas! Why does not my friend the partridge come home tonight? I am much afraid he is caught in some trap, or has even been killed." And many days passed while I grieved in this way.

Now one evening a rabbit named Speedy made himself at home in the partridge's old nest in the hole. Nor did I say him nay, for I despaired of seeing the partridge again.

However, one fine day the partridge, who had grown extremely plump from eating rice, remembered his old home and returned. This, indeed, is not to be wondered at.

> No mortal has such joy, although
> In heaven's fields he roam,
> As in his city, in his land,
> And in his humble home.

Now when he saw the rabbit in the hole, he said reproachfully: "Come now, rabbit, you have done a shabby thing in occupying my apartment. Please begone, and lose no time about it."

"You fool!" said the rabbit, "don't you know that a dwelling is yours only while you occupy it?" "Very well, then," said the partridge, "suppose we ask the neighbors. For, to give you a legal quotation,

For ownership of cisterns, tanks,
  Wells, groves, and houses, too,
The neighbors' testimony goes—
  Such is the legal view.

And again:

When house or field or well or grove
  Or land is in dispute,
A neighbor's testimony is
  Decisive of the suit."

Then the rabbit said: "You fool! Are you ignorant of the consecrated tradition which says:

Suppose beside your neighbor you
  For ten long years abide,
What weight have learnèd arguments?
  Eyewitnesses decide.

Fool! Fool! Did you never hear the dictum of the sage Narada?

The title to possession is
  A ten years' habitation
With men. But with the birds and beasts
  Mere present occupation.

"Hence, even supposing this apartment to be yours, still it was unoccupied when I moved in, and now it is mine."

"Well, well!" replied the partridge, "if you appeal to consecrated tradition, come with me, and we will consult the specialists. It shall be yours or mine according to their decision." "Very well," said the other, and together they started off to have their suit decided. I, too, was at their heels, out of curiosity. "I will just see what comes of all this," I said to myself.

Now they had not traveled far when the rabbit asked the partridge: "My good fellow, who is to pass judgment on our disagreement?" And the partridge answered: "On a sand-bank by the sacred Ganges—where there is sweet music from the dancing waves that intercross and break when the water is swept by nimble breezes—there dwells a tomcat whose name is Curd-Ear. He abides unshaken in his vow of penance and self-denial, and character has begotten compassion."

But when the rabbit spied the cat, his soul staggered with terror, and he said: "No, no! He is a seedy rascal. You must have heard the proverb:

> Oh, never trust a rogue for all
> His pharisaic puzzling:
> At holy shrines some saints are found
> Quite capable of guzzling."

Upon hearing this, Curd-Ear, whose manner of life had been assumed for the purpose of making an easy livelihood, desired to win their confidence. He therefore gazed straight at the sun, stood on his hind-legs, lifted his fore-paws, blinked his eyes, and in order to deceive them by pious sentiments, delivered the following moral discourse. "Alas! Alas! All is vanity. This fragile life passes in a moment. Union with the beloved is an empty dream. Family endearments are a conjurer's trick. But for the moral law, there would be no escape. Oh, listen to Scripture!

> Each transitory day, O man,
> To moral living give;
> Else, like the blacksmith's bellows, you
> Suck air, but do not live.

And furthermore:

> Non-moral learning is a curse,
> A dog's tail, nothing less,
> That does not save from flies and fleas,
> Nor cover nakedness.

And yet again:

> A rotten ear among the wheat,
> Among the birds a bat,
> Is he who spurns the moral law;
> The merest living gnat.
>
> The flowers and fruit are better than the tree;
> Better than curds is butter said to be;
> Better than oil-cake, oil that trickles free;
> Better than mortal man, morality.
>
> The praise of constant steadfastness
> Some wise professors sing;
> But moral earnestness is swift,
> Though many fetters cling.
>
> Forget your prosings manifold;
> The moral law is briefly told:
> To help your neighbor—this is good;
> To injure him is devilhood."

Having listened to this moral discourse, the rabbit said: "Friend partridge, here on the river-bank is the saint who expounds the moral law. Let us ask him."

But the partridge said: "After all, he is our natural enemy. Let us ask him from a distance." So together they began to question him: "O holy moralist, a dispute has arisen between us. Pray give judgment in accordance with the moral law. And whichever of us is found to speak falsely, him you may eat."

"Dear friends," said the cat, "I implore you not to speak thus. My soul abhors every act of cruelty, that street-sign pointing to hell. Surely, you know the Scripture:

> The holy first commandment runs—
> Not harsh, but kindly be—
> And therefore lavish mercy on
> Mosquito, louse, and flea.
>
> Why speak of hurting innocence?
> For he, with purpose fell
> Who injures even noxious beasts,
> Is plunged in ghastly hell.

"Nay, even those who slay living creatures in the act of sacrifice are befuddled, and their hermeneutic theology is at fault. And if you object to me the passage, 'One should sacrifice with goats,' in that passage the word 'goats' signifies grain that has aged seven years. 'Go, oats'—such is the true exegesis. And then, consider the passage:

> If he who cuts down trees or cattle,
> Or makes a bloody slime in battle,

Should thereby win to heaven—well,
Who (let me ask you) goes to hell?

"No, no. I shall eat nobody. However, I am somewhat old and do not readily distinguish your voices from a distance. So how am I to determine winner and loser? In view of this, pray draw near and make me acquainted with the case. Then I can pronounce a judgment that discriminates the essence of the matter, and thus causes no impediment in my march to the other world. You know the stanza:

If any man, from pride or greed,
Timidity or wrath,
Judge falsely, he has set his foot
On hell's down-sloping path.

And again:

Who wrongs a sheep, slays kinsmen five;
Who wrongs a cow, slays ten;
A hundred die for maidens wronged;
A thousand die for men.

"Therefore confide in me and speak clearly at the edge of my ear."

Why spin it out? That seedy rogue won their trust so fully that both drew near him. Then, of course, he seized them simultaneously, one with his paw, the other with the saw of his teeth. And when they were dead, he ate them both.

"And that is why I say:

A seedy umpire is not very. . . .

and the rest of it.

"Just so, you, too, being blind at night, if you take as overlord this seedy fellow who is blind in the daytime, will go the way of the rabbit and the partridge. Reflect on this, then do what seems proper."

And all the birds, after listening to the crow's remarks, said: "He speaks well," and they flew to their homes, planning to reassemble for consultation on the question of a king. Only the owl remained with his consort, for he was blind in the daytime. There he sat in his chair of state, awaiting the anointing. And he called out: "Ho, there! Who takes my orders? Why is the ceremony delayed?"

Thereupon his consort said: "My dear sir, the crow has found means to hold up the ceremony. And the birds have gone flying away. Only that crow, for some reason or other, remains here all alone. Rise at once, and I will conduct you home."

Then the owl was deeply disappointed, and he said: "You monster! Why have you wronged me by preventing the regal anointing? From this day there is enmity between us. For the proverb says:

> When arrows pierce or axes wound
> A tree, it grows together sound;
> From cruel, ugly speech you feel
> A wound that time will never heal."

Thereupon he went home with his consort, while the crow reflected: "Dear me! I have burdened myself with a needless enmity by speaking so. I should have remembered:

All spoken words, if harsh and heedless
And inappropriate and needless,
Are self-condemnatory slips
That turn to poison on the lips.

And again:

However wise and strong you be,
Beware the needless enemy:
You would not swallow poison down
Because a doctor lives in town.

No man of sense vituperates
Another, while the public waits;
For even truth should be concealed,
If causing sorrow when revealed.

And finally:

Reflect with many a chosen friend;
Reflect alone, and to the end;
Then act. You are intelligent,
And fame's and wealth's recipient."

After these reflections, the crow also left the spot.

"For this cause, my son, we have an inherited feud with the crows."

"Father," said Cloudy, "what should we do under the circumstances?" And Live-Strong answered: "Even in these circumstances there is an effective procedure other than the six expedients. This I will adopt, and will myself lead the way to conquer the enemy. I will deceive them and put them in a fatal situation. For the saying goes:

The strong, deft, clever rascals note,
Who robbed the Brahman of his goat."

"How was that?" asked Cloudy. And Live-Strong told the story of

THE BRAHMAN'S GOAT

In a certain town lived a Brahman named Friendly who had undertaken the labor of maintaining the sacred fire. One day in the month of February, when a gentle breeze was blowing, when the sky was veiled in clouds and a drizzling rain was falling, he went to another village to beg a victim for the sacrifice, and said to a certain man: "O sacrificer, I wish to make an offering on the approaching day of the new moon. Pray give me a victim." And the man gave him a plump goat, as prescribed in Scripture. This he put through its paces, found it sound, placed it on his shoulder, and started in haste for his own city.

Now on the road he was met by three rogues whose throats were pinched with hunger. These, spying the plump creature on his shoulder, whispered together: "Come now! If we could eat that creature, we should have the laugh on this sleety weather. Let us fool him, get the goat, and ward off the cold."

So the first of them changed his dress, issued from a by-path to meet the Brahman, and thus addressed that man of pious life: "O pious Brahman, why are you doing a thing so unconventional and so ridiculous? You are carrying an unclean animal, a dog, on your shoulder. Are you ignorant of the verse:

The dog and the rooster,
  The hangman, the ass,
The camel, defile you:
  Don't touch them, but pass."

At that the Brahman was mastered by anger, and he said: "Are you blind, man, that you impute doghood to a goat?" "O Brahman," said the rogue, "do not be angry. Go whither you will."

But when he had traveled a little farther, the second rogue met him and said: "Alas, holy sir, alas! Even if this dead calf was a pet, still you should not put it on your shoulder. For the proverb says:

Touch not unwisely man or beast
  That lifeless lie;
Else, gifts of milk and lunar fast
  Must purify."

Then the Brahman spoke in anger: "Are you blind, man? You call a goat a calf." And the rogue said: "Holy sir, do not be angry. I spoke in ignorance. Do as you will."

But when he had walked only a little farther through the forest, the third rogue, changing his dress, met him and said: "Sir, this is most improper. You are carrying a donkey on your shoulder. Yet the proverb tells you:

If you should touch an ass—be it
  In ignorance or not—
You needs must wash your clothes and bathe,
  To cleanse the sinful spot.

Pray drop this thing, before another sees you."

So the Brahman concluded that it was a goblin in quadruped form, threw it on the ground, and made for home, terrified. Meanwhile, the three rogues met, caught the goat, and carried out their plan.

"And that is why I say:

> The strong, deft, clever rascals note, ...

and the rest of it.

"Moreover, there is sound sense in this:

> Is any man uncheated by
> New servants' diligence,
> The praise of guests, the maiden's tears,
> And roguish eloquence?

Furthermore, one should avoid a quarrel with a crowd, though the individuals be weak. As the verse puts it:

> Beware the populace enraged;
> A crowd's a fearsome thing:
> The ants devoured the giant snake
> For all his quivering."

"How was that?" asked Cloudy. And Live-Strong told the story of

THE SNAKE AND THE ANTS

In a certain ant-hill lived a prodigious black snake, and his name was Haughty. One day, instead of following the beaten path out of his hole, he tried to crawl through a narrower crevice. In doing so, he suffered a wound, because his body was huge, and the opening was small, and fate willed it so.

Then the ants gathered about him, drawn by the odor of blood from the wound, and drove him frantic. How many did he kill? Or how many crush? Yet their uncounted phalanx stung him in every member, and enlarged the numerous wounds. And Haughty perished.

"And that is why I say:

> Beware the populace enraged, ...

and the rest of it.

"Furthermore, O King, I have something to tell you, which you must consider, and ponder, and do."

"Father," said Cloudy, "tell me what you have in mind." And Live-Strong said: "Listen, my son. I have discovered a fifth device, different from the well-known four—conciliation, intrigue, bribery, and fighting. And it is this. You must turn against me, revile me with the hardest-hearted words you can find, smear me with blood (which you will provide) in order to deceive the enemy's spies, throw me out at the foot of this banyan tree, and depart yourself to Antelope Mountain. And there you must stay with your retinue until by clever planning I win the trust of all the enemy, discover the heart of their fortress, and kill them—for they are blind in the daytime. This plan I devised on the assumption that their fortress is of simple construction, without egress at the rear. For the saying goes:

A fort must have for egress, say
  The specialists, a gap;
If this be lacking, it is not
  A fortress, but a trap.

Nor should you feel any pity for me. For the proverb says:

Pet and pamper servants well;
  Love them as you love your life:
Yet consider them as dry
  Tinder in the hour of strife.

Nor must you balk me in my design. For once more:

Cherish servants like yourself;
  Guard them as you guard your life
Every day for one sole day,
  When you meet your foe in strife."

With these words he started a sham fight with the king. And Cloudy's retinue, seeing Live-Strong jabber with unbridled license at the king, started up to kill him. But Cloudy said: "Out of my path, you. I take upon myself the chastisement of this traitorous scoundrel." With this he pounced upon him, pecked at him gently, smeared him with blood (which he had provided), and departed with his retinue for Antelope Mountain, as Live-Strong had recommended.

At this juncture the owl's consort, acting as spy for the enemy, went and reported in detail to the owl-king the disgrace of Cloudy's prime minister. And the owl-king, informed of the occurrence, started with his retainers at sundown on a crow-hunt. And he said: "Hasten, friends, hasten! The enemy is panic-stricken, is in full flight, and can be readily caught. For the proverb says:

> In flight, a fort becomes a trap
>   Where all defense is lacking;
> 'Tis easy then to beat a king
>   Whose men are busy packing."

With this battle-cry they flew to attack the banyan tree. And failing to find a single crow, King Foe-Crusher gleefully perched on a branch, and while the court poets chanted flatteries, he gave orders: "Ho there! Discover their line of retreat. Before they establish themselves in a fort, I will be at their heels and will kill them."

At this point Live-Strong reflected: "If the enemy simply go home after learning what we have done, I shall have accomplished nothing. For the proverb says:

> The first or second evidence
> Of genuine intelligence
> Is—leave a business unbegun,
> Or, if begun, then see it done.

It would have been better not to undertake this than to see the undertaking fail. I will reveal myself by letting them hear me caw."

So he cawed with a feeble squeak. And the owls, hearing this, started up to kill him. But Live-Strong said: "Gentlemen, I am Cloudy's minister, Live-Strong, reduced to this state by Cloudy himself. Pray inform your own king. I have much to discuss with him."

So the owl-king, informed by his followers, came, beheld with astonishment the scars of many wounds, and said: "Well, sir! How did you fall into this condition? Tell me."

And Live-Strong said: "O King, listen. Yesterday that rascal Cloudy, seeing how many crows you had killed, was distracted by wrath and grief, and started for your fortress. Whereupon I said: 'You should not march against him. For they are strong, and we are weak. Now the proverb advises those who wish to thrive:

> Do not, even in thought, offend
> Stronger foes who will not bend;
> They will feel no loss or shame;
> You will die, a moth in flame.

You should seek peace by paying him tribute.' When he heard this, he was made furious by rascally advisers, suspected me of being a partisan of yours, and reduced me to this state. Therefore your royal feet are now my sole refuge. In a word, so long as I can stir, I will conduct you to his abode, and cause the total destruction of the crows."

On hearing this, Foe-Crusher took counsel with the counselors who had served his father and his grandfather. They were five in number, and their names were Red-Eye, Fierce-Eye, Flame-Eye, Hook-Nose, and Wall-Ear.

So first he questioned Red-Eye: "My worthy sir, what is to be done under the circumstances?" And

Red-Eye said: "O King, what is there to consider here? Kill him without hesitation. For the proverb says:

> Kill a weakling, lest he grow
> Hard to smite;
> Later, with augmented power
> He will fight.

Besides, you know how common people say: 'A lost chance brings a curse.' And again:

> He who will not when he may,
> When he will, he shall have nay.

And this too:

> The lighted funeral pile you may
> Break up and fling apart;
> But love, when torn and patched again,
> Lives in an aching heart."

"How was that?" asked Foe-Crusher. And Red-Eye told the story of

THE SNAKE WHO PAID CASH

There was once a Brahman in a certain place. His time was wholly spent in unproductive farming.

Now one day, toward the end of summer, the heat was too much for him, and he dozed in the shade of a tree in the middle of his field. Not far away he saw, peering over an ant-hill, a terrifying snake that thrust forward a great, swelling hood. And he reflected: "Surely, this is the guardian deity of the field, and I never paid him honor. That is why my farm-work is unproductive. I will pay him honor."

Thereupon he begged milk from somebody, put it in a saucer, went to the ant-hill, and said: "O guardian of the field! All this long time I did not know that you were living here. Therefore I paid you no honor. From now on, please be gracious to me." With this he presented the milk and went home.

Now when he came back in the morning and looked about, he found a gold dinar in the saucer. So he went there every day alone, and offered milk, receiving a dinar each time. One day, however, the Brahman went to town, instructing his son to carry milk to the ant-hill. And the boy took the milk there, set it down, and went home again.

The next day he went there, found a single dinar, and thought: "Surely, this ant-hill is full of dinars. I will kill that fellow and get them all." With this purpose, while offering milk the next day, the Brahman's boy struck the snake on the head with a cudgel. Yet somehow—for fate willed it so—the snake did not die. Instead, he furiously struck the boy with his sharp fangs to such effect that the boy died at once. And the relatives cremated him on a woodpile near the field.

On the second day the father returned. And learning from his relatives the cause of his son's death, he found the facts as stated. And he said:

Be generous to all that lives;
Receive the needy guest:
If not, your own life fades away
Like swans from lotus nest.

"How was that?" asked the men. And the Brahman told the story of

THE UNSOCIAL SWANS

There was once a king named Gay-Chariot in a certain place. He owned a lake named Lotus Lake, which his soldiers guarded carefully. For many golden swans lived there, and they gave one tail-feather apiece every six months.

Now to that lake came a great bird, all of gold. And they told him: "You cannot live among us. For we have rented this lake at the rate of a tail-feather for six months." And so, to cut a long story short, a dispute arose.

Then the great bird sought the king's protection, saying: "O King, those birds ask: 'What will our king do? We give lodging to nobody.' And I said: 'You are not very polite. I will go and tell the king.' This is the situation. The king must decide."

Then the king said to his men: "Go, you. Kill all the birds and bring them here at once." And they started immediately, obeying the king's command.

Now one old bird saw the king's men with clubs in their hands, and he said: "Well, kinsmen, this is rather unpleasant. We must all hang together. Let us fly up and away." And they did so.

"And that is why I say:

> Be generous to all that lives, . . .

and the rest of it."

So in the morning the Brahman took milk again, went to the spot, and called out, in an effort to win the snake's confidence: "My son met the death that suited his intelligence." Then the snake said:

The lighted funeral pile you may
  Break up and fling apart;
But love, when torn and patched again,
  Lives in an aching heart.

"Thus, when he is dead, you will without effort enjoy a thornless kingdom."

Having listened to this proposal, the king asked Fierce-Eye: "My worthy sir, what is your opinion?" And Fierce-Eye said: "O King, his advice is heartless. For one does not kill a suppliant. No doubt you have heard the old story:

The dove (there mentioned) entertained
His suppliant foeman slaughter-stained;
Paid honor due, his guest to greet;
And sacrificed himself for meat."

"How was that?" asked Foe-Crusher. And Fierce-Eye told the story of

THE SELF-SACRIFICING DOVE

A ghastly fowler plied his trade
Of horror in a forest; made
All living creatures hold their breath:
He seemed to them the god of death.

He had no comrade on the earth,
No friend, no relative by birth.
They all renounced him; he had made
Them do so by his horrid trade.

For you know

The dreadful wretches bringing death
On those who love their living breath,
With natural repulsion (like
Fierce serpents) fill before they strike.

To snare, to imprison, and to drub
He took a net, a cage, a club,
And wandering daily in the wood,
He brought all creatures harm, not good.

While he was in the wood one day,
The sky grew black with clouds straightway;
So wild the wind, so fierce the rain,
It seemed the world dissolved in pain.

Then, as the heart within him quivered,
And every limb grew numb and shivered,
He sought where might a refuge be,
And chanced to come upon a tree.

Now as he rested, near and far
In sudden-clearing skies, each star
Shone bright; and he had wit to pray:
"O Lord, be kind to me today."

There was a dove upon the tree
Whose nest was in a cavity;
And since his wife was absent long,
He grieved for her in mournful song:

"The wind and rain were very great,
And my belovèd wife is late
In coming home. When she is not
At home, home is an empty spot.

"The house is not the home; but where
The wife is found, the home is there.
The home without the wife is less
To me than some wild wilderness.

"Some wives their life's devotion give,
And in and for the husband live;
Whatever man has such a wife
Is heaped with blessings all his life."

From fowling-cage the female dove
Had caught the speech of grief and love;
And she was deeply gratified,
And to her husband thus replied:

"No woman earns the name of bride
Whose husband is not satisfied.
If he is happy, she may know
The gods she venerates are so.

"That woman should be burned entire
(Like vines that fade in forest-fire
While blossoms drop from clustered side)
Whose husband is not satisfied."

And she continued:

"Oh, harken heedfully, my dear;
My words are good for you to hear;
Though it should cost your life, defend
The guest who seeks in you a friend.

"Here lies a fowler; as a guest
He asks for comfort at your nest.
Since cold and hunger press him sore,
Begrudge him not from honor's store.

And the Scripture says:

"Whoever does not give his best
To cheer the late-arriving guest
Will see his merit borne away,
And for the other's sins will pay.

"Oh, let no hate against him rise
Who caged the wife you idolize;
It is my sins of former lives
That, fateful, hold me in the gyves.

For well you know:

"Disease, and poverty, and pain,
With woe that prison brings amain,
Are all the fruit of one sole tree,
Our own, our past iniquity.

"Abandon, therefore, thoughts of hate
Deriving from my captive state;
On virtue set your heart; and pay
This man such honor as you may."

On listening to his darling, who
Seemed virtue-woven through and through,
An unknown courage fired the dove;
He gave the fowler words of love.

"A hearty welcome, sir, to you;
What for your service may I do?
No more let anxious fancies roam,
For here with me you are at home."

In answer to his kindly words
Replied the murderer of birds:
"Well, dove, the cold is in me still;
Give me a remedy for chill."

The dove then brought a bonfire's sole
Surviving ember—one live coal,
And where a pile of dry leaves lay,
He kindled it to fire straightway.

"Now, sir, take heart; forgetting fear,
Resuscitate your members here;
Alas! I cannot put to flight
The cravings of your appetite.

"One patron feeds a thousand men;
One feeds a hundred; one feeds ten.
But I, whose virtue does not thrive,
Scarce keep my puny self alive.

"Ah, if you have not in your nest
Provision for a single guest,
Why occupy today, tomorrow
A nest that harbors naught but sorrow?

"I shall destroy my body, fain
To end its living with its pain,
That nevermore I stand confessed
Powerless to aid a needy guest."

And thus he blamed himself, you see;
The greedy fowler went scot-free:
Then—"I may yet your craving sate,
If one mere moment you will wait."

Whereat that creature free from sin,
Joy-quivering his soul within,
Walked round the fire, as it had been
His cherished home, and entered in.

When this the greedy fowler saw,
Compassion filled his soul, and awe.

He, while the dove was cooking, spoke
What from his heart a passage broke:

"None loves his soul, 'tis very plain,
Who smears it with a sinful stain.
The soul commits the sin; and late
Or soon, the soul must expiate.

"My thoughts are evil; my desire
Is ever set on what is dire:
It needs but little wit to tell
I steer my course for ghastly hell.

"A moral lesson let me draw
From what my savage spirit saw.
The high-souled dove, that I may eat,
Has sacrificed himself for meat.

"Henceforth let all enjoyment be
An unfamiliar thing to me;
I'll share the shallow water's fate
In August; will evaporate.

"Cold, wind, and heat I will embrace,
Grow thin and dirty, form and face,
Will fast by every method known,
Seek virtue, perfect and alone."

The fowler then apieces tore
Club, peg, net, cage—and what is more,
Set free the wretched female dove
Who sorrowed for her perished love.

But she, released from clutches dire,
Beheld her husband in the fire;
Whereat she gave expression so
To thoughts of horror and of woe:

"My lord! My love! What shall I do
With life that drags, apart from you?
What profit has a wretched wife,
Without a husband, of her life?

"For self-esteem, respect, and pride,
The family honor paid a bride,
Authority with all the brood
Of servants, die with widowhood."

Now after this lamenting sore,
This sorrow bitter evermore,
She went where lay her heart's desire,
Walked straight into the blazing fire.

And lo! She sees her husband shine—
Oh, wonder!—in a car divine;
Her body wears a heavenly gown;
And heavenly gems hang pendent down.

While he, become a god, addressed
True consolation to her breast:
"The deed that you have done, is meet
In following your husband, sweet.

"There grow upon a man alive
Some thirty million hairs and five;
So many years in heaven spend
Wives following husbands to the end."

So he joyfully took her into the chariot, embraced her, and lived happily. But the fowler sank into the deepest despondency, and plunged into a great forest, meditating death.

And there he saw a forest-fire
And entered it; for all desire

Was dead. His sins were burned away;
He went to heaven, there to stay.

"And that is why I say:

The dove (there mentioned) entertained, ...

and the rest of it."

Having listened to this, Foe-Crusher asked Flame-Eye: "What is your opinion, sir, things standing as they do?" And Flame-Eye said:

"She who always shrank from me
Hugs me to her breast.
Thank you, benefactor! Take
What you like the best."

And the thief replied:

"Nothing here that I should like;
Should I want a thing,
I'll return if she does not
Passionately cling."

"But," asked Foe-Crusher, "who is she that does not cling? And who is the thief? I should like to hear this one in detail." And Flame-Eye told the story of

THE OLD MAN WITH THE YOUNG WIFE

There was once an aged merchant in a certain town, and his name was Lovelorn. To such an extent had love clouded his reason that, when his wife died, he gave much money in order to marry the daughter of a penniless shopkeeper. But the girl was heart-broken and could not bear to look at the old merchant. This, indeed, might have been anticipated.

The silvered head will sue in vain,
  A maiden's love beseeching;
The maid, despising it, is fain
  To flee afar with screeching;
Like Hangman's Well it causes pain,
  Where dead men's bones are bleaching.

And furthermore:

Slow, tottering steps the strength exhaust;
  The eye unsteady blinks;
From driveling mouth the teeth are lost;
  The handsome figure shrinks;
The limbs are wrinkled; relatives
  And wife contemptuous pass;
The son no further honor gives
  To doddering age. Alas!

Now one night, while she was turning her back to him in bed, a thief entered the house. And she was terrified at seeing a thief, and embraced her husband, old as he was. He, for his part, felt every limb thrill with astonishment and love, and he thought: "Gracious me! Why does she hug me tonight?" Then, peering narrowly about, he discovered the thief in a corner, and reflected: "No doubt she embraces me from fear of him." So he said to the thief:

"She who always shrank from me,
  Hugs me to her breast;
Thank you, benefactor! Take
  What you like the best."

And the thief made reply:

"Nothing here that I should like;
  Should I want a thing,

I'll return if she does not
Passionately cling."

"Thus advantage may be anticipated from a benefactor, thief though he be. How much more from a suppliant guest? Besides, having been maltreated by them, he will labor for our success, or for the revelation of their vulnerable point. In view of this, he should not be killed."

Having listened to this view, Foe-Crusher questioned another counselor, namely, Hook-Nose. "My worthy sir, what should be done under the present circumstances?" And Hook-Nose answered: "O King, he should not be killed. For

From enemies expect relief,
If discord pierce their host;
Thus, life was given by the thief
And cattle by the ghost."

"How was that?" asked Foe-Crusher. And Hook-Nose told the story of

THE BRAHMAN, THE THIEF, AND THE GHOST

There was once a poor Brahman in a certain place. He lived on presents, and always did without such luxuries as fine clothes and ointments and perfumes and garlands and gems and betel-gum. His beard and his nails were long, and so was the hair that covered his head and his body. Heat, cold, rain, and the like had dried him up.

Then someone pitied him and gave him two calves. And the Brahman began when they were little and fed them on butter and oil and fodder and other things that he begged. So he made them very plump.

Then a thief saw them and the idea came to him at once: "I will steal these two cows from this Brahman." So he took a rope and set out at night. But on the way he met a fellow with a row of sharp teeth set far apart, with a high-bridged nose and uneven eyes, with limbs covered with knotty muscles, with hollow cheeks, with beard and body as yellow as a fire with much butter in it.

And when the thief saw him, he started with acute fear and said: "Who are you, sir?"

The other said: "I am a ghost named Truthful. It is now your turn to explain yourself."

The thief said: "I am a thief, and my acts are cruel. I am on my way to steal two cows from a poor Brahman."

Then the ghost felt relieved and said: "My dear sir, I take one meal every three days. So I will just eat this Brahman today. It is delightful that you and I are on the same errand."

So together they went there and hid, waiting for the proper moment. And when the Brahman went to sleep, the ghost started forward to eat him. But the thief saw him and said: "My dear sir, this is not right. You are not to eat the Brahman until I have stolen his two cows."

The ghost said: "The racket would most likely wake the Brahman. In that case all my trouble would be vain."

"But, on the other hand," said the thief, "if any hindrance arises when you start to eat him, then I cannot steal the two cows either. First I will steal the two cows, then you may eat the Brahman."

So they disputed, each crying "Me first! Me first!" And when they became heated, the hubbub waked the Brahman. Then the thief said: "Brahman, this is a ghost who wishes to eat you." And the ghost said: "Brahman, this is a thief who wishes to steal your two cows."

When the Brahman heard this, he stood up and took a good look. And by remembering a prayer to his favorite god, he saved his life from the ghost, then lifted a club and saved his two cows from the thief.

"And that is why I say:

> From enemies expect relief, ...

and the rest of it. Besides:

> The Scriptures tell a holy tale
> Of sacrificial love,
> How Shibi gave the hawk his flesh
> As ransom for the dove—

showing that it is contrary to religion to slay a suppliant."

Having listened to this opinion, the king asked

Wall-Ear: "What is your view, sir? Tell me." And Wall-Ear said: "O King, he certainly should not be killed. For if you spare his life, you two may well grow fond of each other, and spend the time pleasantly. There is a saying:

Be quick with mutual defense
In honest give-and-take;
Or perish, like the ant-hill beast
And like the belly-snake."

"How was that?" asked Foe-Crusher. And Wall-Ear told the story of

THE SNAKE IN THE PRINCE'S BELLY

In a certain city dwelt a king whose name was Godlike. He had a son who wasted daily in every limb because of a snake that used his belly as a home instead of an ant-hill. So the prince became dejected and went to another country. In a city of that country he begged alms, spending his time in a great temple.

Now in that city was a king named Gift, who had two daughters in early womanhood. One of these bowed daily at her father's feet with the greeting: "Victory, O King," while the other said: "Your deserts, O King."

At this the king grew angry, and said: "See, counselors. This young lady speaks malevolently. Give her to some foreigner. Let her have her own deserts." To this the counselors agreed, and gave the princess, with very few maid-servants, to the prince who made his home in the temple.

And she was delighted, accepted her husband like a god, and went with him to a far country. There by the edge of a tank in a distant city she left the prince to look after the house while she went with her maids to buy butter, oil, salt, rice, and other supplies. When her shopping was done, she returned and found the prince with his head resting on an ant-hill. And from his mouth issued the head of a hooded snake, taking the air. Likewise another snake crawled from the ant-hill, also to take the air.

When these two saw each other, their eyes grew red with anger, and the ant-hill snake said: "You villain! How can you torment in this way a prince who is so perfectly handsome?" And the snake in the prince's mouth said: "Villain yourself! How can you bemire those two pots full of gold?" In this fashion each laid bare the other's weakness.

Then the ant-hill snake continued: "You villain! Doesn't anybody know the simple remedy of drinking black mustard and so destroying you?" And the belly-snake retorted: "And doesn't anybody know the simple way to destroy you, by pouring in hot water?"

Now the princess, hiding behind a branch, overheard their conversation, and did just as they suggested. So she made her husband sound and well, and acquired vast wealth. When she returned to her own country, she was highly honored by father, mother, and relatives, and lived happily. For she had her deserts.

"And that is why I say:

> Be quick with mutual defense, ...

and the rest of it."

Now Foe-Crusher, having heard their advice, agreed. But Red-Eye, perceiving that the matter was decided, continued his remarks with a quiet sneer: "Alas! Alas! Our lord the king has been wickedly done to death by you gentlemen. For the proverb says:

> Where honor is withheld or paid
> Mistakenly, 'tis clear
> Three things have unrestricted course:
> Famine, and death, and fear.

And again:

> It argues utter want of sense
> To pardon obvious offense:
> The carpenter upon his head
> Took wife and him who fouled his bed."

"How was that?" asked the counselors, and Red-Eye told the story of

THE GULLIBLE CARPENTER

There was once a carpenter in a certain village. His wife was a whore, and reputed to be such. So he, desiring to test her, thought: "How can I put her to the test? For the proverb says:

> Fire chills, rogues bless, and moonlight burns
> Before a wife to virtue turns.

"Now I know from popular gossip that she is unfaithful. For the saying goes:

> All things that are not seen or heard
> In science or the Sacred Word,
> All things in interstellar space
> Are known among the populace."

After these reflections, he said to his wife: "Tomorrow morning, my dear, I am going to another village, where I shall be detained several days. Please put me up a nice lunch." And her heart quivered when she heard this; she eagerly dropped everything to make delicious dishes, almost pure butter and sugar. In fact, the old saw was justified:

> When lowering clouds
> Shut in the day,
> When streets are mired
> With sticky clay,
> When husband lingers
> Far away,
> The flirt becomes
> Supremely gay.

Now at dawn the carpenter rose and left his house. When she had made sure that he was gone, with laughing countenance she spent the dragging day in trying on all her best things. Then she called on an old lover and said: "My husband has gone to another village—the rascal! Please come to our house when the people are asleep." And he did so.

Now the carpenter spent the day in the forest, stole into his own house at twilight by a side entrance, and hid under the bed. At this juncture the other fellow arrived and got into bed. And when the carpenter saw him, his heart was stabbed by wrath, and he thought: "Shall I rise and smite him? Or shall I wait until they are asleep and kill them both without effort? Or again, shall I wait to see how she behaves, listen to what she says to him?" At this moment she softly locked the door and went to bed.

But as she did so, she stubbed her toe on the carpenter's body. And she thought: "It must be that carpenter—the rascal!—who is testing me. Well, I will give him a taste of woman's tricks."

While she was thinking, the fellow became insistent. But she clasped her hands and said: "Dear and honored sir, you must not touch me." And he said: "Well, well! For what purpose did you invite me?"

"Listen," said she. "I went this morning to Gauri's shrine to see the goddess. There all at once I heard a voice in the sky, saying: 'What am I to do, my daughter? You are devoted to me, yet in six months' time, by the decree of fate, you will be a widow.' Then I said: 'O blessèd goddess, since you are aware of the calamity, you also know the remedy. Is there any means of making my husband live a hundred years?' And the goddess replied: 'Indeed there is—a remedy depending on you alone.' Of course I said: 'If it cost my life, pray tell me, and I will do it.' Then the goddess said: 'If you go to bed with another man, and embrace him, then the untimely death that threatens your husband will pass to him. And your husband will live another hundred years.' For this purpose I invited you. Now do what you had in mind. The words of a goddess must not be falsified—so much is certain." Then his face blossomed with noiseless laughter, and he did as she said.

Now the carpenter, fool that he was, felt his body thrill with joy on hearing her words, and he issued from under the bed, saying: "Bravo, faithful wife! Bravo, delight of the family! Because my heart was troubled by the gossip of evil creatures, I pretended a trip to another village in order to test you, and lay hidden under the bed. Come now, embrace me!"

With these words he embraced her and lifted her to his shoulder, then said to the fellow: "My dear and honored sir, you have come here because my good deeds earned this happiness. Through your favor I have won a full hundred years of life. You, too, must mount my shoulder."

So he forced the fellow, much against his will, to mount his shoulder, and then went dancing about to the doors of the houses of all his relatives.

"And that is why I say:

> It argues utter want of sense
> To pardon obvious offense, ...

and the rest of it.

"We are certainly uprooted and undone. For the proverb is right in saying:

> Shrewd men unmask a foe
> Who seems a friend,
> Whose speech is kind, whose acts
> To hatred tend.

And again:

> Before fools' counsel flees
> Prosperity, though won;
> Its place and time are lost,
> Like dark before the sun."

But they all disregarded his advice, picked Live-Strong up, and started to carry him to their fortress. And on the journey Live-Strong said: "O King, I have done nothing yet, and I am in a sad state. Why are you so kind to me? Nay, I desire to enter the blazing fire. Pray put me under obligations by providing fire."

Now Red-Eye pierced his purpose and said: "Why do you wish to enter fire?" And Live-Strong replied: "For your sake I have been plunged into this calamity by Cloudy. Therefore I wish to be reborn as an owl in order to requite their enmity." Now Red-Eye, being a master of diplomacy, rejoined: "My dear sir, you are wily and plausible. Even if reborn as an owl, you would highly esteem your corvine provenience. There is a story that illustrates the point:

> Though mountain, sun, and cloud, and wind
> Were suitors at her feet,
> The mouse-maid turned a mouse again—
> Nature is hard to beat."

"How was that?" asked Live-Strong. And Red-Eye told the story of

MOUSE-MAID MADE MOUSE

The billows of the Ganges were dotted with pearly foam born of the leaping of fishes frightened at hearing the roar of the waters that broke on the rugged, rocky shore. On the bank was a hermitage crowded with holy men devoting their time to the performance of sacred rites—chanting, self-denial, self-torture, study, fasting, and sacrifice. They would take purified water only, and that in measured sips. Their bodies wasted under a diet of bulbs, roots, fruits, and moss. A loin-cloth made of bark formed their scanty raiment.

The father of the hermitage was named Yajnavalkya. After he had bathed in the sacred stream and had begun to rinse his mouth, a little female mouse dropped from a hawk's beak and fell into his hand. When he saw what she was, he laid her on a banyan leaf, repeated his bath and mouth-rinsing, and performed a ceremony of purification. Then through the magic power of his holiness, he changed her into a girl, and took her with him to his hermitage.

As his wife was childless, he said to her: "Take her, my dear wife. She has come into life as your daughter, and you must rear her carefully." So the wife reared her and spoiled her with petting. As soon as the girl reached the age of twelve, the mother saw that she was ready for marriage, and said to her husband: "My dear husband, how can you fail to see that the time is passing when your daughter should marry?"

And he replied: "You are quite right, my dear. The saying goes:

> Before a man is gratified,
> These gods must treat her as a bride—
> The fire, the moon, the choir of heaven;
> In this way, no offense is given.
>
> Holiness is the gift of fire;
> A sweet voice, of the heavenly choir;
> The moon gives purity within:
> So is a woman free from sin.
>
> Before nubility, 'tis said
> That she is white; but after, red;
> Before her womanhood is plain,
> She is, though naked, free from stain.
>
> The moon, in mystic fashion, weds
> A maiden when her beauty spreads;
> The heavenly choir, when bosoms grow;
> The fire, upon the monthly flow.

To wed a maid is therefore good
Before developed womanhood;
Nor need the loving parents wait
Beyond the early age of eight.

The early signs one kinsman slay;
The bosom takes the next away;
Friends die for passion gratified;
The father, if she ne'er be bride.

For if she bides a maiden still,
She gives herself to whom she will;
Then marry her in tender age:
So warns the heaven-begotten sage.

If she, unwed, unpurified,
Too long within the home abide,
She may no longer married be:
A miserable spinster, she.

A father then, avoiding sin,
Weds her, the appointed time within
(Where'er a husband may be had)
To good, indifferent, or bad.

Now I will try to give her to one of her own station. You know the saying:

Where wealth is very much the same,
And similar the family fame,
Marriage (or friendship) is secure;
But not between the rich and poor.

And finally:

Aim at seven things in marriage;
All the rest you may disparage:

"But

> Get money, good looks,
> And knowledge of books,
> Good family, youth,
> Position, and truth.

"So, if she is willing, I will summon the blessèd sun, and give her to him." "I see no harm in that," said his wife. "Let it be done."

The holy man therefore summoned the sun, who appeared without delay, and said: "Holy sir, why am I summoned?" The father said: "Here is a daughter of mine. Be kind enough to marry her." Then, turning to his daughter, he said: "Little girl, how do you like him, this blessèd lamp of the three worlds?" "No, father," said the girl. "He is too burning hot. I could not like him. Please summon another one, more excellent than he is."

Upon hearing this, the holy man said to the sun: "Blessèd one, is there any superior to you?" And the sun replied: "Yes, the cloud is superior even to me. When he covers me, I disappear."

So the holy man summoned the cloud next, and said to the maiden: "Little girl, I will give you to him." "No," said she. "This one is black and frigid. Give me to someone finer than he."

Then the holy man asked: "O cloud, is there anyone superior to you?" And the cloud replied: "The wind is superior even to me."

So he summoned the wind, and said: "Little girl,

I give you to him." "Father," said she, "this one is too fidgety. Please invite somebody superior even to him." So the holy man said: "O wind, is there anyone superior even to you?" "Yes," said the wind. "The mountain is superior to me."

So he summoned the mountain and said to the maiden: "Little girl, I give you to him." "Oh, father," said she. "He is rough all over, and stiff. Please give me to somebody else."

So the holy man asked: "O kingly mountain, is there anyone superior even to you?" "Yes," said the mountain. "Mice are superior to me."

Then the holy man summoned a mouse, and presented him to the girl, saying: "Little girl, do you like this mouse?"

The moment she saw him, she felt: "My own kind, my own kind," and her body thrilled and quivered, and she said: "Father dear, turn me into a mouse, and give me to him. Then I can keep house as my kind of people ought to do."

And her father, through the magic power of his holiness, turned her into a mouse, and gave her to him.

"And that is why I say:

> Though mountain, sun, and cloud, and wind, ...

and the rest of it."

But they paid no heed to Red-Eye's reasoning, and took the crow to their fortress, to the destruction of their race. And on the journey Live-Strong laughed in his heart and said:

> The secrets of diplomacy
> To him alone were plain
> Who, instant in his master's cause,
> Advised that I be slain.

"Now if they were to take his advice, not even the slightest misfortune would befall them."

When they came to the fortress gate, Foe-Crusher said: "Come, my friends! Give this Live-Strong whatever chamber he prefers—for he wishes us well."

And Live-Strong, hearing this, reflected: "I must now devise a plan for their destruction. This is not possible if I live in their midst. For they would observe motions betraying my purpose, and would keep their eyes open. Only by remaining near the gate can I accomplish my desire."

He therefore said to the owl-king: "O King, what the king has said, is eminently right. Yet I, too, am a student of diplomacy and a well-wisher. I know that even one who is loyal and pure in purpose should not dwell in the heart of a fortress. I will therefore take my place here at the fortress gate and pay daily homage, my body sanctified by the dust from your lotus feet."

To this the owl-king agreed, and his efficient caterers daily gave Live-Strong, by special command of the king, the pick of the viands. So that in a very few days he grew strong as a peacock.

But Red-Eye, seeing how Live-Strong was being pampered, was amazed, and he said to the counselors and to the king himself: "Dear me! These counselors are a pack of fools, and you, too, sir. I cannot think otherwise. Then there is the saying:

> I played the fool at first; then he
> Who had me on his tether;
> And then the king and counselor—
> We all were fools together."

"How was that?" they asked. And Red-Eye told the story of

THE BIRD WITH GOLDEN DUNG

There was once a great tree on a mountain side. On it lived a bird in whose dung gold appeared.

One day a hunter came to the spot, and directly in front of him the bird dropped its dung, which at the moment of falling turned to gold. At this the hunter was amazed.

"Well, well!" said he. "For eighty years, man and boy, I have had bird-trapping on the brain, and I never once saw gold in a bird's dung." So he set a snare in the tree. And the bird, fool that he was, forgot the danger, and perched on the customary spot. Of course, he was caught immediately.

Then the hunter freed him from the snare, put him in a cage and took him home. But he reflected: "What am I to do with this bird of ill omen? If anybody should ever discover his peculiarity, it would be reported to the king. In that case my very life would be in genuine danger. I will take the bird and report to the king myself." And he did so.

Now when the king saw the bird, his lotus eyes blossomed and he felt supremely gratified. "Come now, guardsmen," said he. "Look after this bird with anxious care. Give him everything he wants to eat and drink."

Then a counselor said: "He was hatched from an egg. Why keep him? You have no evidence save the mere incredible assurance of a hunter. Is gold ever present in bird-dung? Take this bird from the cage and set him free."

So the king, taking the counselor's advice, freed the bird, who perched on the lofty arch of the doorway long enough to drop dung which was of gold. Then he recited the stanza:

> I played the fool at first; then he
> Who had me on his tether;
> And then the king and counselor—
> We all were fools together.

After which he took his carefree flight through the atmosphere.

"And that is why I say:

> I played the fool at first, ...

and the rest of it."

But once more—for fate was hostile—they neglected Red-Eye's counsel, sound as it was, and pampered Live-Strong further with varied viands, including plenty of meat.

Then Red-Eye called together his personal adherents, and said to them privately: "The end is at hand. The welfare of our king, and his fortress, are things of the past. I have given him such counsel as an ancestral counselor should give. Let us now, for our part, seek another fortress in the mountains. For the saying goes:

> Joy comes from knowing what to dread,
> And sorrow smites the dunderhead:
> A long life through, the woods I've walked,
> But never heard a cave that talked."

"How was that?" they asked. And Red-Eye told the story of

THE CAVE THAT TALKED

There was once a lion in a part of a forest, and his name was Rough-Claw. One day he found nothing whatever to eat in his wanderings, and his throat was pinched by hunger. At sunset he came to a great mountain cave and went in, for he thought: "Surely, some animal will come into this cave during the night. I will hide and wait."

Presently the owner of the cave, a jackal named Curd-Face, came to the door and began to sing: "Cave ahoy! Cave aho-o-oy!" Then after a moment's silence, he continued in the same tone: "Hello! Don't you remember how you and I made an agreement that I was to speak to you when I came back from the world outside, and that you were to sing out to me? But you won't speak to me today. So I am going off to that other cave, which will return my greeting."

Now when he heard this, the lion thought: "I see. This cave always calls out a greeting when the fellow returns. But today, from fear of me, it doesn't say a word. This is natural enough. For

> The feet and hands refuse to act
> When peril terrifies;
> A trembling seizes every limb;
> And speech unuttered dies.

"I will myself call out a greeting, which he will follow to its source, so providing me with a dinner."

The lion thereupon called out a greeting. But the cave so magnified the roar that its echo filled the circuit of the horizon, thus terrifying other forest creatures as well, even those far distant. Meanwhile the jackal made off, repeating the stanza:

> Joy comes from knowing what to dread,
> And sorrow smites the dunderhead:
> A long life through, the woods I've walked,
> But never heard a cave that talked.

"Take this to heart and come with me." And Red-Eye, having made his decision, departed for another fortress, accompanied by a retinue of followers.

At Red-Eye's departure, Live-Strong was overjoyed. And he reflected: "Very good, indeed. Red-Eye's flight is a blessing to us. For he was farsighted, while the rest are numskulls. I can easily destroy them now. For the proverb says:

> If no farsighted counselors,
> Long-tried, secure,
> Aid him, the downfall of a king
> Is swift and sure.

And there is sound reasoning in this:

> The shrewd discover enemies
> Disguised as friends
> In senseless counselors whose speech
> To evil tends."

After these reflections, he dropped each day one fagot from the forest into his own nest, with the ultimate purpose of setting the cave afire. Nor did the owls, poor fools, perceive that he was building up his nest in order to burn them alive. Well, there is sense in the saying:

> Cause your friends no bitter woes;
> Do not fraternize with foes:
> Friends, when lost, are friends no more;
> Enemies were lost before.

Thus, pretending to build a nest, Live-Strong constructed a woodpile at the fortress gate. Then at sunrise, when the owls became blind, he hastened away and reported to Cloudy: "My lord and king, I have prepared the enemy's cave for burning. Come with your retainers, each bringing a lighted fagot from the forest, to throw on my nest at the gate of the cave. Thus all your foes will die in torments like those in Pot-baking Hell."

At this Cloudy was delighted and said: "Father, tell me your adventures. It is long since we met." "No, my son," said Live-Strong. "This is no time for talk. Some enemy spy might possibly report my journey hither. And our blind enemy, thus informed, might make his escape. Make haste, make haste. For the proverb says:

> When speed is needful, ne'er permit
> Delay, but do it pat;
> Else, wrathful gods are sure to strike
> The undertaking flat.

And again:

> Whatever deed you have in mind
> (Especially when fate is kind),
> Do quickly. If you wait a bit,
> Then time will suck the juice of it.

"Later, when your enemies are slain, and you have returned to your home, I will tell the whole story in carefree humor."

So Cloudy and his followers, taking Live-Strong's advice, seized one lighted fagot apiece in their bills, flew to the gate of the cave, and threw their fagots upon Live-Strong's nest. Then all the owls (being blind in the daytime) remembered Red-Eye's counsels as they suffered the torments of Pot-baking Hell. In this fashion Cloudy exterminated his foes and returned to his old fortress in the banyan tree.

There he mounted the lion-throne and, his heart

overflowing with joy, he questioned Live-Strong in full session of his court: "Father, how did you pass the time in the midst of the enemy? For the proverb says:

> Better a plunge in blazing fire
> (The righteous know)
> Than momentary contact with
> A wicked foe."

And Live-Strong said: "My lord and king!

> Whatever path provides escape
> When danger's face is seen,
> With clear decision follow, if
> It noble seem, or mean:
> Two arms like trunks of elephants,
> Fight-calloused, skilled to wield
> The bow of heaven, Arjun felt
> To woman's bracelets yield.
>
> The wise and strong, awaiting days
> More prosperous, must grant
> Obedience to wicked lords
> Whose speech is adamant:
> Gigantic Bhima, smoke-begrimed,
> Puffing at labor, and
> A ladle flourished in his fist,
> Was cook in Matsya land.
>
> The prudent, hopeful man should act
> As suits an evil case,
> Should steel his heart to carry through
> A holy deed, or base:
> Great Arjun with a calloused arm
> From twanging bow divine
> Effeminately danced, and saw
> His tinkling girdle shine.

The wise, alert, ambitious man,
  If he expect success,
Must wait on fortune, watch his step,
  And curb his stateliness:
Yudhishthir King, with pilgrim's staff,
  Long drew his painful breath,
Though worshiped by his brothers, great
  As War, and Wealth, and Death.

So Kunti's handsome, powerful twins,
  High birth writ on their brows,
Were menials at Virata's court,
  And lived by counting cows.

So queenly Draupadi, with youth's
  And matchless beauty's seal,
In charm most like a goddess, fell
  By turn of fortune's wheel;
And haughty maidens called her slave
  And sneered at her for sport,
What time she powdered sandalwood
  In Matsya's royal court."

"Father," said Cloudy, "this dwelling with an enemy seems to me like the sword-blade ordeal." "So it is," said Live-Strong. "But I never saw such a pack of fools anywhere. Not one was sensible except Red-Eye. He, indeed, has great capacity, an intelligence not blunted by his extensive scientific attainments. He discovered my exact purpose. But as for the other counselors, they were great fools, making a living by a mere pretense of giving good counsel, with no flair for verity. They were not even aware of this:

'Tis ruinous to trust the scamps
Who come to you from hostile camps;
Such rivals you should chase away,
For constant trouble does not pay.

The foeman serving as a scout,
Who knows (by bobbing in and out)
Your favored chair, familiar bed,
And how you drink, and what you're fed,
Your travels to another town—
Will strike his heedless foeman down.

The prudent therefore guards himself—
The source of virtue, love, and pelf—
With every effort, strain, and stress:
For death will follow heedlessness.

And there is plenty of sense in this:

Who, ill-advised, does not commit
  Grave faults of *savoir faire?*
What glutton has not much unrest
  Within himself to bear?
Whom does not fortune render proud?
  Whom does not death lay low?
To whom do not possessions bring
  Abundant harm and woe?

The steady forfeit glory, while
  The restless forfeit friends;
The bankrupt forfeits family,
  The banker, better ends;
The man of passion forfeits books,
  The fawner, friendship's flower;
The king with careless counselors
  Must forfeit kingly power.

"Yes, O King, I have experienced in person what you were kind enough to put into words: that association with the enemy is equal to the sword-blade ordeal. As the old verse puts it:

> Bear even foes upon your back;
> When fortune clogs
> Your path, endure. The great black snake
> Slew many frogs."

"How was that?" asked Cloudy. And Live-Strong told the story of

THE FROGS THAT RODE SNAKEBACK

There was once an elderly black snake in a certain spot, and his name was Slow-Poison. He considered the situation from this point of view: "How in the world can I get along without overtaxing my energies?" Then he went to a pond containing many frogs, and behaved as if very dejected.

As he waited thus, a frog came to the edge of the water and asked: "Uncle, why don't you bustle about today for food as usual?"

"My dear friend," said Slow-Poison, "I am afflicted. Why should I wish for food? For this evening, as I was bustling about for food, I saw a frog and made ready to catch him. But he saw me and, fearing death, he escaped among some Brahmans intent upon holy recitation, nor did I perceive which way he went. But in the water at the edge of the pond was the great toe of a Brahman boy, and stupidly deceived by its resemblance to a frog, I bit it, and the boy died immediately. Then the sorrowing father cursed me in these terms: 'Monster! Since you bit my harmless son, you shall for this sin become a vehicle for frogs, and shall subsist on whatever they choose to allow you.' Consequently, I have come here to serve as your vehicle."

Now the frog reported this to all the others. And every last one of them, in extreme delight, went and reported to the frog-king, whose name was Water-Foot. He in turn, accompanied by his counselors, rose hurriedly from the pond—for he thought it an extraordinary occurrence—and climbed upon Slow-Poison's hood. The others also, in order of age, climbed on his back. Yet others, finding no vacant spot, hopped along behind the snake. Now Slow-Poison, with an eye to making his living, showed them fancy turns in great variety. And Water-Foot, enjoying contact with his body, said to him:

> I'd rather ride Slow-Poison than
> The finest horse I've seen,
> Or elephant, or chariot,
> Or man-borne palanquin.

The next day, Slow-Poison was wily enough to move very slowly. So Water-Foot said: "My dear Slow-Poison, why don't you carry us nicely, as you did before?"

And Slow-Poison said: "O King, I have no carrying power today because of lack of food." "My dear fellow," said the king, "eat the plebeian frogs."

When Slow-Poison heard this, he quivered with

joy in every member and made haste to say: "Why, that is a part of the curse laid on me by the Brahman. For that reason I am greatly pleased at your command." So he ate frogs uninterruptedly, and in a very few days he grew strong. And with delight and inner laughter he said:

> The trick was good. All sorts of frogs
>   Within my power have passed.
> The only question that remains,
>   Is: How long will they last?

Water-Foot, for his part, was befooled by Slow-Poison's plausibilities, and did not notice a thing.

At this moment another black snake, a tremendous fellow, arrived on the scene. And being amazed at the sight of Slow-Poison used as a vehicle by frogs, he said: "Partner, they are our natural food, yet they use you as a vehicle. This is repellent." And Slow-Poison said:

> I know I should not carry frogs;
>   I have it well in mind;
> But I am marking time, as did
>   The Brahman butter-blind.

"How was that?" asked the snake. And Slow-Poison told the story of

THE BUTTER-BLINDED BRAHMAN

There was once a Brahman named Theodore in a certain town. His wife, being unchaste and a pursuer of other men, was forever making cakes with sugar and butter for a lover, and so cheating her husband.

Now one day her husband saw her and said: "My dear wife, what are you cooking? And where are you forever carrying cakes? Tell the truth."

But her impudence was equal to the occasion, and she lied to her husband: "There is a shrine of the blessèd goddess not far from here. There I have undertaken a fasting ceremony, and I take an offering, including the most delicious dishes." Then she took the cakes before his very eyes and started for the shrine of the goddess, imagining that after her statement, her husband would believe it was for the goddess that his wife was daily providing delicious dishes. Having reached the shrine, she went down to the river to perform the ceremonial bath.

Meanwhile her husband arrived by another road and hid behind the statue of the goddess. And his wife entered the shrine after her bath, performed the various rites—laving, anointing, giving incense, making an offering, and so on—bowed before the goddess, and prayed: "O blessèd one, how may my husband be made blind?"

Then the Brahman behind the goddess' back spoke, disguising his natural tone: "If you never stop giving him such food as butter and butter-cakes, then he will presently go blind."

Now that loose female, deceived by the plausible revelation, gave the Brahman just that kind of food every day. One day the Brahman said: "My dear, I don't see very well." And she thought: "Thank the goddess."

Then the favored lover thought: "The Brahman has gone blind. What can he do to me?" Whereupon he came daily to the house without hesitation.

But at last the Brahman caught him as he entered, seized him by the hair, and clubbed and kicked him to such effect that he died. He also cut off his wicked wife's nose, and dismissed her.

"And that is why I say:

> I know I should not carry frogs ....

and the rest of it."

Then Slow-Poison, with noiseless laughter, hummed over the verse:

> The trick was good. All sorts of frogs ....

and the rest of it. And Water-Foot, hearing this, was conscience stricken, and wondering what he meant, inquired: "My dear sir, what do you mean by reciting that repulsive verse?" "Nothing at all," said Slow-Poison, desiring to mask his purpose. And Water-Foot, befooled by his plausible manner, failed to perceive his treachery.

Why spin it out? He ate them all so completely that not even frog-seed was left.

"And that is why I say:

> Bear even foes upon your back, ...

and the rest of it. Thus, O King, just as Slow-Poison destroyed the frogs through the power of intelligence, so did I destroy all the enemy. There is much wisdom in this:

> The forest-fire leaves roots entire,
> Though trunks remain a shell;
> The flooding pool of water cool
> Uproots the roots as well."

"Very true," said Cloudy. "And besides:

> This is the greatness of the great
> Whom gems of wisdom decorate;
> Despite what hurts and hinders, too,
> They see an undertaking through."

"Very true," said Live-Strong. "And once again:

> The final penny of a debt,
> The final foeman dire,
> The final twinges of disease,
> The final spark of fire—
> Finality on these imposed
> Leaves nothing to desire.

"O King, you are truly fortunate. For your undertaking has had final success. Indeed, valor is not sufficient to end a matter. Victory is wisdom's business. As the proverb says:

> 'Tis not the sword destroys a foe,
> 'Tis wit that utterly lays low:
> Swords kill the body; wit destroys
> Fame, family, and regal joys.

"Thus, success comes with minimum effort to a man of wisdom and manliness. For

Wisdom broods o'er the inception;
Memory does not fail;
Means appear to predilection;
Counsels wise prevail;
Sparkles fruitful meditation;
Mind attains its height;
Joy achieves its consummation
In a worthy fight.

"Thus kingship belongs to the man possessing prudence, capacity for self-sacrifice, and courage. As the verse puts it:

Associate in full delight
With someone who is wise,
Self-sacrificing, brave; thereby
Win virtue as a prize;
On virtue follows money; and
On money follows fame;
Then, personal authority;
And then, the kingly name."

And Cloudy replied: "It is wonderful how immediate is the reward of knowing social ethics. By virtue of which you penetrated and exterminated Foe-Crusher with his retinue." Whereupon Live-Strong said:

"Where at last you need sharp measures,
First try gentle measures there:
Thus the lofty, lordly tree-trunk
Is not felled without a prayer.

"And yet, O my king, why say of a future matter either that it involves no effort or that it is not readily attainable? There is wisdom in the saying:

Since words with actions fail to suit,
The timidly irresolute
Who see a thousand checks and blocks
Turn into public laughingstocks.

Nor are thoughtful men heedless even in minor matters. For

The negligent who say:
'Some day, some other day—
The thing is petty, small;
Demands no thought at all,'
Are, heedless, headed straight
For that repentant state
That ever comes too late.

"But as for my master, who has overcome his foes, he may sleep tonight as soundly as ever he did. You know the saying:

In houses where no snakes are found,
One sleeps; or where the snakes are bound:
But perfect rest is hard to win
With serpents bobbing out and in.

"And again:

A noble purpose to attain
Desiderates extended pain,
Asks man's full greatness, pluck, and care,
And loved ones aiding with a prayer.
Yet if it climb to heart's desire,
What man of pride and fighting fire,

Of passion, and of self-esteem
Can bear the unaccomplished dream?
His heart indignantly is bent
(Through its achievement) on content.

"Therefore my heart is at peace. For I saw the undertaking through. Therefore may you now long enjoy this kingdom without a thorn—intent on the safeguarding of your people—your royal umbrella, throne, and glory unshaken through the long succession of son, grandson, and beyond. Remember:

A king should bring his people ease,
But he should also aim to please;
His reign is else of little note,
A neck-teat on a female goat.

And once again:

Love of virtue, scorn of vice,
Wisdom—make a kingdom's price.
Then is Glory proud as slave,
Then her plumes and pennons brave
Near the white umbrella wave.

"Nor must you, in the thought, 'My kingdom is won,' shatter your soul with the intoxication of glory. And this because the power of kings is a thing uncertain. Kingly glory is hard to climb as a bamboo-stem; hard to hold, being ready to tumble in a moment, with whatever effort it be held upright; even though conciliated, yet sure to slip away at last; fidgety as the bandar-log; unequilibrated as water on a lotus-leaf; mutable as the wind's path; untrustworthy as rogues' friendship; hard to tame as a serpent; gleaming but a moment like a strip of evening cloud; fragile by nature, like the bubbles on water; ungrateful as the substance of man's body; lost in the moment of attainment, like the treasure of a dream. And furthermore:

> Whenever kings anointed are,
> Let wit spy trouble from afar;
> Anointing-jars too often spill,
> With holy water, pending ill.

"And no man in the wide world is beyond the clutch of pending ill. As the poet sings:

> Remember Rama, wandering far;
> Remember Nala's sinking star;
> With Bali's bonds, the Vrishnis' tomb,
> And Lanka's monster-monarch's doom;
> The Pandus' forest-borne disaster,
> And knightly Arjun, dancing-master.
> Time brings us woe in countless shapes.
> What savior is there? Who escapes?

> Ah, where is Dasharath, who rose to heaven
> And dwelt its king beside?
> Ah, where King Sagar, he to whom 'twas given
> To bind the ocean's tide?
> Where arm-born Prithu? Where is Manu gone,
> Sun-child (yet suns still rise)?
> Imperious Time awakened them at dawn,
> At evening closed their eyes.

And again:

> Where is Mandhatar, conqueror supreme?
> Where Satyavrat, the king?
> God-ruling Nahush? Keshav, e'er the gleam
> Of science following?

They and their lordly elephants, I ween,
  Their cars, their heavenly throne,
By lofty Time conferred, in Time were seen,
  And lost through Time alone.

And yet again:

The king, his counselors,
  His maidens gay,
His golden groves, Fate stings.
  They sink away.

"Thus, having won kingly glory, quivering like the ear of a rogue elephant, take delight in her, but trust in wisdom only."

Here ends Book III, called "Crows and Owls," which treats of peace, war, and the other four expedients. The first verse runs:

Reconciled although he be,
Never trust an enemy.
For the cave of owls was burned,
When the crows with fire returned.

BOOK IV

LOSS OF GAINS

BOOK IV

LOSS OF GAINS

Here, then, begins Book IV, called "Loss of Gains." The first verse runs:

Blind folly always has to pay
For giving property away
Because of blandishments and guile—
The monkey tricked the crocodile.

"How was that?" asked the princes. And Vishnu-sharman told the story of

THE MONKEY AND THE CROCODILE

On the shore of the sea was a great rose-apple tree that was never without fruit. In it lived a monkey named Red-Face.

Now one day a crocodile named Ugly-Mug crawled out of the ocean under the tree and burrowed in the soft sand. Then Red-Face said: "You are my guest, sir. Pray eat these rose-apples which I throw you. You will find them like nectar. You know the proverb:

A fool or scholar let him be,
Pleasant or hideous to see,
A guest, when offerings are given,
Is useful as a bridge to heaven.

Ask not his home or education,
His family or reputation,

But offer thanks and sacrifice:
For so prescribes the lawbook wise.

And again:

By honoring the guests who come
Wayworn from some far-distant home
To share the sacrifice, you go
The noblest way that mortals know.

And once again:

If guests unhonored leave your door,
And sadly sighing come no more,
Your fathers and the gods above
Turn from you and forget their love."

Thus he spoke and offered rose-apples. And the crocodile ate them and enjoyed a long and pleasant conversation with the monkey before returning to his home. So the monkey and the crocodile rested each day in the shade of the rose-apple tree. They spent the time in cheerful conversation on various subjects, and were happy.

Now the crocodile went home and gave his wife the rose-apples which he had not eaten. And one day she asked him: "My dear husband, where do you get such fruits? They are like nectar."

"My dear," he said, "I have an awfully good friend, a monkey named Red-Face. He gives me these fruits in the most courteous manner."

Then she said: "If anyone eats such nectar fruit every day, his heart must be turned to nectar. So, if you value your wife, give me his heart, and I will eat it. Then I shall never grow old or sick, but will be a delightful companion for you."

But he objected: "In the first place, my dear, he is our adopted brother. Secondly, he gives us fruit. I cannot kill him. Please do not insist. Besides, there is a proverb:

> To give us birth, we need a mother;
> For second birth we need another:
> And friendship's brothers seem by far
> More dear than natural brothers are."

But she said: "You have never refused me before. So I am sure it is a she-monkey. You love her and spend the whole day with her. That is why you will not give me what I want. And when you meet me at night, your sighs are hot as a flame of fire. And when you hold me and kiss me, you do not hug me tight. I know some other woman has stolen into your heart."

Then the crocodile was quite dejected, and said to his wife:

> When I am at your feet
> And at your service, sweet,
> Why do you look at me
> With peevish jealousy?

But her face swam in tears when she heard him, and she said:

> "You love her, you deceiver;
> Your wishes never leave her;

Her pretty shamming steals upon your heart.
My rivalry is vain, sir;
And so I pray abstain, sir,
From service that is only tricky art.

"Besides, if you do not love her, why not kill her when I ask you? And if it is really a he-monkey, why should you love him? Enough! Unless I eat his heart, I shall starve myself to death in your house."

Now when he saw how determined she was, he was distracted with anxiety, and said: "Ah, the proverb is right:

Remember that a single grab
Suffices for a fish or crab,
For fool or woman; and 'tis so
For sot, cement, or indigo.

"Oh, what shall I do? How can I kill him?" With these thoughts in mind, he visited the monkey.

Now the monkey had missed his friend, and when he saw him afflicted, he said: "My friend, why have you not been here this long time? Why don't you speak cheerfully, and repeat something witty?"

The crocodile replied: "My friend and brother, my wife scolded me today. She said: 'You ungrateful wretch! Do not show me your face. You are living daily at a friend's expense, and make him no return. You do not even show him the door of your house. You cannot possibly make amends for this. There is a saying:

The Brahman-murderer or thief,
Drunkard or liar, finds relief;
While for ingratitude alone
No expiation will atone.

"'I regard this monkey as my brother-in-law. So bring him home, and we will make some return for his kindness. If you refuse, I will see you later in heaven.' Now I could not come to you until she had finished her scolding. And this long time passed while I was quarreling with her about you. So please come home with me. Your brother's wife has set up an awning. She has fixed her clothes and gems and rubies and all that, to pay you a fitting welcome. She has hung holiday garlands on the doorposts. And she is waiting impatiently."

"My friend and brother," said the monkey, "your lady is very kind. It is quite according to the proverb:

Six things are done by friends:
  To take, and give again;
To listen, and to talk;
  To dine, to entertain.

"But we monkeys live in trees, and your home is in the water. How can I go there? Rather bring your lady here, brother, that I may bow down and receive her blessing."

The crocodile said: "My friend, our home is on a lovely sand-bank under the water. So climb on my back and travel comfortably with nothing to fear."

When the monkey heard this, he was delighted and said: "If that is possible, my friend, then hasten. Why delay? Here I am on your back."

But as he sat there and saw the crocodile swimming in the bottomless ocean, the monkey was terribly frightened and said: "Go slow, brother. My whole body is drenched by the great waves."

And the crocodile thought when he heard this: "If he fell from my back, he could not move an inch, the water is so deep. He is in my power. So I will tell him my purpose, and then he can pray to his favorite god."

And he said: "Sir, I have deceived you and brought you to your death, because my wife bade me do it. So pray to your favorite god."

"Brother," said the monkey, "what harm have I done her or you? Why have you planned to kill me?"

"Well," replied the crocodile, "those nectar fruits tasted so sweet that she began to long to eat your heart. That is why I have done this."

Then the quick-witted monkey said: "If that is the case, sir, why didn't you tell me on shore? For then I might have brought with me another heart, very sweet indeed, which I keep in a hole in the rose-apple tree. As it is, I am forlorn in this heart, at being taken to her in vain, without my sweet heart."

When he heard this, the crocodile was delighted and said: "If you feel so, my friend, give me that other heart. And my cross wife will eat it and give up starving herself. Now I will take you back to the rose-apple tree."

So he turned back and swam toward the rose-apple tree, while the monkey murmured a hundred prayers to every kind of a god. And when at last he came to shore, he hopped and jumped farther and farther, climbed up the rose-apple tree, and thought: "Hurrah! My life is saved. Surely, the saying is a good one:

> We dare not trust a rogue; nor must
> We trust in those deserving trust:
> For danger follows, and we fall
> Destroyed and ruined, roots and all.

So today is my rebirthday."

The crocodile said: "My friend and brother, give me the heart, so that my wife may eat it and give up starving herself."

Then the monkey laughed, and scolded him, saying: "You fool! You traitor! How can anyone have two hearts? Go home, and never come back under the rose-apple tree. You know the proverb:

> Whoever trusts a faithless friend
> And twice in him believes,
> Lays hold on death as certainly
> As when a mule conceives."

Now the crocodile was embarrassed when he heard this, and he thought: "Oh, why was I such a fool as to tell him my plan? If I can possibly win his confidence again, I will do it." So he said: "My friend, she has no need of a heart. What I said was just a joke to test your sentiments. Please come to our house as a guest. Your brother's wife is most eager for you."

The monkey said: "Rascal! Go away this moment. I will not come. For

> The hungry man at nothing sticks;
> The poor man has his heartless tricks.
> Tell Handsome, miss, that Theodore
> Will see him in the well no more."

"How was that?" asked the crocodile. And the monkey told the story of

HANDSOME AND THEODORE

There was once a frog-king in a well, and his name was Theodore. One day when tormented by his relatives, he climbed from bucket to bucket up the water-wheel, and finally emerged. Then he thought: "How can I pay those relatives back? For the proverb says:

> While one brings comfort in distress,
> Another jeers at pain;
> By paying both as they deserve,
> A man is born again."

With this in mind, he saw a black snake named Handsome crawling out of his hole. And on seeing him, he thought once more: "I will invite that black snake into the well, and clean out all my relatives. For the saying goes:

A sliver draws a sliver out;
  Just so the wise employ
Grim foes to slaughter foes; and thus
  Turn danger into joy."

Having come to this conclusion, he went to the mouth of the hole and called: "Come out! Come out, Handsome! Come out!" But when the snake heard this, he thought: "Whoever he may be that is calling me, he does not belong to my race. That is no snake's voice. And I have no alliance with anyone else in the living world. So I will just stay here until I am sure who he may be. For the proverb says:

Until you have full information
Of prowess, character, and station,
To no man let your trust be given—
Such is the current saw in heaven.

Perhaps it is some conjurer or druggist who is calling me in order to put me in a cage. Or a man who bears a grudge and summons me in the interest of his friend."

So he said: "Who are you?" The other said: "I am a frog-king named Theodore, and I have come to make friends with you."

When the snake heard this, he said: "Why, it is incredible. Does grass make friends with fire? You know the proverb:

You do not, even in a dream,
  Approach the kind of foe
Who kills at sight. What can you mean?
  Why should you babble so?"

But Theodore said: "You are quite right, sir. You are my born enemy. And yet I come to you because I have been insulted. You know well:

> When all your property is gone
> And life itself at stake—
> To save that life and property
> You grovel to a snake."

The snake said: "Well, who insulted you?" And the frog answered: "My relatives." "But where is your home?" asked the snake. "In a pond? or a well? or a cistern? or a tank?" "My home is in a well," said the frog. "But," said the snake, "I can't get in. And if I could, there is no place for me to lie while killing your relatives. Begone. Besides, you know:

> Eat only what will swallow
> And gratify the hollow
> Within with good digestion—
> Put not your health in question."

But Theodore replied: "No, sir. Come with me. I will show you an easy way into the well. And inside there is a very attractive hole at water-level. There you can lie, and you will find it child's play to finish my relatives."

Then the snake reflected: "Yes, I am old. Now and then, with great effort, I catch one mouse. And often I don't. Yes, yes. The proverb is right:

> When strength is ebbing, dying,
> When friends are gone, and wife,

The prudent should be trying
A carpet-slippery life."

After these reflections, he said: "Well, Theodore, if you really mean it, lead the way. We will go together." "Friend Handsome," said Theodore, "I will take you there by an easy way and show you the resting-place. But you must spare my family. You must not eat any except those I point out."

"My dear fellow," said the snake, "you and I are now friends. Have no fear. I will do nothing but what you wish."

Then he came out of his hole, hugged the frog, and started off with him. So they came to the edge of the well, and the snake went in with the frog by way of the buckets on the water-wheel. Then Theodore settled the black snake in the hole and showed him the relatives. And he ate them all one after another. And lacking relatives, he made up to a few of the friends, and ate them, too, with much circumspection.

Then the snake said: "My dear fellow, I have disposed of your enemies. Please give me something to eat, for you brought me here."

"But, my dear fellow," said Theodore, "you have done what a friend should do. Pray return by way of the buckets."

"Friend Theodore," said Handsome, "you make a serious mistake. How can I go home? My hole was my fortress, and it is surely occupied by strangers.

Here I stay, and you must give me a frog at a time, even from your own family. If not, I will eat every one."

At this, Theodore was disturbed in spirit, and reflected: "Oh, what was I about when I brought him here? And if I deny him now, he will eat every one. Yes, the proverb is right:

> Whoever fraternizes with
> Too vigorous a foe,
> Is eating poison, and will soon
> Perceive it to be so.

"So I will give him one a day, even if it must be a friend. For they say:

> Calm with a prudent, petty bribe
> A foe who may desire
> To seize your all. So calms the sea
> Its fierce subaqueous fire.

And again:

> 'Tis wise, when all is threatened,
> To give a half, and guard
> The other half to win one's ends;
> For total loss is hard.

And yet again:

> No prudent soul would lose
> Much good for little use;
> Prudence implies much gain
> Acquired with little pain."

So he made up his mind, and assigned a frog a day. And the snake ate this one and another, too, behind the frog-king's back. Ah, it is too true:

As muddied garments dirty
  All that you sit upon,
So, when one virtue tumbles,
  The rest are quickly gone.

Now one day, while eating frogs, he ate a frog named Theodosius, the son of Theodore. And Theodore, seeing him do it, wailed with piercing shrillness. But his wife said:

"Why so shrill? You were still
While you worked your cruel will.
Hope has fled with your dead;
Who will save your hapless head?

So think out a plan of escape this very day, or else a scheme to kill him."

Now in course of time the frogs were finished one and all; only Theodore remained. And then Handsome said: "My dear Theodore, I am hungry and all the frogs are finished. Please give me something to eat, for you brought me here."

Theodore said: "My friend, feel no anxiety on that head while I am alive. If you permit me to leave, I will persuade the frogs in other wells, and bring them all here."

The snake said: "Well, I can't eat you, for you are like a brother. Now if you do as you say, you will be like a father."

So the frog planned his escape, and left the well, while Handsome waited there, impatient for his return. But after a long time Handsome said to a lizard that lived in another hole in the same well: "My dear madam, do me a small favor, since Theodore is an old friend of yours. Please go and find him in some pool or other, and take him a message from me. Tell him to return quickly, alone if need be, if no other frogs will come. I cannot live here without him. And tell him that if I hurt him, he may have all the merit I have acquired in a lifetime."

So the lizard did as she was bid, quickly hunted Theodore out, and said: "My dear sir, your friend Handsome is waiting, waiting for your return. Please hurry back. And furthermore, in case of his doing you any harm, he pledges you the merit acquired in a lifetime. So drop all anxious thoughts, and come home." But Theodore said:

> The hungry man at nothing sticks;
> The poor man has his heartless tricks.
> Tell Handsome, miss, that Theodore
> Will see him in the well no more.

And so he sent her back.

"So then, you rascally water-beast! Like Theodore, I will never, never enter your house."

When he heard this, the crocodile said: "My good friend, you are quite wrong. I beg of you to come to my house, and so wipe out my sin of ingratitude. Otherwise, I shall starve myself to death on your doorstep."

"You fool!" said the monkey, "shall I go there like Flop-Ear, in full sight of the danger, and let myself be killed?"

"But who was Flop-Ear?" asked the crocodile. "And how did he perish in full sight of the danger? Please tell me." So the monkey told the story of

FLOP-EAR AND DUSTY

There was once a lion named Fierce-Mane, who lived in a part of a forest. And for servant he had a jackal, a faithful drudge named Dusty.

Now one day the lion fought with an elephant, and took such cruel wounds on his body that he could not stir a foot. And since the master could not stir, Dusty grew feeble, for his throat was pinched by hunger. Then he said to the lion: "O King, I am tortured with hunger until I cannot drag one foot after another. So how can I serve you?" "My good Dusty," said the lion, "hunt out some animal that I can kill even in my present state."

So the jackal went hunting, and dragging himself to a nearby village, he saw beside a tank a donkey named Flop-Ear who was choking over the thin and prickly grass. And he drew near and said: "Uncle, my respects to you. It is long since we met. How have you grown so feeble?"

And Flop-Ear answered: "What am I to do, nephew? The laundryman is merciless, and tortures me with dreadful burdens. And he never gives me a handful of fodder. I eat nothing but this prickly grass flavored with dust, and I do not thrive."

"Well, uncle," said the jackal, "I know a lovely spot by a river, all covered with emerald grass. Come there and live with me. I promise you the pleasure of witty conversation."

"Very well said, nephew," answered Flop-Ear, "but village beasts are likely to be killed by forest animals. So what good is your charming spot to me?"

"No, no," said the jackal. "My paws form a cage to protect the spot, and no stranger has entrance there. Besides, there are three unmarried she-donkeys who were tormented just like you by laundrymen. They have now grown plump; they are young and frisky; they said to me: 'Uncle dear, go to some village and bring us a proper husband.' That is why I came to fetch you."

Now when he heard the jackal's words, Flop-Ear felt his limbs quiver with love, and he said: "In that case, my dear sir, lead the way. We will hurry there." For the poet hits the mark when he says:

> You are our only nectar; you,
> O woman, are our poison, too.
> For union with you is the breath
> Of life; and absence from you, death.

So the poor creature went with the jackal into the lion's presence. But the lion was dreadfully foolish. When he saw the donkey actually within range of his spring, he was so overjoyed that he jumped over him and landed on the other side. And the donkey wondered: "What, oh, what can this be?" For to him it seemed like the fall of a thunderbolt. Yet somehow—for fate was kind to him—he escaped quite unhurt. But when he looked back, he saw the egregious creature, cruel, horrifying, with bloodshot eyes, and he beat a hasty, terrified retreat to his own city.

Then the jackal said to the lion: "Well, what does this mean? I saw your heroic exhibition." And the lion was dumfounded, and he said: "But I could not prepare for a spring. So what was I to do? Could an elephant, even, escape, if he came within range of my spring?"

The jackal said: "Have your spring prepared next time. For I am going to bring him to you again." "My dear fellow," said the lion, "he saw me face to face and escaped. How can he be enticed here again? Bring me some other animal."

But the jackal said: "Why should you worry about that? I am wide awake on that point." So the jackal followed the donkey's tracks, and found him grazing in the old place.

Now when he saw the jackal, the donkey said: "Well, nephew, it was a charming spot you took me to. I was lucky to escape with my life. Tell me, what was that horrible creature? He was a thunderbolt, but he missed me."

Then the jackal laughed and said: "Uncle, that

was a she-donkey. She was unspeakably lovesick, and seeing you, she rose up passionately to embrace you. But you were shy, and ran away. And as you disappeared, she stretched out a hand to detain you. That is the whole story. So come back. She has resolved to starve to death for your sake, and she says: 'If Flop-Ear does not marry me, I will plunge into fire or water, or will eat poison. Anyhow, I cannot bear to be separated from him.' So have mercy, and return. If not, you will be a woman-murderer, and the god of love will be angry. For you know:

> Woman is Love's victorious seal,
> Confers all good. If for their weal
> (Supposed) in heaven or for salvation
> Dull men hold her in detestation,
> Love strikes them for their sins forlorn,
> And some turn naked monks, some shorn;
> Some have red garments; others wear
> Skull-necklaces, or frowsy hair."

So the donkey, persuaded by this reasoning, started off with him once more. Indeed, the proverb is right:

> Men, knowing better, oft commit
> A shabby deed—so strong is fate.
> But where are they who relish it,
> When once it is irrevocate?

Thereupon the donkey, deceived by a hundred arguments of the rascal, came again into the presence, and was straightway killed by the lion, who had prepared his spring beforehand. And then the lion set the jackal on guard, and went himself to the river to bathe. Whereupon the greedy jackal ate the donkey's ears and heart. Now when the lion returned after bathing and repeating the proper prayers, he found the donkey minus ears and heart, and his soul was suffused with wrath, and he said to the jackal: "You scoundrel! What is this unseemly deed? You have eaten ears and heart, and my share is your leavings."

"O King," said the jackal respectfully, "do not speak so. This creature was born without ears and heart. Otherwise, how could he have come here, have seen you with his own eyes, have run in terror, and then come back? Why, it goes into poetry:

> He came, he saw, he fled
> From your appearance dread,
> Returned, forgot his fears—
> The fool lacked heart and ears."

So the lion was convinced by the jackal's argument, divided with him, and ate his own share without suspicion.

"And that is why I say that I shall not be like the donkey Flop-Ear. You see, you foolish fellow, you played a trick, but spoiled it by telling the truth, just like Fight-Firm. The saying is correct:

> The heedless trickster who forgets
> His own advantage, and who lets
> The truth slip out, like Fight-Firm, he
> Is sure to lose his victory."

"How was that?" asked the crocodile. And the monkey told the story of

THE POTTER MILITANT

There was once a potter in a certain place. One day he carelessly ran with all his might into the jagged edge of a broken pot, and tumbled. And though the jagged edge tore his forehead, he struggled to his feet, blood streaming over his body. Now as the wound was unskilfully treated, the scar cicatrized horribly.

After some time the land was afflicted with famine, and he felt the pinch of hunger. So he joined certain life-guards, went to another country, and became a life-guard.

Now the king noticed on his brow the horrible scar from the potsherd, and he thought: "Surely, this man is a great hero. He took a wound in front, on his brow." So he bestowed honors and gifts and the like, regarding him more graciously than all others. Even the princes, observing the exceptional favor shown him, cherished an extreme jealousy, yet they feared the king and said not a word.

Now one day there was a review of picked troops. While the elephants were being accoutered and the horses caparisoned and the men inspected, the king took occasion to say to the potter: "O Prince, what is your name? And what your family? In what battle was this wound printed on your brow?"

"Your Majesty," he replied, "by birth I am a potter, and my name is Fight-Firm. This is not a sword-wound. But when I was unsteady with liquor, I was hurrying through a courtyard littered with broken pots, and tumbled over one. Later the scar from the potsherd became a horrible cicatrice."

Then the king reflected: "Good heavens! I was taken in by this potter who seemed a prince. Let a cuffing be administered."

When this had been done, the potter said: "Your Majesty, do not treat me thus, but witness my adroitness in battle." "No, my friend," said the king, "you may be a treasure-house of all the virtues. Yet you must begone. You may have heard the stanza:

Handsome you are, and valorous;
You have a scholar's brain:
But in your family, my boy,
No elephants are slain."

"How was that?" asked the potter. And the king told the story of

THE JACKAL WHO KILLED NO ELEPHANTS

In a part of a forest lived a lion and his wife. One day the lioness gave birth to twins. And the lion killed deer and things every day, and gave them to the lioness.

But one day as he ranged the forest, he had met nothing when the blessèd sun sank to his setting. As he trotted home, he found a baby jackal on the trail. And he pitied it because it was a baby. So he held it between his teeth and carefully carried it home, giving it to the lioness alive.

Then the lioness said: "Have you brought any food, sweetheart?" And he answered: 'My dear, I didn't find a thing today except this jackal cub. Even him I did not kill, for I thought: 'He is a creature much like us, and a baby at that.' You know the proverb:

> Never strike a hermit mild,
> Woman, clergyman, or child:
> Give your life, if needs you must—
> Do not falsify their trust.

"Now suppose you eat him, and feel better. In the morning I will bring something else."

"Sweetheart," said she, "you did not kill him because you thought: 'He is a baby.' So how can I destroy him for my belly's sake? You know the verse of Scripture:

> No man may plead the death-god's might
> For doing wrong, or shirking right.

So he shall be my third son."

After this reply, she gave him her own milk and made him very fat. So the three cubs spent their babyhood in the same business and amusements, not recognizing any difference in parentage.

Now one day a wild elephant came wandering into that forest. The two lion-cubs, when they saw him, wrathfully started for him, eager to kill. But the jackal-cub said: "Brothers, that is an elephant, an enemy of your race. Don't go near him." With this he ran home. And the other two, seeing their elder brother routed, felt their pluck ooze away. The well-known proverb is right:

> One bold and plucky fighter
> Will give an army pluck:
> One broken, routed blighter
> Diffuses evil luck.

And, indeed,

> This is the very reason why
> Kings look for sturdy fighters,
> Heroic, dauntless, stone-wall men,
> And shun the cowardly blighters.

Later the twin brothers went home, and humorously told their parents how their elder brother had behaved. "Why, you know," said they, "the minute he saw him, he couldn't get far enough quick enough."

When the jackal heard this, wrath entered his spirit. His blossom-lip quivered, his eyes grew red, and a frown made two deep wrinkles on his brow. And he spoke harshly, scolding the twins.

Then the lioness took him aside and admonished him: "You must never, never speak so, my dear. They are your brothers." But her patient pleading filled him with greater anger, and he burst upon her, too: "Do you think me their inferior in courage or beauty or science or application or skill? What right have they to ridicule me? I am certainly going to kill them."

When she heard this outburst, the lioness laughed quietly— for she did not wish him to die—and said:

"Handsome you are, and valorous;
You have a scholar's brain:
But in your family, my boy,
No elephants are slain.

Now listen carefully, my dear. Your mother was a jackal, and I fattened you with my own milk because I pitied you. Now while my twins are babies and do not know you for a jackal, hurry away and join your own people. If not, they will fight you, and you will tread the path of death." When the jackal heard this, he was terror stricken, and softly stole away to join his own people.

"Just so you, too, had best decamp before these veterans learn that you are a potter. If not, you will be hooted and killed." And the potter, hearing this, absconded.

"And that is why I say:

The heedless trickster who forgets, ...

and the rest of it. Oh, fool, fool! To undertake such a thing for your wife! Never trust a woman. You must have heard the pat little anecdote:

I left my family for her;
I gave her half my life;
She leaves me now without a thought;
What man can trust his wife?"

"How was that?" asked the crocodile, and the monkey told the story of

THE UNGRATEFUL WIFE

There was once a Brahman in a certain city who loved his wife more than his life. But she squabbled with his family every day, and never rested. Since he could not endure the squabbling, yet was devoted to his wife, he left his family and started for another country far away.

In the middle of a great forest, the Brahman's wife said: "My dear, I am tortured by thirst. Please look about for water." And he did as she requested, but when he returned with water, he found her dead.

Since he loved her dearly, he fell into despair, but as he lamented, he heard a voice from heaven, saying: "Brahman, if you will give half your own life, your wife may live." So he performed a ceremony of purification, then gave a half of his own life by repeating the three magic words: "I give life." The moment he spoke, his wife stood up, alive.

So together they drank the water, ate forest-fruits, and started on. Finally, they entered a flower-garden near a city, where the Brahman said to his wife: "Belovèd, please stay here until I return with food." And he left her.

Now in the garden was a cripple, turning a water-wheel and singing with a heavenly voice. When she heard the song, she was smitten with love, went to him, and said: "Dear friend, if you do not give me your love, you will be the murderer of a Brahman woman." "But what can you do with an invalid like me?" asked the cripple. "Be still," said she, "you must make me your bride." And hearing her words, he did so. Thereupon she said: "From this moment I give you my person for life. You must accompany us with this understanding." "Very well," said he.

Then when the Brahman returned with food and began to eat with her, she said: "This cripple is hungry. Please give him a bite, too." When this was done, the lady said: "Brahman, when you go alone to another village, I have no one to talk to. Suppose we take this cripple with us." But he replied: "I cannot even carry myself, to say nothing of this cripple." "I will carry him," said she, "if he will get into a basket." And the Brahman agreed, his judgment being bewildered by her artful argument.

One day thereafter, as they rested near a well, the wife, aided by the cripple, gave the Brahman a push and plunged him in. And she took the cripple and went to a city. There the policemen, making their rounds to attend to taxes, robberies, and protection, saw the basket on her head, snatched it from her, and took it to the king. And as soon as the king had it opened, he saw the cripple.

Presently the Brahman's wife arrived, weeping and wailing, for she had followed on the heels of the policemen. And when the king asked, "What does this mean?" she said: "This is my invalid husband who was tormented by countless relatives, until, distracted by love, I put him on my head and brought him before you." And the king said: "You are my sister. Receive two villages, enjoy their delights with your husband, and make yourself comfortable."

At this point the Brahman arrived in the same city, for a certain holy man, as it happened, had drawn him from the well, and he had wandered on. When the wicked wife saw him, she denounced him to the king. "O King," she said, "there comes my husband's enemy."

And the king sentenced him to death.

But the Brahman said: "Your Majesty, this woman has something which she received from me. If you love justice, make her give it back." "My good woman," said the king, "restore whatever you may have that belongs to him." And she replied: "Your Majesty, I have nothing."

Then the Brahman said: "With three magic words I gave you half my life. Give me that." And from fear of the king she murmured, just as he had done, the three words "I give life," and fell dead.

Then the king was amazed and said: "What does this mean?" And the Brahman related to him all that had gone before.

"And that is why I say:

> I left my family for her, ...

and the rest of it."

Then the monkey continued: "There is another little anecdote that is very pat:

> What will not man for woman do,
> When heads are shorn—at odd times, too?
> What will not man for woman say,
> When those who are not horses, neigh?"

"How was that?" asked the crocodile. And the monkey told the story of

KING JOY AND SECRETARY SPLENDOR

There was once a king named Joy, lord of the sea-girdled earth, whose power and manliness were famed afar, whose footstool was reticulated with interlacing beams of light from the diadems of uncounted hosts of kneeling princes, whose glory was unspotted as the autumn moonbeams. He had a secretary named Splendor, who had absorbed the total truth of all the scientific textbooks, but whose wife pouted in a lovers' quarrel.

"Belovèd," said her husband, "tell me the means of appeasing you. I will adopt it without fail." And it cost her a struggle to say: "If you will shave your head and fall at my feet, then I will think of relenting." When he did so, she did so.

Now Joy's wife became angry in just the same way, and would not be appeased though he begged her pardon. Then he said: "Belovèd, I cannot live a moment without you. I will fall at your feet and beg your pardon." She said: "If you hold a bit in your mouth and let me climb on your back and drive you, and if, when driven, you neigh like a horse, then I will relent." And this was done.

Next morning Splendor came before the king as he sat in council. And the king asked, when he saw him: "Good Splendor, why is your head shaved at this odd time?" And Splendor answered:

What will not man for woman do,
When heads are shorn—at odd times, too?
What will not man for woman say,
When those who are not horses, neigh?

"You simpleton! You, too, are henpecked just like Joy and Splendor. You tried to find a means of killing me, because your wife asked it. But you were betrayed by your own speech. Yes, the proverb is right:

The parrots and the grackle birds
Are caged because they utter words:
The stupid herons go scot-free—
For silence is a master-key.

And again:

However skilful in disguise,
However frightful to the eyes,
Although in tiger-skin arrayed,
The ass was killed—because he brayed."

"How was that?" asked the crocodile. And the monkey told the story of

THE ASS IN THE TIGER-SKIN

There was once a laundryman named Clean-Cloth in a certain town. He had a single donkey who had grown very feeble from lack of fodder.

As the laundryman wandered in the forest, he saw a dead tiger, and he thought: "Ah, this is lucky. I will put this tiger-skin on the donkey and let him loose in the barley fields at night. For the farmers will think him a tiger and will not drive him out."

When this was done, the donkey ate barley to his heart's content. And at dawn the laundryman took him back to the barn. So as time passed, he grew plump. He could hardly squeeze into the stall.

But one day the donkey heard the bray of a she-donkey in the distance. At the mere sound he himself began to bray. Then the farmers perceived that he was a donkey in disguise, and killed him with blows from clubs and stones and arrows.

"And that is why I say:

> However skilful in disguise, ...

and the rest of it."

Now while the monkey was telling these stories to the crocodile, another water-beast came up and said: "Friend crocodile, your wife has starved herself to death."

When the crocodile heard this, he was bewildered in spirit, and lamented: "Oh, what has come upon me, upon hapless me? For the proverb says:

> Where a mother does not dwell
> And a wife who flatters well,
> Better leave the house, and roam
> Forests not so wild as home.

Oh, my friend! Forgive my sins toward you. For I have lost her, and I plan to burn myself alive."

When the monkey heard this, he laughed and said: "Come now! I knew from the very beginning that you were henpecked and in leading-strings. And this proves it. You dunderhead! You despair when you ought to be happy. When a wife like that dies, you ought to give a party. For the proverb says:

A wife forever nagging
  And falling in a rage,
Is not a wife, say sages,
  But premature old age.

Therefore with patient effort
  Avoid the very name
Of every earthly woman,
  If comfort be your aim.

For what she feels, she does not say;
She speaks and looks a different way;
Far from her looks her actions veer:
Oh, woman, woman! You are queer.

But enough!

One fact suffices. Cite no more!
They kill the children that they bore.

And yet:

Though girls are tasteless, hard, and selfish,
Boys think them sweet and soft and elfish."

"True enough," said the crocodile, "but what am I to do? Two calamities have befallen me. First, my home is ruined. And second, I have quarreled with my friend. Yet so it goes with the unfortunate. You know the stanza:

> The cleverness that you have shown,
> You naked thing! is twice my own;
> Your husband and your lover fair
> Are lost. But why this vacant stare?"

"How was that?" asked the monkey. And the crocodile told the story of

THE FARMER'S WIFE

There was once a farmer who lived with his wife in a certain place. And because the husband was old, the wife was forever thinking of lovers, and could not possibly be contented at home. Her one idea was strange men.

Now a rogue who lived by pilfering, noticed her and said: "You lovely creature, my wife is dead, and I am smitten with love at the sight of you. Pray enrich me with love's perfect treasure."

And she said: "You beautiful man, if you feel that way, my husband has a great deal of money, and he is so old that he cannot stir. I will bring it, so that I may go somewhere with you and enjoy the delights of love."

"That is satisfactory to me," he replied. "Suppose you hasten to this spot at dawn, so that we may go together to some fascinating city where life may bear for me its perfect fruit." "Very well," she agreed, and went home with laughing countenance.

Then at night, while her husband slept, she took all the money, and reached the rendezvous at dawn. The rogue, for his part, put her in front, started south, and traveled two leagues, gaily enjoying the delights of conversation with her. But when he saw a river ahead, he reflected: "What am I to do with this middle-aged female? Besides, someone might perhaps pursue her. I will just take her money and be off."

So he said to her: "My dear, this is a great river, hard to cross. I will just take the money and put it safe on the far bank, then return to carry you alone on my back, and so transport you in comfort." "Do so, my belovèd," said she.

So he took the money to the last penny, and then he said: "Dearest, hand me your dress and your wrap, too, so that you may travel through the water unembarrassed." And when she did so, the rogue took the money and the two garments and went to the place he had in mind.

Then the farmer's wife sat down woebegone on the river-bank, digging her two hands into her throat. At that moment a she-jackal came to the spot, carrying a piece of meat. As she came up and peered about, a great fish leaped from the water and was stranded on the bank. On spying him, she dropped the meat and darted at the fish. Whereupon a vulture swooped from the sky and flew off with the meat. And the fish, perceiving the jackal, struggled into the river.

So the she-jackal had her pains for nothing, and as she gazed after the vulture, the naked woman smiled and said:

"You poor she-jackal!

> The vulture has your meat;
> The water holds your fish:
> Of fish and flesh forlorn,
> What further do you wish?"

And the she-jackal, perceiving that the woman was equally forlorn, having lost her husband's money and her lover, said with a sneer:

"You naked thing!

> Your cleverness is twice
> As great as mine, 'twould seem;
> Lover and husband lost,
> You sit beside the stream."

While the crocodile was telling this story, a second water-beast arrived and reported: "Alas! Your house has been occupied by another crocodile—a big fellow." And the crocodile became despondent on hearing this, anxiously considering how to drive him from the house. "Alas, my friends!" said he. "See how unlucky I am. For you must know,

> A stranger occupies my house;
> My friend is sadly vexed;
> On top of that, my wife is dead.
> Oh, what will happen next?

"How true it is that misfortunes never come singly! Well, shall I fight him? Or shall I address him with soft conciliation, and get him out of the house? Or shall I try intrigue? Or bribery? Ah, here is my monkey friend. I will ask him. For the proverb says:

> Ask aid of kindly teachers, man,
> The kind you ought to ask.
> Their counsel leads to sure success,
> Whatever be your task."

After these reflections, he put the question to the monkey, who had climbed back into the rose-apple tree. "Oh, my friend," said he, "see how unlucky I am. For now my very house is seized and held by a powerful crocodile. Therefore I put it to you. Tell me, what am I to do? Is this the place for soft conciliation or one of the other three devices?"

But the monkey said: "You ungrateful wretch! Why do you still pursue me, though I asked you not to? You are a fool, therefore I will not even give you good advice. For the proverb says:

> Give counsel only when it fits
> To such as seek the best.
> The foolish monkey broke to bits
> The sparrow's cozy nest.

"How was that?" asked the crocodile. And the monkey told the story of

THE PERT HEN-SPARROW

In a certain wood lived a sparrow and his wife who had built their nest on the branch of a tree.

One day in the month of February a monkey took shelter under the tree; for he had been caught in an unseasonable hail-storm, and his body shivered to the slightest breeze. Since his teeth were making music and his face was woebegone and his hands and feet were tightly clenched, the hen-sparrow said to him compassionately:

> With hands and feet of human plan,
> Almost you seem to be a man.
> So, if you find the weather cool,
> Why not construct a house, you fool?

When the monkey heard this, he reflected: "Well, well, some people fancy themselves. Here is this paltry hen-sparrow who has a good opinion of her own judgment. The well-known saying is correct:

> Of self-conceit all creatures show
> An adequate supply:
> The plover lies with claws upstretched
> To prop the falling sky."

Thereupon he said to her:

> You slut! You wench! You smarty!
> You needle-face! Be still,
> Or I will spoil the party;
> I will, I will, I will.

But she continued to ply him with excellent advice concerning the construction of a house, even after he had thus requested her not to do so. So he climbed the tree and destroyed her nest, breaking it to bits.

"And that is why I say:

> Give counsel only when it fits, ...

and the rest of it."

Then the crocodile said: "Oh, my friend, I did wrong, but please remember our old friendship and give me good advice."

"I will not tell you a thing," said the monkey, "because you took your wife's advice and carried me out to sea in order to drop me in. However much you love your wife, why throw friends, relatives, and such into the ocean just because she asks it?"

And the crocodile answered: "My dear fellow, it is all true. Yet consider the maxim, 'Seven words make friendship,' and give me a bit of good advice. For there is a saying:

> Disaster cannot threaten
> The man of sterling worth
> Who offers helpful counsel—
> In heaven, or on earth.

So, though I did you a wrong, I beg you to show forgiveness by giving good advice. You know the proverb:

> And is there any saintlihood
> In recompensing good with good?
> But worthy men go seeking still
> The saints returning good for ill."

Then the monkey said: "Well, well, my good fellow, I advise you to go and fight him. For there is a saying:

Sway patrons with obeisance;
In heroes raise a doubt;
Fling petty bribes to flunkeys;
With equals, fight it out."

"How was that?" asked the crocodile. And the monkey told

HOW SUPERSMART ATE THE ELEPHANT

There was once a jackal named Supersmart in a part of a forest. One day he came upon an elephant that had died a natural death in the wood. But he could only stalk about the body; he could not cut through the tough hide.

At this moment a lion, in his wanderings to and fro, came to the spot. And the jackal, spying him, obsequiously rubbed his scalp in the dust, clasped his lotus paws, and said: "My lord and king, I am merely a cudgel-bearer, guarding this elephant in the king's interest. May the king deign to eat it."

Then the lion said: "My good fellow, under no circumstances do I eat what another has killed. I graciously bestow this elephant upon you." And the jackal joyfully replied: "It is only what our lord and king has taught his servants to expect."

When the lion was gone, a tiger arrived. And the jackal thought when he saw him: "Well, I sent one rascal packing by doing obeisance. Now, how shall I dispose of this one? To be sure, he is a hero, and therefore can be managed only by intrigue. For there is a saying:

Where bribes and flattery would fail,
Intrigue is certain to avail.

And indeed, all creatures are held in bondage by heart-piercing intrigue. As the saying goes:

Even a pearl, so smoothly hard and round,
Is fastened by a thread and safely bound,
After a way to pierce its heart is found."

So he took his decision, went to meet the tiger, and slightly stiffening his neck, he said in an agitated tone: "Uncle, how could you venture into the jaws of death? This elephant was killed by a lion, who put me on guard while he went to bathe. And as he went, he gave me my orders. 'If any tiger comes this way,' he said, 'creep up and tell me. I have to clear this forest of tigers, because once, when I had killed an elephant, a tiger helped himself while my back was turned, and I had the leavings. From that day I have been death on tigers.' "

On hearing this, the tiger was terrified, and said: "My dear nephew, make me a gift of my life. Even if he is slow in returning, don't give him any news of me." With these words he decamped.

When the tiger had gone, a leopard appeared. And the jackal thought when he saw him: "Here comes Spot. He has powerful teeth. So I will use him to cut into this elephant-hide."

With this in mind, he said: "Well, nephew, where have you been this long time? And why do you seem so hungry? You come as my guest, according to the proverb:

A guest in need
Is a guest indeed.

Now here lies this elephant, killed by a lion who appointed me its guardian. But for all that, you may enjoy a square meal of elephant-meat, provided you cut and run before he gets back."

"No, uncle," said the leopard, "if things stand so, this meat is not healthy for me. You know the saying:

A man to thrive
Must keep alive.

Never eat a thing that doesn't sit well on the stomach. So I will be off." "Don't be timid," said the jackal. "Pluck up courage and eat. I will warn you of his coming while he is yet a long way off." So the leopard did as suggested, and the jackal, as soon as he saw the hide cut through, called out: "Quick, nephew, quick! Here comes the lion." Hearing this, the leopard vanished also.

Now while the jackal was eating meat through the opening cut by the leopard, a second jackal came on the scene in a great rage. And Supersmart, esteeming him an equal whose prowess was a known quantity, recited the stanza:

Sway patrons with obeisance;
In heroes raise a doubt;
Fling petty bribes to flunkeys;
With equals, fight it out—

made a dash at him, tore him with his fangs, made him seek the horizon, and himself comfortably enjoyed elephant-meat for a long time.

"Just so you, too, should fight it out with a natural enemy, one of your own race, and send him to the horizon. If you don't, he will presently strike his roots deep and will destroy you. You know the saying:

> From cows expect subsistence;
>   From Brahmans, self-denial;
> From women, fickle conduct;
>   From relatives, a trial.

"And the further saying:

> The food is very good to eat
>   And does not lack variety;
> While easy-going women meet
>   You in the town's society:
> But kinsmen in that foreign street
>   Are wanting in sobriety."

"How was that?" asked the crocodile. And the monkey told the story of

THE DOG WHO WENT ABROAD

There was once a dog named Spot in a certain town which was afflicted by a long famine. And as food gave out, dogs and others began to lose their homes. In fear of this, Spot felt his throat pinched by hunger, and he went to another country far away.

In a city of that country he found a citizen's wife

who was slipshod in her housekeeping, so he entered her house every day, and ate his fill from a diversified bill of fare. But as he left the house, other dogs, drunk with aristocratic spleen, closed in from all sides, and tore him in every limb with their fangs.

Then he thought: "Better one's native land, where one lives at peace even in times of famine, and no one picks a quarrel. It is better to return to my own city." Having thus reasoned it through, he returned to his own place.

Then his relatives asked him questions, as one returning from foreign parts: "Come now, tell us about it. What is the country like? How do the people behave? What do they eat? And what are their habits?"

And he replied: "Why speak of the country?

> The food is very good to eat
> And does not lack variety;
> While easy-going women meet
> You in the town's society:
> But kinsmen in that foreign street
> Are wanting in sobriety."

So the crocodile, having received his friend's advice, resolved to die if need be, said farewell to the monkey, and went to his own house. There he joined battle with the desperate ruffian who had forced a way in, put his reliance in resolute valor, and killed him. So he recovered his home and lived there happily for a long time.

Yes, the proverb is right:

> Shun pleasant days that listless pass,
>   The joy that hides
> In sloth. For deer can eat the grass
>   That fate provides.

Here ends Book IV, called "Loss of Gains." The first verse runs:

> Blind folly always has to pay
> For giving property away
> Because of blandishments and guile—
> The monkey tricked the crocodile.

BOOK V

ILL-CONSIDERED ACTION

BOOK V

ILL-CONSIDERED ACTION

Here, then, begins Book V, called "Ill-considered Action." The first verse runs:

> Deeds ill-known, ill-recognized,
> Ill-accomplished, ill-devised—
> Thought of these let no man harbor;
> Take a warning from the barber.

"How was that?" asked the princes. And Vishnusharman told the following story.

In the southern country is a city called Trumpet-Flower. In it lived a merchant named Jewel, who lost his fortune by the decree of fate, though his life was given to the pursuit of virtue, money, love, and salvation. The loss of property led to a series of humiliations, so that he sank into utter despondency. And one night he reflected: "A curse, a curse upon this state of poverty! For the proverb says:

> Conduct, patience, purity,
> Manners, loving-kindness, birth,
> After money disappears,
> Cease to have the slightest worth.
>
> Wisdom, sense, and social charm,
> Honest pride and self-esteem,
> After money disappears,
> All at once become a dream.

To the wisdom of the wise
  Constant household worries bring
Daily diminution, like
  Winter breathed upon by spring.

After money disappears,
  Keenest wisdom is at fault,
Choked by daily fuel and clothes,
  Oil and butter, rice and salt.

Poor and paltry neighbors scarce
  Waken sentiments of scorn,
Like the bubbles on a stream,
  Ever dying, ever born.

Yet the rich have license for
  All things vulgar and debased:
When the ocean bellows, none
  Reprobate his faulty taste."

Having thus set his mind in order, he concluded: "Under these circumstances, I will abandon life by self-starvation. What can be made of this calamity—life without money?" With his resolve taken, he went to sleep.

Now as he slept, a trillion dollars appeared in the form of a Jain monk, and said: "Good merchant, do not lose interest. I am a trillion, earned by your ancestors. Tomorrow morning I will come to your house in this same form. Then you must club me on the head, so that I may turn to gold and prove inexhaustible."

On awaking in the morning, he spent some time pondering on his dream: "Let me think. Will this dream prove true or false? I cannot tell. No doubt it will prove false, for I think of nothing but money all day and all night. And the proverb says:

> Dreams that do not mean a thing
> Come to sick and sorrowing,
> Lovelorn, drunk, and worrying."

At this moment a barber arrived to manicure his wife's nails. And while the barber was busy with his manicuring, the Jain monk suddenly appeared. When Jewel perceived the monk, he was delighted and struck him on the head with a stick of wood that lay handy. Whereupon the monk turned to gold and immediately fell to the ground.

The merchant then set him up in the middle of the house, and said to the barber, after handing him a tip: "My good fellow, you must not tell anybody what has happened in our house." To this the barber assented, but when he reached home, he thought: "Surely, all these naked fellows turn to gold when clubbed on the head. So tomorrow morning I, too, will invite a lot of them and club them to death, in order to get a lot of gold." And the day and the night dragged away as he meditated his plan.

In the morning he rose and went to a Jain monastery, arranged his upper garment, circumambulated the Conqueror thrice, sought the ground with his knees, laid his garment's hem over the gateway of his mouth, made a profound obeisance, and with an ear-piercing voice intoned the following hymn:

"The saints victorious endure
Who live by saving knowledge pure,
Who sterilize the mind within
By mind, against the seed of sin.

And further:

The tongue that praiseth Him is blest;
The heart, in Him that seeketh rest;
The hands are blest, and only they,
That e'er to Him due homage pay."

After chanting other hymns also to the same effect, but in great variety, he sought out the abbot and dropped on his knees and hands, saying: "Greetings, Your Reverence." From the abbot he received a benediction for the increase of his virtue, likewise instructions for a vow that involved the practice of celibacy. Then he said devoutly: "Holy sir, when you take your pious walk today, pray come to my house with your whole company of monks."

"My dear neophyte," replied the abbot, "you know the holy law. How can you speak so? Do you take us for Brahmans, that you invite us to eat? Nay, we wander each day just as it happens, and when we meet a pious neophyte, enter his house. Begone. Never speak so again."

"Holy sir," said the barber, "I know it well. I will do as you say. However, you have many neophytes engaged in pious labors; while I, for my part, have made ready strips of canvas adapted to the wrapping of manuscripts. And for the copying of manuscripts and the payment of scribes, sufficient money is provided. In view of this, pray do what seems proper." And so he started home.

When he arrived there, he got ready cudgels of acacia wood, placed them in a corner behind the door, then toward noon he returned to the monastery gate and waited there. Then as they all came forth in order of dignity, he besought them as teachers, and led them to his house. For their part, in their greed for book-covers and money they passed by their familiar neophytes, even the pious ones, and joyfully flocked behind him. Well, there is sense in the verse:

Behold a wonder! Even he
Who lives alone, from kindred free,
With hand for spoon, and air for dress,
Is overcome by greediness.

Then the barber conducted them well into the house and clubbed them. Under the clubbing some died, others had their heads broken and began to bawl. But when the soldiers in the citadel heard the howling, they said: "Well, well! What is this tremendous hubbub in the middle of town? Come along!" So they all scampered and saw the monks rushing from the barber's house, blood streaming over their bodies. And being asked what it meant, they told exactly how the barber had behaved.

So the soldiers fettered the barber and carried him off to court together with such monks as had survived the slaughter. There the judges questioned him: "Come, sir! What means this shameful deed by you committed?" And he replied: "Gentlemen, what else could I do?" And with this he related the behavior of Jewel.

The judges therefore despatched a summonser, who returned with Jewel. And they questioned him: "Merchant, why did you kill a certain Jain monk?" And he in turn gave a full account of the original monk. Whereupon they said: "Well, well! Let this villainous barber be impaled. For his act was ill advised."

When this had been done, they observed:

> Deeds ill-known, ill-recognized,
> Ill-accomplished, ill-advised—
> Thought of these let no man harbor;
> Take a warning from the barber.

And there is sound sense in this:

> Let the well-advised be done;
> Ill-advised leave unbegun:
> Else, remorse will be let loose,
> As with lady and mungoose.

"How was that?" asked Jewel. And they told the story of

THE LOYAL MUNGOOSE

There was once a Brahman named Godly in a certain town. His wife mothered a single son and a mungoose. And as she loved little ones, she cared for the mungoose also like a son, giving him milk from her breast, and salves, and baths, and so on. But she did not trust him, for she thought: "A mungoose is a nasty kind of creature. He might hurt my boy." Yes, there is sense in the proverb:

> A son will ever bring delight,
> Though bent on folly, passion, spite,
> Though shabby, naughty, and a fright.

One day she tucked her son in bed, took a water-jar, and said to her husband: "Now, Professor, I am going for water. You must protect the boy from the mungoose." But when she was gone, the Brahman went off somewhere himself to beg food, leaving the house empty.

While he was gone, a black snake issued from his hole and, as fate would have it, crawled toward the baby's cradle. But the mungoose, feeling him to be a natural enemy, and fearing for the life of his baby brother, fell upon the vicious serpent halfway, joined battle with him, tore him to bits, and tossed the pieces far and wide. Then, delighted with his own heroism, he ran, blood trickling from his mouth, to meet the mother; for he wished to show what he had done.

But when the mother saw him coming, saw his bloody mouth and his excitement, she feared that the villain must have eaten her baby boy, and without thinking twice, she angrily dropped the water-jar upon him, which killed him the moment that it struck. There she left him without a second thought, and hurried home, where she found the baby safe and sound, and near the cradle a great black snake, torn to bits. Then, overwhelmed with sorrow because she had thoughtlessly killed her benefactor, her son, she beat her head and breast.

At this moment the Brahman came home with a dish of rice gruel which he had got from someone in his begging tour, and saw his wife bitterly lamenting her son, the mungoose. "Greedy! Greedy!" she cried. "Because you did not do as I told you, you must now taste the bitterness of a son's death, the fruit of the tree of your own wickedness. Yes, this is what happens to those blinded by greed. For the proverb says:

Indulge in no excessive greed
(A little helps in time of need)—
A greedy fellow in the world
Found on his head a wheel that whirled."

"How was that?" asked the Brahman. And his wife told the story of

THE FOUR TREASURE-SEEKERS

In a certain town in the world were four Brahmans who lived as the best of friends. And being stricken with utter poverty, they took counsel together: "A curse, a curse on this business of being poor! For

The well-served master hates him still;
His loving kinsmen with a will
Abandon him; woes multiply,
While friends and even children fly;
His high-born wife grows cool; the flash
Of virtue dims; brave efforts crash—
For him who has no ready cash.

And again:

Charm, courage, eloquence, good looks,
And thorough mastery of books
(If money does not back the same)
Are useless in the social game.

"Better be dead than penniless. As the story goes:

A beggar to the graveyard hied
And there 'Friend corpse, arise,' he cried;
'One moment lift my heavy weight
Of poverty; for I of late
Grow weary, and desire instead
Your comfort: you are good and dead.'
The corpse was silent. He was sure
'Twas better to be dead than poor.

"So let us at any cost strive to make money. For the saying goes:

Money gets you anything,
Gets it in a flash:
Therefore let the prudent get
Cash, cash, cash.

"Now this cash comes to men in six ways. They are: (1) begging for charity, (2) flunkeyism at a court, (3) farmwork, (4) the learned professions, (5) usury, (6) trade.

"However, among all these methods of making money, trade is the only one without a hitch in it. For

Kings' favor is a thing unstable;
Crows peck at winnings charitable;
You make, in learning the professions,
Too many wearisome concessions
To teachers; farms are too much labor;
In usury you lend your neighbor

The cash which is your life, and therefore
You really live a poor man. Wherefore
I see in trade the only living
That can be truly pleasure-giving.
Hurrah for trade!

"Now profitable trade has seven branches. They are: (1) false weights and balances, (2) price-boosting, (3) keeping a pawnshop, (4) getting regular customers, (5) a stock company, (6) *articles de luxe* such as perfumes, (7) foreign trade.

"Now the economists say:

False weights and boosting prices to
An overshameless sum
And constant cheating of one's friends
Are fit for social scum.

And again:

Deposits in the house compel
The pawnshop man to pray:
If you will kill the owner, Lord,
I'll give you what you say.

Likewise:

The holder of a stock reflects
With glee, though one of many:
The wide world's wealth belongs to me;
No other gets a penny.

Furthermore:

Perfumery is first-class ware;
Why deal in gold and such?
Whate'er the cost, you sell it for
A thousand times as much.

"Foreign trade is the affair of the capitalist. As the book says:

> Wild elephants are caught by tame:
>   So money-kings, devising
> A trap for money, capture it
>   With far-flung advertising.
>
> The brisk commercial traveler,
>   Who knows the selling game,
> Invests his money, and returns
>   With twice or thrice the same.

And again:

> The crow, or good-for-naught, or deer,
>   Afraid of foreign lands,
> In heedless slothfulness is sure
>   To perish where he stands."

Having thus set their minds in order, and resolved on foreign travel, they said farewell to home and friends, and started, all four of them. Well, there is wisdom in the saying:

> The man whose mind is money mad,
>   From all his kinsmen flees;
> He hastens from his mother dear;
>   He breaks his promises;
> He even goes to foreign lands
>   Which he would not elect
> And leaves his native country. Well,
>   What else do you expect?

So in time they came to the Avanti country, where they bathed in the waters of the Sipra, and adored the great god Shiva. As they traveled farther, they met a master-magician named Terror-Joy. And having greeted him in proper Brahman fashion, they all accompanied him to his monastery cell. There the magician asked them whence they came, whither they were going, and what was their object. And they replied: "We are pilgrims, seeking magic power. We have resolved to go where we shall find enough money, or death. For the proverb says:

> While water is given
> By fate out of heaven,
> If men dig a well,
> It bubbles from hell.
> Man's effort (sufficiently great)
> Can equal the wonders of fate.

And again:

> Success complete
> In any feat
> Is sure to bless
> True manliness.
> Man's effort (sufficiently great)
> Is just what a dullard calls fate.

> There is no toy
> Called easy joy,
> But man must strain
> To body's pain.
> Even Vishnu embraces his bride
> With arms that the churn-stick has tried.

"So disclose to us some method of getting money, whether crawling into a hole, or placating a witch, or living in a graveyard, or selling human flesh, or anything. You are said to have miraculous magic, while we have boundless daring. You know the saying:

Only the great can aid the great
To win their heart's desire:
Apart from ocean, who could bear
The fierce subaqueous fire?"

So the magician, perceiving their fitness as disciples, made four magic quills, and gave one to each, saying: "Go to the northern slope of the Himalaya Mountains. And wherever a quill drops, there the owner will certainly find a treasure."

Now as they followed his directions, the leader's quill dropped. And on examining the spot, he found the soil all copper. So he said: "Look here! Take all the copper you want." But the others said: "Fool! What is the good of a thing which, even in quantity, does not put an end to poverty? Stand up. Let us go on." And he replied: "You may go. I will accompany you no farther." So he took his copper and was the first to turn back.

The three others went farther. But they had traveled only a little way when the leader's quill dropped. And when he dug down, he found the soil all silver. At this he was delighted, and cried: "Look! Take all the silver you want. No need of going farther." "Fool!" said the other two. "The soil was copper first, then silver. It will certainly be gold ahead. This stuff, even in quantity, does not relieve poverty so much." "You two may go," said he. "I will not join you." So he took his silver and turned back.

The two went on until one quill dropped. When

the owner dug down, he found the soil all gold. Seeing this, he was delighted, and said to his companion: "Look! Take all the gold you want. There is nothing beyond better than gold." "Fool!" said the other. "Don't you see the point? First came copper, then silver, and then gold. Beyond there will certainly be gems. Stand up. Let us go farther. What is the good of this stuff? A quantity of it is a mere burden." "You may go," he replied. "I will stay here and wait for you."

So the other went on alone. His limbs were scorched by the rays of the summer sun and his thoughts were confused by thirst as he wandered to and fro over the trails in the land of the fairies. At last, on a whirling platform, he saw a man with blood dripping down his body; for a wheel was whirling on his head. Then he made haste and said: "Sir, why do you stand thus with a wheel whirling on your head? In any case, tell me if there is water anywhere. I am mad with thirst."

The moment the Brahman said this, the wheel left the other's head and settled on his own. "My very dear sir," said he, "what is the meaning of this?" "In the very same way," replied the other, "it settled on my head." "But," said the Brahman, "when will it go away? It hurts terribly."

And the fellow said: "When someone who holds in his hand a magic quill such as you had, arrives and speaks as you did, then it will settle on his head." "Well," said the Brahman, "how long were you here?" And the other asked: "Who is king in the world at present?" On hearing the answer, "King Vinavatsa," he said: "When Rama was king, I was poverty stricken, procured a magic quill, and came here, just like you. And I saw another man with a wheel on his head and put a question to him. The moment I asked a question (just like you) the wheel left his head and settled on mine. But I cannot reckon the centuries."

Then the wheel-bearer asked: "My dear sir, how, pray, did you get food while standing thus?" "My dear sir," said the fellow, "the god of wealth, fearful lest his treasures be stolen, prepared this terror, so that no magician might come so far. And if any should succeed in coming, he was to be freed from hunger and thirst, preserved from decrepitude and death, and was merely to endure this torture. So now permit me to say farewell. You have set me free from a sizable misery. Now I am going home." And he went.

After he had gone, the gold-finder, wondering why his companion delayed, eagerly followed his footprints. And having gone but a little way, he saw a man whose body was drenched with blood, a man tortured by a cruel wheel whirling on his head—and this man was his own companion. So he came near and asked with tears: "My dear fellow, what is the meaning of this?" "A whim of fate," said the other. "But tell me," said he, "what has happened." And in answer to his question, the other told the entire history of the wheel.

When the friend heard this, he scolded him, saying: "Well, I told you time and again not to do it. Yet from lack of sense you did not do as I said. Indeed, there is wisdom in the saying:

> Scholarship is less than sense;
> Therefore seek intelligence:
> Senseless scholars in their pride
> Made a lion; then they died."

"How was that?" asked the wheel-bearer. And the gold-finder told the story of

THE LION-MAKERS

In a certain town were four Brahmans who lived in friendship. Three of them had reached the far shore of all scholarship, but lacked sense. The other found scholarship distasteful; he had nothing but sense.

One day they met for consultation. "What is the use of attainments," said they, "if one does not travel, win the favor of kings, and acquire money? Whatever we do, let us all travel."

But when they had gone a little way, the eldest of them said: "One of us, the fourth, is a dullard, having nothing but sense. Now nobody gains the favorable attention of kings by simple sense without scholarship. Therefore we will not share our earnings with him. Let him turn back and go home."

Then the second said: "My intelligent friend, you lack scholarship. Please go home." But the third said: "No, no. This is no way to behave. For we have played together since we were little boys. Come along, my noble friend. You shall have a share of the money we earn."

With this agreement they continued their journey, and in a forest they found the bones of a dead lion. Thereupon one of them said: "A good opportunity to test the ripeness of our scholarship. Here lies some kind of creature, dead. Let us bring it to life by means of the scholarship we have honestly won."

Then the first said: "I know how to assemble the skeleton." The second said: "I can supply skin, flesh, and blood." The third said: "I can give it life."

So the first assembled the skeleton, the second provided skin, flesh, and blood. But while the third was intent on giving the breath of life, the man of sense advised against it, remarking: "This is a lion. If you bring him to life, he will kill every one of us."

"You simpleton!" said the other, "it is not I who will reduce scholarship to a nullity." "In that case," came the reply, "wait a moment, while I climb this convenient tree."

When this had been done, the lion was brought to life, rose up, and killed all three. But the man of sense, after the lion had gone elsewhere, climbed down and went home.

"And that is why I say:

> Scholarship is less than sense, ...

and the rest of it."

But the wheel-bearer, having heard the story, retorted: "Not at all. The reasoning is at fault. For creatures of very great sense perish if stricken by fate, while those of very meager intelligence, if protected by fate, live happily. There is a stanza:

> While Hundred-Wit is on a head,
> While Thousand-Wit hangs limp and dead,
> Your humble Single-Wit, my dear,
> Is paddling in the water clear."

"How was that?" asked the gold-finder. And the wheel-bearer told the story of

HUNDRED-WIT, THOUSAND-WIT, AND SINGLE-WIT

In a certain pond lived two fishes whose names were Hundred-Wit and Thousand-Wit. And a frog named Single-Wit made friends with them. Thus all three would for some time enjoy at the water's edge the pleasure of conversation spiced with witticisms, then would dive into the water again.

One day at sunset they were engaged in conversation, when fishermen with nets came there, who said to one another on seeing the pond: "Look! This pond appears to contain plenty of fish, and the water seems shallow. We will return at dawn." With this they went home.

The three friends felt this speech to be dreadful as the fall of a thunderbolt, and they took counsel together. The frog spoke first: "Hundred-Wit and Thousand-Wit, my dear friends, what should we do now: flee or stick it out?"

At this Thousand-wit laughed and said: "My good friend, do not be frightened merely because you have heard words. An actual invasion is not to be anticipated. Yet should it take place, I will save you and myself by virtue of my wit. For I know plenty of tricks in the water." And Hundred-Wit added: "Yes, Thousand-Wit is quite right. For

Where wind is checked, and light of day,
The wise man's wit soon finds a way.

One cannot, because he has heard a few mere words, abandon his birthplace, the home of his ancestors. You must not go away. I will save you by virtue of my wit."

"Well," said the frog, "I have only a single wit, and that tells me to flee. My wife and I are going to some other body of water this very night."

So spoke the frog and under cover of night he went to another body of water. At dawn the next day came the fish-catchers, who seemed the servants of Death, and inclosed the pond with nets. And all the fishes, turtles, frogs, crabs, and other water-creatures were caught in the nets and captured. Even Hundred-Wit and Thousand-Wit fell into a net and were killed, though they struggled to save their lives by fancy turns.

On the following day the fishermen gleefully started home. One of them carried Hundred-Wit, who was heavy, on his head. Another carried Thousand-Wit tied to a cord. Then the frog, safe in the throat of a cistern, said to his wife: "Look, darling, look!

While Hundred-Wit is on a head,
While Thousand-Wit hangs limp and dead,
Your humble Single-Wit, my dear,
Is paddling in the water clear."

"And that is why I say that intelligence is not the sole determinant of fate."

Then the gold-finder said: "It may be so. Yet a friend's advice should not be disregarded. But what happened? Spite of my dissuasion, you would not stop, such was your greed and pride in your scholarship. Yes, there is sense in the stanza:

Well sung, uncle! Why would you
Not stop when I told you to?
What a necklace! Yes, you wear
Music medals rich and rare."

"How was that?" asked the wheel-bearer. And the other told the story of

THE MUSICAL DONKEY

In a certain town was a donkey named Prig. In the daytime he carried laundry packages, but was at liberty to wander anywhere at night. One night while wandering in the fields he fell in with a jackal and made friends. So the two broke through a hedge into cucumber-beds, and having eaten what they could hold of that comestible, parted at dawn to go home.

One night the egotistical donkey, standing among the cucumbers, said to the jackal: "See, nephew! The night is marvelously fine. I will contribute a song. What sentiment shall my song express?" "Don't, uncle," said the jackal. "It might make trouble, seeing that we are on thieves' business. Thieves and lovers should keep very quiet. As the proverb says:

> No sleepyhead should pilfer fur,
> No invalid, rich provender,
> No sneezer should become a thief—
> Unless they wish to come to grief.

"Besides, your vocal music is not agreeable, since it resembles a blast on a conch-shell. The farmers would hear you from afar, would rise, and would fetter or kill you. Better keep quiet and eat."

"Come, come!" said the donkey. "Your remarks prove that you live in the woods and have no musical taste. Did you never hear this?

> Oh, bliss if murmurs sweet to hear
> Of music's nectar woo your ear
> When darkness flees from moonlight clear
> In autumn, and your love is near."

"Very true, uncle," said the jackal. "But your bray is harsh. Why do a thing that defeats your own purpose?" "Fool, fool!" answered the donkey. "Do you think me ignorant of vocal music? Listen to its systematization, as follows:

Seven notes, three scales, and twenty-one
  Are modulations said to be;
Of pitches there are forty-nine,
  Three measures, also pauses three;

Caesuras three; and thirty-six
  Arrangements of the notes, in fine;
Six apertures; the languages
  Are forty; sentiments are nine.

One hundred songs and eighty-five
  Are found in songbooks, perfect, pure,
With all accessories complete,
  Unblemished in their phrasing sure.

On earth is nothing nobler found,
  Nor yet in heaven, than vocal song;
The singing Devil soothes the Lord,
  When quivering strings the sound prolong.

"After this, how can you think me lacking in educated taste? How can you try to hinder me?"

"Very well, uncle," said the jackal. "I will stay by the gap in the hedge, and look for farmers. You may sing to heart's content."

When he had done so, the donkey lifted his neck and began to utter sounds. But the farmers, hearing the bray of a donkey, angrily clenched their teeth, snatched cudgels, rushed in, and beat him so that he fell to the ground. Next they hobbled him by fastening on his neck a mortar with a convenient hole, then went to sleep. Presently the donkey stood up, forgetting the pain as donkeys naturally do. As the verse puts it:

With dog, and ass, and horse,
  And donkey more than most,
The pain from beatings is
  Immediately lost.

Then with the mortar on his neck, he trampled the hedge and started to run away. At this moment the jackal, looking on from a safe distance, said with a smile:

Well sung, uncle! Why would you
Not stop when I told you to?
What a necklace! Yes, you wear
Music medals rich and rare.

"Just so, you would not stop when I advised it."

After listening to this, the wheel-bearer said: "O my friend, you are quite right. Yes, there is much wisdom in the verse:

He who, lacking wit, does not
  Harken to a friend,
Just like weaver Slow, inclines
  To a fatal end."

"How was that?" asked the gold-finder. And the wheel-bearer told the story of

SLOW, THE WEAVER

In a certain town lived a weaver named Slow. One day all the pegs in his loom broke. So he took an axe, and in his search for wood, came to the seashore. There he found a great sissoo tree, and he thought: "This seems a good-sized tree. If I cut it down, I can make plenty of weaving-tools." He therefore lifted his axe upon it.

Now there was a fairy in the tree who said: "My friend, this tree is my home. Please spare it. For I live here in utter happiness, since my body is caressed by breezes cool from contact with ocean billows."

"But, sir," said the weaver, "what am I to do? While I lack apparatus made of wood, my family is pinched by hunger. Therefore, please move elsewhere, and quickly. I intend to cut it down."

"Sir," said the fairy, "I have taken a liking to you. Ask anything you like, but spare this tree."

"In that case," said the weaver, "I will go home and return after asking my friend and my wife." And when the fairy consented, the weaver started home. On entering the town, he encountered his particular friend, the barber, and said: "My friend, I have won the favor of a fairy. Tell me what to ask for."

And the barber said: "My dear fellow, if it is really so, ask for a kingdom. You can be king, and I will be prime minister. So we shall both taste the delights of this world before those of the world to come."

"Quite so, my friend," replied the weaver. "However, I shall ask my wife, too." "Don't," said the barber. "It is a mistake to consult women. As the saying goes:

Give a woman food and dresses
(Chiefly when her trouble presses);
Give her gems and all things nice;
Do not ask for her advice.

And again:

Where a woman, gambler, child,
As a guide is domiciled,
Death advances, stage by stage—
So declares the ancient sage.

And once again:

Only while he does not hear
Woman's whisper in his ear,
May a man a leader be,
Keeping due humility.

Women seek for selfish treasures,
Think of nothing but their pleasures,
Even children by them reckoned
To their selfish comfort second."

And the weaver rejoined: "You may be right. Still, I shall ask her. She is a good wife."

So he made haste and said to her: "My dear wife, today we won the favor of a fairy. He offers anything we want. So I have come to ask you to tell me what to say to him. Here is my friend, the barber, who tells me to ask for a kingdom."

"Dear husband," said she, "what sense have barbers? Do not take his advice. For the proverb says:

All advice you may discard
From a barber, child, or bard,

Monk or hermit or musician,
Or a man of base condition.

"Besides, this king-business means a series of dreadful troubles and involves worry about peace, war, change of base, entrenchment, alliance, duplicity, and other matters. It never gives satisfaction. And even worse,

His very sons and brothers wish
The slaughter of a king;
As this is kingship's nature, who
Would not reject the thing?"

"Yes," said the weaver, "you are right. But tell me what to ask for." And she replied: "As it is, you turn out one piece of cloth a day, and this meets all our expenses. Now ask for a second pair of arms and an extra head, so that you may produce one piece of cloth in front and another behind. The price of one meets the household expenses, with the price of the other you may put on style and spend the time in honor among your peers."

On hearing this, he was delighted and said: "Splendid, my faithful wife! You have made a splendid suggestion. I am determined to follow it."

So the weaver went and laid his request before the fairy: "Well, sir, if you offer what I wish, pray give me a second pair of arms and an extra head." And in the act of speaking he became two-headed and four-armed.

But as he came home, delight in his heart, the

people thought he was a fiend, and beat him with clubs and stones and things so that he died.

"And that is why I say:

He who, lacking wit, does not, ...

and the rest of it."

Then the wheel-bearer continued: "Yes, any man becomes ridiculous when bitten by the demon of extravagant hope. There is sense in this:

Do not indulge in hopes
Extravagantly high:
Else, whitened like the sire
Of Moon-Lord, you will lie."

"How was that?" asked the gold-finder. And the other told the story of

THE BRAHMAN'S DREAM

In a certain town lived a Brahman named Seedy, who got some barley-meal by begging, ate a portion, and filled a jar with the remainder. This jar he hung on a peg one night, placed his cot beneath it, and fixing his gaze on the jar, fell into a hypnotic reverie.

"Well, here is a jar full of barley-meal," he thought. "Now if famine comes, a hundred rupees will come out of it. With that sum I will get two she-goats. Every six months they will bear two more she-goats. After goats, cows. When the cows calve, I will sell the calves. After cows, buffaloes; after buffaloes, mares. From the mares I shall get plenty of horses. The sale of these will mean plenty of gold. The gold will buy a great house with an inner court. Then someone will come to my house and offer his lovely daughter with a dowry. She will bear a son, whom I shall name Moon-Lord. When he is old enough to ride on my knee, I will take a book, sit on the stable roof, and think. Just then Moon-Lord will see me, will jump from his mother's lap in his eagerness to ride on my knee, and will go too near the horses. Then I shall get angry and tell my wife to take the boy. But she will be busy with her chores and will not pay attention to what I say. Then I will get up and kick her."

Being sunk in his hypnotic dream, he let fly such a kick that he smashed the jar. And the barley-meal which it contained turned him white all over.

"And that is why I say:

> Do not indulge in hopes, ...

and the rest of it."

"Very true, indeed," said the gold-finder. "For

> Greedy folk who do not heed
> Consequences of a deed,
> Suffer disappointment soon;
> For example take King Moon."

"How was that?" asked the wheel-bearer. And the other told the story of

THE UNFORGIVING MONKEY

In a certain city was a king named Moon, who had a pack of monkeys for his son's amusement.

They were kept in prime condition by daily provender and pabulum in great variety.

For the amusement of the same prince there was a herd of rams. One of them had an itching tongue, so he went into the kitchen at all hours of the day and night and swallowed everything in sight. And the cooks would beat him with any stick or other object within reach.

Now when the chief of the monkeys observed this, he reflected: "Dear me! This quarrel between ram and cooks will mean the destruction of the monkeys. For the ram is a regular guzzler, and when the cooks are infuriated, they hit him with anything handy. Suppose some time they find nothing else and beat him with a firebrand. Then that broad, woolly back will very easily catch fire. And if the ram, while burning, plunges into the stable near by, it will blaze—for it is mostly thatch—and the horses will be scorched. Now the standard work on veterinary science prescribes monkey-fat to relieve burns on horses. This being so, we are threatened with death."

Having reached this conclusion, he assembled the monkeys and said:

"A quarrel of the ram and cooks
Has lately come about;
It threatens every monkey life
Without a shade of doubt.

"Because, if senseless quarrels rend
A house from day to day,

The folk who wish to keep alive
Had better move away.

"For quarrels end a happy home;
And slander, friendship's story;
While evil kings their kingdoms end;
And meanness, manly glory.

"Therefore let us leave the house and take to the woods before we are all dead."

But the conceited monkeys laughed at his warning and said: "Oho! You are old and your mind is slipping. Your words prove it. We have no intention of foregoing the heavenly dainties which the princes give us with their own hands, in order to eat fruits peppery, puckery, bitter, and sour from the trees out there in the forest."

Having listened to this, the monkey chief made a wry face and said: "Come, come! You are fools. You do not consider the outcome of this pleasant life. Just at present it is sweet, at the last it will turn to poison. At any rate, I will not behold the death of my household. I am off for that very forest. As the proverb says:

Blest are they who do not see
Death upon the family,
Friend in trouble, stolen wife,
Ruin of the nation's life."

With these words the chief left them all behind, and went to the forest.

One day after he had gone, the ram entered the

kitchen. And the cook, finding nothing else, picked up a firebrand, half-consumed and still blazing, and struck him. Whereat, with half his body blazing, he plunged bleating into the stable near by. There he rolled until flames started up on all sides—for the stable was mostly thatch—and of the horses tethered there some died, their eyes popping, while some, half-burned to death and whinnying with pain, snapped their halters, so that nobody knew what to do.

In this state of affairs, the saddened king assembled the veterinary surgeons and said: "Prescribe some method of giving these horses relief from the pain of their burns." And they, recalling the teachings of their science, said: "O King, the blessèd master of our craft prescribed for this emergency as follows:

> Let monkey-fat be freely used;
> Like dark before the dawn,
> The pain that horses feel from burns,
> Will very soon be gone.

Pray adopt this remedy before they perish miserably."

When the king heard this, he ordered the slaughter of the monkeys. And, not to waste words, every one was killed.

Now the monkey chief did not with his own eyes see this outrage perpetrated on his household. But he heard the story as it passed from one to another, and did not take it tamely. As the proverb says:

If foes commit an outrage on
A house, and one forgives—
Be it from fear or greed—he is
The meanest man that lives.

Now as the elderly monkey wandered about thirsty, he came to a lake made lovely by clusters of lotuses. And as he observed it narrowly, he noticed footprints leading into the lake, but none coming out. Thereupon he reflected: "There must be some vicious beast here in the water. So I will stay at a safe distance and drink through a hollow lotus-stalk."

When he had done so, there issued from the water a man-eating fiend with a pearl necklace adorning his neck, who spoke and said: "Sir, I eat everyone who enters the water. So there is none shrewder than you, who drink in this fashion. I have taken a liking to you. Name your heart's desire."

"Sir," said the monkey, "how many can you eat?" And the fiend replied: "I can eat hundreds, thousands, myriads, yes, hundreds of thousands, if they enter the water. Outside, a jackal can overpower me."

"And I," said the monkey, "I live in mortal enmity with a king. If you will give me that pearl necklace, I will awaken his greed with a plausible narrative, and will make that king enter the lake along with his retinue." So the fiend handed over the pearl necklace.

Then people saw the monkey roaming over trees

and palace-roofs with a pearl necklace embellishing his throat, and they asked him: "Well, chief, where have you spent this long time? Where did you get a pearl necklace like that? Its dazzling beauty dims the very sun."

And the monkey answered: "In a spot in the forest is a shrewdly hidden lake, a creation of the god of wealth. Through his grace, if anyone bathes there at sunrise on Sunday, he comes out with a pearl necklace like this embellishing his throat."

Now the king heard this from somebody, summoned the monkey, and asked: "Is this true, chief?" "O King," said the monkey, "you have visible proof in the pearl necklace on my throat. If you, too, could find a use for one, send somebody with me, and I will show him."

On hearing this, the king said: "In view of the facts, I will come myself with my retinue, so that we may acquire numbers of pearl necklaces." "O King," said the monkey, "your idea is delicious."

So the king and his retinue started, greedy for pearl necklaces. And the king in his palanquin clasped the monkey to his bosom, showing him honor as they traveled. For there is wisdom in the saying:

> The educated and the rich,
> Befooled by greed,
> Plunge into wickedness, then feel
> The pinch of need.

And again:

A hundred's mine? A thousand, please.
Thousand? A lakh would give me ease.
A kingdom's power would satisfy
The lakh-lord. Kings would own the sky.

The hair grows old with aging years;
The teeth grow old, the eyes and ears.
But while the aging seasons speed,
One thing is young forever—greed.

At dawn they reached the lake and the monkey said to the king: "O King, fulfilment comes to those who enter at sunrise. Let all your attendants be told, so that they may dash in with one fell swoop. You, however, must enter with me, for I will pick the place I found before and show you plenty of pearl necklaces." So all the attendants entered and were eaten by the fiend.

Then, as they lingered, the king said to the monkey: "Well, chief, why do my attendants linger?" And the monkey hurriedly climbed a tree before saying to the king: "You villainous king, your attendants are eaten by a fiend that lives in the water. My enmity with you, arising from the death of my household, has been brought to a happy termination. Now go. I did not make you enter there, because I remembered that you were the king. But the proverb says:

Having suffered an offense,
Give an evil recompense;

For I deem it righteous still,
Evil to repay with ill.

Thus you plotted the death of my household, and I of yours."

When the king heard this, he hastened home, grief-stricken. And when the king had gone, the fiend, fully satisfied, issued from the water, and gleefully recited a verse:

Very good, my monkey-o!
You won a friend, and killed a foe,
And kept the pearls without a flaw,
By sucking water through a straw.

"And that is why I say:

Greedy folk who do not heed, ...

and the rest of it."

Then the gold-finder continued: "Please bid me farewell. I wish to go home." But the wheel-bearer answered: "How can you go, leaving me in this plight? You know the proverb:

Whoever through hard-heartedness
Deserts a friend in his distress,
For such ingratitude must pay—
To hell he treads the certain way."

"That is true," said the gold-finder, "in case one able to aid deserts a friend in a remediable situation. But this situation has no human remedy, and I shall never have the ability to set you free. Besides, the more I gaze at your face, distorted with pain from the whirling wheel, the surer I feel that I am going to leave this spot at once, lest perchance the same calamity befall me, too. There is some point in this:

> To judge by the expression,
> Friend monkey, on your face,
> You have been caught by Twilight—
> He lives who wins the race."

"How was that?" asked the wheel-bearer. And the other told the story of

THE CREDULOUS FIEND

In a certain city lived a king whose name was Fine-Army. He had a daughter named Pearl, blessed with the thirty-two marks of perfect beauty.

Now a certain fiend, who wished to carry her off, came every evening and abused her, but he could not carry her off because she protected herself by drawing a magic circle. However, at the hour when he embraced her, she experienced trembling, fever, and the like, the feelings that arise in the presence of a fiend.

While matters were in this state, the fiend once took his stand in a corner and revealed himself to the princess, who thereupon said to a girl friend: "Look, my dear! This is the fiend who comes every evening at twilight's hour and torments me. Is there any means of keeping the ruffian at a distance?"

When he heard this, the fiend thought: "Aha! I am not the only one. There is someone else—and his name is Twilight—who comes every day to carry her off. But he cannot do it either. Suppose I take the form of a horse, go to the stable, and find out what he looks like and what power he has."

When he had done so, a horse-thief came to the palace at dead of night. He examined all the horses, found the fiend-horse the finest, put a bit in his mouth, and mounted. Meanwhile the fiend was thinking: "I presume this is the fellow named Twilight. He thinks me a vile creature, he is angry, he has come to kill me. What shall I do?"

While he was thinking, the horse-thief struck him with a whip. And he was terrified and started to run. The thief, for his part, after traveling some distance, tried to stop him by tugging at the bit. And he thought: "Now if he were a horse, he would mind the bit. Instead, he goes faster and faster."

When the thief perceived how little he minded the tugging at the bit, he reflected: "Well, well! Horses are not like this. This must be a fiend in equine form. So if I find a spot thick with dust, I will drop. It is my one chance of life."

While the horse-thief was thinking and praying to his favorite god, the fiend-horse passed under a banyan tree. And the thief caught a branch and stuck. So both of them gained the hope of life from their separation, and were filled with extreme delight.

Now in the banyan was a monkey, a friend of the fiend, who said when he saw the fiend making off:

"Look here! Why do you run from an imaginary danger? This is your natural food, a man. Eat him."

On hearing this, the fiend took his own form and turned about—but his mind was disturbed and his purpose shaky. And when the thief saw that the monkey had called him back, he was angry. As the monkey sat above, and his tail hung down, the thief took it in his mouth and started to chew very hard. Then the monkey concluded that he was dealing with one more powerful than the fiend, and was too frightened to utter a word. In dreadful pain, he could only shut his eyes tight, clench his teeth, and wait. And the fiend, observing him in this state, recited the stanza:

> To judge by the expression,
> Friend monkey, on your face,
> You have been caught by Twilight—
> He lives who wins the race.

Then the gold-finder continued: "Bid me farewell. I desire to go home. You may stay here and taste the fruit of the tree of your waywardness."

"Oh," said the wheel-bearer, "that is uncalled for. Good or evil comes by fate's decree to men well-behaved or wayward. As the old verse puts it:

> Blind man, hunchback, and unblest
> Princess with an extra breast—
> Waywardness is prudence, when
> Fortune favors wayward men."

"How was that?" asked the gold-finder. And the wheel-bearer told the story of

THE THREE-BREASTED PRINCESS

In the north country was a city called Honey-Town, where the king was named Honey-Host. And once there was born to him a daughter with three breasts. As soon as he learned of the birth of a three-breasted girl, he summoned the chamberlain and said: "Sir, let this girl be exposed in the forest, so that not a single soul may learn the fact."

To this the chamberlain replied: "O king of kings, it is a well-known fact that a three-breasted daughter brings misfortune. In spite of this, the Brahmans should be summoned and their opinion asked, in order that no law be offended, whether human or divine. For the proverb says:

> A prudent man should always ask
> What is beyond his ken:
> A dreadful fiend the Brahman caught,
> But let him go again."

"How was that?" asked the king. And the chamberlain told the story of

THE FIEND WHO WASHED HIS FEET

In a certain forest lived a fiend named Cruel. One day he met a Brahman in his wanderings, climbed on his shoulder, and said: "Now go ahead."

So the terrified Brahman started off with him.

But on observing that the fiend's feet were soft as a lotus-heart, he asked him: "Sir, why are your feet so tender?"

And the fiend replied: "I am under a vow never to touch the ground with my feet until I have washed them." Soon the Brahman, while meditating a plan of escape, came to a lake. Here the fiend said: "Sir, do not stir from this spot until I come forth from the lake after bathing and worshiping the god."

Thereupon the Brahman thought: "He will be sure to eat me after his worship. I will hurry away. For he will not follow me with unwashen feet."

And when he did so, the fiend, not daring to break his vow, did not follow.

"And that is why I say:

> A prudent man should always ask, ...

and the rest of it."

After listening to this, the king summoned the Brahmans and said: "Brahmans, a three-breasted daughter has been born to me. Are any remedial measures to be taken, or not?" And they replied: "O King, listen.

> A daughter fitted out with limbs
> Too numerous or few,
> Will lose her character, and will
> Destroy her husband, too.
>
> But if the father sees a girl
> With triple breast about,

She dooms him to a speedy death
Without a shade of doubt.

"Therefore, O King, shun the sight of her. Give her to anyone who will marry her, but banish him from the country. If this is done, there is no offense to laws human or divine."

When the king had listened to this opinion, he ordered a proclamation to be made everywhere with beat of drum, as follows: "Hear ye! There is a three-breasted princess. To anyone who marries her the king will give a hundred thousand gold-pieces, but will exile him." For a long time this proclamation was made without anyone marrying the princess, who remained in seclusion and grew to young womanhood.

Now there was a blind man in the city, and as companion he had a hunchback named Slow, who guided him with a staff. These two heard the drum and consulted, saying: "In case we touch that drum, we get girl and gold. With the gold our life will be happy. And even if death results from the girl's deformity, it will put a final end to the wretchedness of poverty. For

Until a mortal's belly-pot
Is full, he does not care a jot
For love or music, wit or shame,
For body's care or scholar's name,
For virtue or for social charm,
For lightness or release from harm,
For godlike wisdom, youthful beauty,
For purity or anxious duty."

After this consultation, the blind man went and touched the drum, saying: "I will marry the girl." Thereupon the king's men went and reported: "O King, a certain blind man has touched the drum. Decision rests with the king."

And the king said: "Listen.

> Blind or deaf, of meanest birth,
> Leprous may he be;
> Let him take the girl and gold
> To a far country."

So the king's men, following their lord's command, took the three-breasted princess to the river-bank, married her to the blind man, and gave him the hundred thousand gold-pieces. Then putting them all in a fishing-boat, they said to the fishermen: "Men, take this blind man, with his wife and the hunchback, to a foreign land, and settle them in some town or other."

So they came to a foreign country, all three of them. There in a certain town they purchased a house and lived comfortably. The blind man, however, spent all his time dozing on a couch. The hunchback did the housework.

In course of time the princess had an intrigue with the hunchback, and she said: "My belovèd, if this blind man happened to be killed, we should live happily together. Please find some poison. I will administer it, will kill him, and will become happy."

Now one day the hunchback picked up a dead

black snake, and joyfully returning home with it, he said to her: "Belovèd, I found this black snake. Please cut it up, season it with delicious tidbits, and give it to that eyeless fellow, telling him it is fish. Then he will die in a hurry." And with this Slow started off for the market.

But she cut up the snake, put it in a kettle with buttermilk, placed it over the fire, and as she was herself occupied with chores about the house, she civilly said to the blind man: "My dear, I got your favorite fish today, and I am cooking them. So while I am busy with other chores, please take the spoon and stir them." And he was delighted to hear it, stood up at once, licking his chops, took the spoon, and started to stir.

But as he did so, the poisoned steam reached his eyes, and the film began to peel off. And he, perceiving its healthful action, intercepted all he could. So his vision cleared, and looking into the kettle, he saw nothing but chopped black snake. And he thought: "Well, what is the meaning of this? She called it fish to my face. But this is chopped snake. I must learn, for certain, whether this is the work of the three-breasted woman or a move to kill me on the part of Slow, or of somebody else."

With this in mind, he concealed his feelings and behaved like a blind man. Presently Slow returned and without hesitation began to hug the wife, to kiss her, and so on. And the blind man saw it all.

Not finding a knife, he went up to Slow in the old way, wrathfully seized him by the feet, whirled him about his head with every bit of strength he could muster, and dashed him against the chest of the three-breasted woman. And the blow from the hunchback's body forced the third breast in, while the hunchback, when his hump smashed against her bosom, became straight.

"And that is why I say:

Blind man, hunchback, ...

and the rest of it."

Then the gold-finder said: "Yes, you are quite right in saying that good fortune always comes through the favor of fate. Yet, after all, a man should make fate his own, and not desert prudence, as you did in rejecting my advice."

With this the gold-finder bade him farewell and started home.

Here ends Book V, called "Ill-considered Deeds." The first verse runs:

Deeds ill-known, ill-recognized,
Ill-accomplished, ill-devised—
Thought of these let no man harbor;
Take a warning from the barber.

PRINTED IN THE U.S.A.